Moral Matters

Moral Matters

FIVE WAYS TO DEVELOP THE MORAL LIFE OF SCHOOLS

Barbara S. Stengel and Alan R. Tom

Foreword by Nel Noddings

Teachers College, Columbia University
New York and London

Published by Teachers College Press, 1234 Amsterdam Avenue, New York, NY 10027

Library of Congress Cataloging-in-Publication Data

Stengel, Barbara Senkowski.
  Moral matters : five ways to develop the moral life of schools / Barbara S. Stengel and Alan R. Tom ; foreword by Nel Noddings.
      p.   cm.
  Includes bibliographical references and index.
  ISBN-13: 978-0-8077-4720-9 (pbk : alk. paper)
  ISBN-10: 0-8077-4720-3 (pbk : alk. paper)
  ISBN-13: 978-0-8077-4721-6 (cloth : alk. paper)
  ISBN-10: 0-8077-4721-1 (cloth : alk. paper)
  1. Moral education—United States.   I. Tom, Alan R., 1937–   II. Title.

  LC311.S74 2007
  370.11'4—dc22

                                                                    2006016063

ISBN-13:   ISBN-10:
978-0-8077-4720–9 (paper)   0-8077-4720-3 (paper)
978-0-8077-4721–6 (cloth)   0-8077-4721-1 (cloth)

Printed on acid-free paper
Manufactured in the United States of America

13   12   11   10   09   08   07   06   8   7   6   5   4   3   2   1

Contents

Foreword by Nel Noddings   *ix*
Acknowledgments   *xiii*

Introduction   1

    "Teach Children Character"   2
    "Not One Way"   4
    "Some Character Flaw"   6
    A Framework for Engagement   7
    Organization of the Book   9

1. The Moral Resurgent   12

    The Rise of Academic Accountability   13
    The Emergence of Character Education   16
    Broadening the Moral in Theory   17
    Broadening the Moral in Practice   20

2. Constructing the Categories   23

    Meaning in Use: The Moral and the Academic 24
    Why the Moral Raises a Red Flag   30
    Uncovering the Moral   35
    Constructing the Categories   36
    Where We Began   43

3. The SEPARATE Category   45

        Making the Case for Character Education   47
        Service Learning   52
        The Ethics of Teaching   56
        Possibilities and Dangers   60

4. The SEQUENTIAL Category   66

        Which Comes First?   66
        Possibilities and Dangers   78

5. The DOMINANT Category   81

        ACADEMIC DOMINANT   81
        MORAL DOMINANT   89
        Possibilities and Dangers   94

6. The TRANSFORMATIVE Category   97

        C-School's Relational Education   98
        Nel Noddings's Caring Curriculum   101
        David Purpel and the Teacher as Prophet   104
        Ted Sizer and Horace's School   107
        Possibilities and Dangers   111

7. The INTEGRATED Category   115

        Teaching for Social Justice   116
        Habits of Mind for Democratic Education   120
        Accessing the "Culture of Power"   122
        Democracy and Christian Tradition   125
        Education as Spiritual Journey   128
        The Moral Inheres in the Practice   129
        Possibilities and Dangers   130

8. Mapping the Moral Terrain   134

        Is That All There Is?   135
        Critical Markers   138
        What the Categories Teach Us   140
        Acting As If the Moral Matters   144

Ideological Standpoint(s) 146
Minding the Gaps 148
Conclusion 149

References 151
Index 163
About the Authors 175

Foreword

We seem to be living today in a morally corrupt world. Lying, fraud, and greed appear everywhere—in government, business, family life, religion, science, and even in education. Recently it was reported that several school principals in New York City had accepted monetary gifts for their schools from private tutoring companies in exchange for granting the companies access to their students. Two of the principals said that they saw nothing wrong in doing this. Similarly, many students confess to cheating quite regularly. "Everyone does it," they say.

It is hard to imagine that any well-informed person today would argue against providing moral education in our schools. Yet there are those who, although they recognize the need for moral education, do not want the public schools to provide it. Moral education, they argue, is a task for family and religious institutions.

But as Barbara Stengel and Alan Tom point out, schools are powerful agents of moral education even when they deny an explicit role in it. Schools establish required courses and rules for attendance, behavior, and dress. Further, they back these rules with rewards and penalties. Teachers assign work, tell students where (and how) to sit, decide when students may talk, assess student work with grades, and make clear that following the rules is "good" and disobeying them is "bad." Clearly, schools inevitably engage in moral education. Stengel and Tom refer to this pattern as "invisible" moral education—moral education as part of a hidden curriculum.

Stengel and Tom are, however, more interested in *visible* moral education, and they set out to make the moral visible—in essence, by showing how educators make the moral visible. To get started, they posit two essential domains within education—the academic and the moral. They then suggest five categories by which to classify approaches to moral education; each category describes the relationship between the academic and the moral: separate, sequential, dominant, transformative, and integrated. These are not stages, and they cannot be placed on a continuum of development. Indeed, Stengel and Tom achieve a laudable level of balance in discussing the categories, each of which has its strengths and weaknesses.

In the "separate" approach, for example, schools may offer special courses in moral education or ethics, or they may locate such instruction in a particular subject, say, reading or language arts. In either case, moral education remains technically separate from other subjects in the curriculum. This approach is common throughout the curriculum in schools. We might call it the "add a course" approach. Whenever an important need is identified, the school responds by adding a course to meet it. Sometimes—as in driver education—this is a reasonable, even necessary, decision. In other cases, it leads to the fragmentation and mindlessness that characterize so much of schooling. I am not accusing those who design and teach special courses in moral education of mindlessness—and Stengel and Tom certainly do not do this. However, despite the best intentions and creative efforts, the result of this separation is often a loss of meaning. Connections are lost, and moral education becomes "moral ed"—just another course. Notice that this criticism might be directed more broadly at an entire system that organizes curriculum into discrete, sharply separate subjects.

The authors admit that their categories are not perfect. True, there is some overlap in categories, and we might take an entirely different approach to the analysis of moral education. However, their categories are ingenious and invite both reflection and further analysis. I had a wonderful time with them.

Consider the "sequential" category. Moral educators in this group begin with either the moral or the academic, and then develop the other on the base of the first. Such a strategy is used widely, even when moral education is "invisible." Teachers are advised to get control of the class, establish rules and expectations, and get everything in order before launching into instruction. Indeed, many of us in the dominant, transformative, and integrated categories agree that the moral is in some way fundamental. For example when teachers ask me how they can attend to caring relations "on top of everything else," I always answer that establishing such relations is not a task "on top" of others; it is one that underlies all we do. However, I would not recommend an explicitly sequential program.

There are, of course, other useful ways to look at moral education. One very popular way, sometimes associated with the "separate" and "dominant" categories is to concentrate on making the kids "good." Strategies designed to do this usually attempt to teach the virtues directly, and there are several attractive programs available, mainly at the elementary school level. Parents, teachers, and philosophers have debated the value of these strategies for centuries—indeed, since the days of Socrates. Research may yet show that teaching the virtues is an effective means of moral education, but we do not have definitive conclusions at this time.

A contrasting approach is to work more on the environment than on the kids. Those who take this line of attack point out that happy kids are usually good kids. Educators, then, should try to establish an educational climate in which it is both desirable and possible to be good. We should reduce competition (eliminate pernicious competition and retain only that which is healthy), get rid of zero-tolerance rules but retain zero-tolerance attitudes ("in this school, we never talk to one another like that"), reduce academic anxiety by concentrating on learning rather than testing, and allow students to stay with one teacher long enough to develop relations of care and trust. Obviously, all of these recommendations require analysis and elaboration. They are ideas to think about, and readers may enjoy trying to locate educators who think this way in the Stengel/Tom categories.

Another important aspect of working on the moral environment is its emphasis on the moral dilemmas of teachers. We must work on ourselves as we encourage students to think about their own moral lives. What rules should I maintain? How should I evaluate student work? How should I connect my subject to moral issues and to other subjects? When should I put formal subject matter aside and address a social issue? How far should I intervene in the personal lives of my students? These are all moral questions, and our answers can improve the moral climate or make it worse.

Just as there is overlap in the categories offered by Stengel and Tom, there are similarities in the two approaches just sketched. Those who would teach the virtues directly usually share the desire to improve the moral climate, and those who emphasize the moral environment engage students in frequent dialogue about virtues and moral dilemmas. The difference is in part a matter of emphasis, but that difference is important.

Stengel and Tom have given us a lot to think about. In their conclusion, they call for a language that incorporates both the academic and the moral. It seems to me that we once—not so long ago—had such a language. It was the *language of education*. It included discussion of aims, of the balance between proactive and interactive curriculum; of content and process, of school and community, of democratic classrooms, of social responsibility, of indoctrination and rationality, of critical thinking, of teaching versus training. We need to recapture, refresh, and extend that language. Stengel and Tom have given us a start.

Nel Noddings
Stanford University

Acknowledgments

This book has taken shape over a 5-year period; in that time, our students, our colleagues, and our institutions have played a significant supporting role and we acknowledge that support.

Good fortune and the generosity of Millersville University and the University of North Carolina at Chapel Hill combined to give us both sabbatical leave at the same time. We are grateful for the significant investment in this work that those sabbaticals represent.

Over the past several years, sets of students—in Philosophy of Education courses at Millersville and in Curriculum Theory courses at UNC—read and responded thoughtfully to various drafts of chapters. We acknowledge careful reading, prodding questions, important clarifications, and useful examples from those students. Their willingness to engage the moral dimensions of their work as educators is a model of the kind of dialogue we hope this book will generate.

On a number of occasions, we have shared the ideas represented here with colleagues at professional conferences: the Curriculum and Pedagogy Conference in Austin, Texas, the American Educational Research Association Conference in New Orleans, and the Association of Moral Education Conference in Cambridge, Massachusetts. We came away from each of those conferences with a clearer sense of what we intended and a better understanding of how to convey our thinking. We thank those colleagues who responded to our presentations and who spent time with us checking our perceptions about the ways of thinking about the relation between the moral and the academic, particularly Landon Beyer, Dwight Boyd, Mary Casey, Dennis Denenberg, David Hansen, Janette Hewitt, Nel Noddings, and Jared Stallones.

Finally, I (Barb) want to acknowledge the loving interest of Tim and Emily, who have been my most effective teachers and most faithful supporters and who are fast becoming my best friends. And I (Alan) want to thank Abbie for her wonderful support over the years and to let her know that this is the last book!

Introduction

If asked to characterize American schooling at the beginning of the 21st century, most educators would point to the development of systems of academic standards and the high-stakes testing plans that thrust those academic standards to the forefront of principals', teachers', and students' minds. But this characterization would miss an important parallel development—a similarly compelling, if less widespread, interest in moral education and the moral nature and implications of schooling. This book has been written to shine a spotlight on this parallel development, a spotlight that is both descriptive and analytic.

Throughout this book, we describe the thought and action of educators who focus on schooling's moral dimensions. Our central claim pushes beyond the inventory and emulation of model programs, however. We maintain that the variety and richness of ideas described here can—and should—be analyzed and better understood through a careful, conscious examination of the way the moral is conceptualized vis-à-vis the academic. To that end, we construct a set of categories that capture the relationship between the moral and the academic—SEPARATE, SEQUENTIAL, DOMINANT, TRANSFORMATIVE, and INTEGRATED—and we use those categories to facilitate analysis. Within each chapter, we offer a sampler of educational thinking and programming representative of a particular relationship between the moral and the academic. We also show when and how the meaning of the moral and the meaning of the academic alter in response to a changing relationship between these two markers of educational phenomena.

The characterizations, the categories, we propose and exemplify here are intended as a heuristic—a map—to aid in individual reflection, to stimulate collaborative consideration of the issues, and, ultimately, to ground defensible action. Such a heuristic is needed because the issues surrounding the moral dimensions of teaching and learning are complex and often obscured. Three vignettes convey the complexity we face when we attend to the moral.

"TEACH CHILDREN CHARACTER"

In November of 1993, Judy Hoffman, school board chair for Wake County in North Carolina, called for the creation of a Character Education Task Force. Concerned that "kids are more and more lacking in respect" and that some young people have "a seeming lack of basic values," Hoffman wanted the task force to agree on such common values as honesty and respect (Silberman, 1993, p. A1). Another school board member, Bill Fisher, a local principal who had been recently elected to the school board on a platform of stronger discipline, was concerned that "kids sometimes don't have a sense of obligation to some entity larger than themselves" (p. A1).

By mid-December, the Wake County School Board had appointed a Character Education Task Force. Assistant principal Annie Lee was its chair, and the task force had 32 members, including county residents, teachers, administrators, and students from the Wake County Public Schools. At its first meeting on January 20, the task force brainstormed 63 specific character traits and behaviors and started to cluster these traits into larger categories. During the task force's February 17 meeting, these core character traits were reviewed and further reduced to eight: courage, good judgment, integrity, kindness, perseverance, respect, responsibility, and self-discipline.

While initially it appeared that the task force had successfully finessed controversy, subsequent events demonstrated otherwise. As soon as the news became public that abstinence from premarital sex was not to be one of the task force's basic virtues, some in Wake County became alarmed. They aired their concerns on radio and television shows and phoned and wrote members of the task force. At a March 10 task force meeting, chair Annie Lee repeated task force member Tami Fitzgerald's (1994) earlier rationale that abstinence, although not a separate character trait, was clearly part of the trait of self-discipline. Lee's comments did not deter Raleigh mayor Tom Fetzer from making the case for stressing abstinence. "We as a society," asserted Fetzer, "have failed to inculcate the responsibility of bringing children into the world" (Silberman, 1994, p. B1).

Mindful of the need for broad support, the task force circulated 105,000 surveys to school district parents; to administrators and teachers; to all fourth-, seventh-, and tenth-grade students; and to interested community members. On the 28,000 completed surveys, approval rates for the eight specific traits were high, ranging from a 77.8% approval rate for perseverance to an 86.3% approval rate for respect (*Character education*, n.d.; Silberman, 1994). However, on 490 written responses, an optional part of the survey, only 64% supported teaching values in the schools at all, 26% were in opposition, and about 10% were undecided. A common response among those opposed to teaching values in the schools was that "the schools should devote more time to instruction in academics" (Silberman, 1994).

This and other concerns were expressed in letters to the Raleigh *News & Observer*. One person wrote that "no citizen would respond negatively to the statements that the schools outlined." The real issue, this person claimed, was that time devoted to teaching values would lessen attention to the academic curriculum (Genovesi, 1994, p. A12). Another person observed that the vast majority of parents in Wake County were raising their children according to an explicit Judeo-Christian morality. He worried youngsters would be taught character education in a secular and often relativistic context that was objectionable to most parents. Perhaps the school district should do no values education at all (Cuddy, 1994). Yet another set of parents found that the definitions of several traits embodied "narrow and controversial moral conclusions as opposed to character traits on which a consensus can truly emerge." The definition of *respect*, for example, included the phrase "high regard for authority," but what would happen if that authority is an incestuous, abusive father? "A good citizen must question authority when necessary and not blindly follow orders" (Risman & Kane, 1994, p. A15).

Opposition was lively but had no apparent effect. When the Wake County Public Schools launched its character education effort in the fall of 1994, the eight traits and their definitions remained unchanged from the original proposal. The avowed goal was to integrate character education into the overall curriculum. Religion was to be respected, but character education would not be taught "in a manner that is unique to a particular tradition" (*Character Education*, n.d.).

It is difficult to know how broadly and how successfully character education ideas have been woven into the academic curriculum of the Wake County schools. How to implement character education was essentially left up to individual teachers. When the entire district was named a National School of Character by the Character Education Partnership, Judy Hoffman, the school board member who had pushed character education from the beginning, summed up her feelings: "The question isn't whether we are going to teach children character, the question is what kind of character are we going to teach them and are we going to teach them in a collaborative, unified way in the community so children hear the same message over and over again" ("Character Educators Applaud," 1999, para. 15).

Robre

"NOT ONE WAY"

Rodney Morris is a middle school history and writing teacher who prides himself on caring for and about his students. Caring for them involves taking a personal interest in each one and taking responsibility for making school interesting, meaningful, and worthwhile. Caring about them requires that he establish his professional authority, setting high standards for student behavior and performance and holding all students to those standards fairly. Morris might be characterized as a "moral steward." He feels he has a responsibility "to facilitate his students' intellectual, moral, and social development so that those students will become skilled and valuable members of the working world, good people, and decent citizens" (Colton, 1998, p. 248). This entails modeling the kind of moral character he wishes to instill in his students, creating a learning environment that promotes prosocial behaviors, and directly teaching moral values. Rodney Morris is pleased to be teaching in a private educational community where dealing with values openly is possible.

Despite his conscious claim of responsibility as a moral educator, and despite his apparent awareness that his interactions with students are morally charged, Morris seems curiously insensitive to the moral impact of his daily curricular, instructional, and disciplinary actions. Amy Colton, a researcher who documented Morris' "professional morality," notes that when asked to share situations in which he had a moral impact on his students, Morris "never talked about his everyday approach to how he taught or disciplined his students. He seemed to talk only about situations that involved breaking the Golden Rule or where students did something he saw as wrong, like lying or cheating. Yet in providing the rationale for his behavior it was clear it was based on moral considerations. Perhaps he does not have the language to discuss the moral aspects of his practice" (Colton, 1998, p. 294).

Colton also introduces us to Mary Brown, like Morris a National Board Certified middle school teacher, teaching math in a public school environment. Where Morris understands himself as a moral steward, Brown defines herself as a "professional servant," carefully avoiding the potential red flag associated with moral matters in a public setting. Brown views herself as professional in that her knowledge and training ground her work as a teacher. She is a servant because that work is facilitating "her students' intellectual, moral, social and emotional development" (Colton, 1998, p. 193) within the framework of the expectations and demands of the different publics with which she is affiliated (State Department of Education, school district, parents, public at large). Thus her primary responsibility is students' academic growth in mathematics. While she cares *personally* about her students' so-cial, moral, and emotional development, these concerns go beyond her *professional* boundaries.

Mary Brown is ever aware of those boundaries. She frames her goals judiciously: first, "to facilitate her students' development of the mathematical understandings as prescribed by the school curriculum" so they will "be adequately prepared for high school," and "be able to solve real-life problems" and, secondarily, to facilitate "students' moral and social development" by modeling such behaviors (p. 273). There is none of the lofty moral mandate offered by Morris. Instead, Brown remains, by her own admission, "value-neutral" (not teaching values directly) while modeling moral and social conventions and norms (p. 294).

Both Brown and Morris are exemplary teachers if National Board Certification is accepted as evidence, but their understanding of the moral dimensions of their work is different. As Amy Colton notes, "There is not one way to describe teachers' professional morality" (Colton, 1999, p. 14). Brown recognizes the moral nature of her work but is constrained to keep moral concerns under wraps by her understanding of public education. Morris, perhaps freed by being in a private setting, claims his work is thoroughly moral in intent and interaction but still does not talk about his everyday academic interactions in moral terms.

By luck or design, Colton's research subjects illustrate well two common conundrums faced by contemporary educators. On the one hand, political context creates pressure to separate academic responsibilities from moral responsibilities, privileging the former and making the latter downright dangerous. On the other hand, even when context or courage empowers an educator to face the moral contours of teaching head-on, there is no readily available language that enables the expression of the everyday intertwining of moral and academic concerns. In either case, the result is the same. Schooling seems, in the public imagination, to be a predominantly value-neutral affair of the mind. Teachers appear, first of all, to be technicians who deliver instruction and assess performance. The irony, of course, is that this putatively neutral vision carries its own moral message, validates particular values, and requires specific kinds of relationships.

As Rodney Morris and Mary Brown both know, teachers are morally influential in the lives of their students. In determining goals, in selecting curricula or instructional methods, in recognizing and responding to student behavior and misbehavior, in constructing environments that are safe, challenging, or both, in evaluating reasonably and fairly, in offering moral direction or moral advice, in acting as a responsible adult in the world, teachers act and interact morally.

"SOME CHARACTER FLAW"

"The first hint of trouble at Potomac School came from the students. Fifth graders whispered to one another on the playground and subsequently told their parents about the strange behavior of their principal, Karen Karch, as she monitored the Maryland state assessments. After some children had finished the test, they were summoned by the principal and urged to 'review' their answers. 'You might want to look at this one again,' Karch would say. ... A 10-year-old boy recounted that he was given extra time on the math test. ... 'I definitely thought that she was cheating, but I thought if I said anything I would get in trouble or something'" (Thomas & Wingert, 2000, pp. 50, 52).

It is understandable that students at Potomac Elementary might be confused by this state of affairs in light of the "Character Counts" board in the front hall of the school, where rainbow-colored letters enumerated the virtues of character, respect, responsibility, perseverance, sympathy, honesty, and self-discipline (Thomas & Wingert, 2000, p. 51). Their parents were confused by the attitudes of both the teachers and the district administration. Administrators focused on minimizing negative publicity and saving face in statements to the press and in community meetings. Teachers neither acknowledged nor honored students' willingness to do the right thing and name dishonesty.

Karen Karch resigned on May 31, 2000, the day before the *Washington Post* broke this story. In a press release, she stated: "I have concluded that I exercised poor judgment in some of my decisions," but insisted that "my resignation is not an admission of guilt" (quoted in Thomas & Wingert, 2000, p. 52). In a June 23 report to superintendent Jerry Weast, cluster administrator Jay Headman determined that Karch had violated state testing laws and that "many current staff members who were aware of the violations have expressed sincere regret in not reporting the violations in a timely and professional manner" (quoted in Schulte, 2000, p. B1).

Something went very wrong at Potomac Elementary School. But what? Commentators saw differing moral situations in the Potomac School incident. Many identified Principal Karch's ethical lapse, and by implication her character, as the crux of the issue. Others focused on the systemic pressure to perform created by state policy that is neither educational nor ethical.

Explaining that Potomac School serves an "upscale" bedroom community near Avenal Country Club, a world-class golf course surrounded by mansions, two *Newsweek* writers noted that graduates of Potomac Elementary School proceed on to Montgomery County high schools, which have the highest SAT scores of any of the nation's 20 largest counties. Pressure on the staff increased in 1998; Potomac Elementary was rated "less productive" by Superintendent Weast because its student scores had leveled off (though still high in relation to other elementary schools). This pressure to "win" was at the root of the moral "breakdown" at Potomac, according to the *Newsweek* authors.

Critics of high-stakes testing go beyond this explanation to argue that the state tests—not administrators' or teachers' lapses—are the core moral issue. "The major problem," notes Monty Neill, executive director of the National Center for Fair & Open Testing, "is the unreasonable, unfair, and inappropriate use of standardized exams" (quoted in Kleiner, 2000, para. 5). Robert Schaefer, a Fair Test director, sums up criticism of high-stakes testing by asserting that when teachers and principals have "their job or future depend on one thing, people do unethical, irrational, and illegal things" (quoted in Magnuson, 2000, para. 14). Neill and Schaefer imply that those who create such accountability policies act immorally by placing educators in an untenable position.

On the other hand, Jeanne Allen, President of the Center for Education Reform in Washington, D.C., insists that the story in instances of such cheating is the ethical failure of an individual. She claims that

> the cause [of cheating] is not the test, not the standards movement, but some character flaw. These tests . . . are challenging, but they reflect what should be taught in various grades, and if educators are cheating, it means they don't have the ability to get these kids to learn, which means they shouldn't be teaching in the first place. (quoted in Kleiner, 2000, para. 6)

What went wrong at Potomac? Answers differ dramatically depending on the way the question is framed. Was this an act of unethical behavior by an individual principal or a symptom of an immoral system of academic accountability?

A FRAMEWORK FOR ENGAGEMENT

Schooling is academic. But it is not *only* academic. Yes, we want kids to be "smart," to be knowledgeable, competent, and culturally literate, but we also want kids to be "good," to be good neighbors, responsible citizens, thoughtful colleagues, caring friends, loving parents. We want our children to reflect our best selves and to take their place in the community. Schooling plays a significant role in this.

The three vignettes illuminate many of the moral challenges of schooling. Two practical questions are at the heart of the matter: How do we take responsibility for children's moral development? And how do we do that without diluting responsibility for their academic development?

Numerous foundational issues underlie these two practical questions—issues about private morality and public responsibility, individual autonomy and accountability, relationship and community, the debatable goodness of social institutions and public policies, the role of religious belief in public endeavors, the relation between rhetoric and reality, the purposes of public schooling, and, of course, what is in the best interests of the children. These are not easy issues to deliberate or decide. For a variety of reasons, some of which we discuss later, we are not well prepared to talk reasonably about moral matters in public settings.

Too often, we defend, disappear behind political ideology, and discount the perspective of the other. Or we prescribe a particular moral system to the exclusion of others. In fact, when one writes about the moral in schooling, it is assumed that the purpose of such writing is to propose and vigorously defend a specific moral point of view to the exclusion of others. And it is not uncommon for critics to offer commentary on the moral ideas of others that borders on personal attack (e.g., Katz, 1997). Those who do manage to avoid bitter disagreement often sidestep real difference to avoid controversy or paper over differences to reach a thin "consensus" that does not support constructive action. None of these responses represent constructive dialogue across difference.

This book is an effort to bring the answer-oriented debate of the past two decades back to the questions that prompt proposals and programs. Specifically, we hope to use the answers educators and others have offered—in the form of programs and platforms—to construct a framework for understanding how those questions fit together. Our framework, as noted earlier, is a set of categories, categories that will help expose the varying ways that the moral can be addressed in schooling and the differing choices available for connecting the moral and the academic. Our primary goal is to provide a conceptual basis for constructive dialogue among educators and the general public about the role of the moral in schooling.

Conceptual schemes can easily get far removed from the realities of schooling practice. We spent a lot of time considering not only how the categories could be based on important distinctions but also whether these distinctions could be seen in existing school-based moral efforts (and the platforms underlying such moral efforts). Our intention, therefore, was to develop a framework that revealed key features of existing schooling practices yet also identified new ways of thinking about these existing practices. In what follows, we include some of the case examples we examined as we developed the five categories. Our intention is to provide careful, sympathetic descriptions of contemporary thinking about the moral contours of schools. In some instances, these cases focus on teaching as a moral endeavor, but we also look at teachers as moral educators and schools as systems of personal and political interaction. In truth, this book might be useful just as a collection of case examples. To gather multiple answers to similar questions in one place enables comparison, contrast, analysis, and, occasionally, insight.

But, as noted at the outset, we offer more; we offer a particular orientation to the task of analysis. We use one seemingly simple conceptual distinction to orient ourselves, to map out the territory. That is the relationship between the academic and the moral in each program or proposal described. The use of this analytic device results in a map with five subdivisions, five categories, three of which are bimodal. We suggest that the relationship between the academic and the moral can be understood as SEPARATE, SEQUENTIAL (ACADEMIC FIRST or MORAL FIRST), DOMINANT (ACADEMIC DOMINANT or MORAL DOMINANT), TRANSFORMATIVE (ACADEMIC TRANSFORMATIVE or MORAL TRANSFORMATIVE), or INTEGRATED.

We begin with simple and inclusive meanings of *moral* and *academic*, but as we shall see, the meaning of each term within our analytic device shifts vis-à-vis the relationship posited for the two domains. Both issues—the relationship between things academic and things moral, and the shifting meanings of *moral* and *academic*—turn out to be important. So is the fact that the subdivisions in our mapping cut across standard political, ideological, cultural, and religious divides. Since these divides often hamper our ability to talk to one another about the role of the moral in schooling, we believe our category system can help foster richer engagement than has been the norm.

As the cases above suggest and the contents of this book will confirm, (1) there has been much contemporary interest in schooling as a means of moral education, as a site of moral action, and as a moral endeavor in itself, and (2) there has not been the kind of sustained, constructive public engagement on the critical educational issues and concerns that underlie the recent rush to fix what's wrong morally in schools and in society. Our purpose here is to encourage just this sort of thoughtful engagement by taking a new look at old issues, by defusing some taken-for-granted political allegiances, and by suggesting a conceptual frame for constructive discussion and action.

ORGANIZATION OF THE BOOK

In Chapter 1, "The Moral Resurgent," we mark the boundaries of the terrain we are surveying: programs and proposals that highlight the moral contours of American schooling (public, private, parochial, home) since 1983. We begin with a general geography of American schooling since *A Nation at Risk*, laying out in broad strokes efforts at moral education in schools and efforts to highlight the moral dimensions of schooling during that time period. We then emphasize a series of specific public actions and events that together constitute a pattern of broad and multidimensional concern with the moral in schools.

Chapter 2, "Constructing the Categories," begins with some exploration of how the terms *academic* and *moral* can be understood and moves to a provisional statement of the meaning of *moral* and *academic* for our purposes. We take a brief detour to consider the perceived danger of indoctrination, the unsettled relationship between church and state, and the continual challenge of constructing unity in conditions of cultural diversity. We follow with a preliminary explanation of the categories, or "ideal types," that we use to demarcate the field of moral/education and conclude with a discussion of our own presuppositions about this territory.

Chapters 3 through 7 each consider a category—SEPARATE, SEQUENTIAL, DOMINANT, TRANSFORMATIVE, and INTEGRATED—in turn and in detail. Each chapter includes sketches of programs, proposals, and positions focused on either moral education efforts, initiatives for the moral renewal of schools, curricula with moral impact, schooling-generated moral issues, or teaching as a moral endeavor. We attempt to present each program, proposal, and position generously and on its own terms.

Our survey of the field constitutes a sampling rather than a complete listing, but we believe it is nonetheless representative. The sketches presented in each chapter gather together typical exemplars of particular ways of regarding the relationship between things moral and things academic in schooling. Exemplars within each category, within each chapter, are distinctive in substance, religious slant, and political perspective, but *as a set* they confirm our categorization and our contention that there are different ways of acting out the relationship between the moral and the academic in schooling. Each chapter concludes with a consideration of the possibilities and dangers that arise out of a particular academic/moral nexus.

Chapter 8, "Mapping the Moral Terrain," brings together possibilities and dangers outlined in each chapter in comparison and contrast. We try to make clear that there is something to be learned from each exemplar considered throughout the previous chapters. We readily acknowledge that the programs, proposals, and positions do not always appear in "pure" form, but that some of the most useful efforts presently available may be eclectic in design. Nonetheless, we assert that there is value in identifying distinguishable conceptual elements as we do in Chapters 3 through 7 and in using those concepts and categories to stimulate novel ways of imagining moral matters in schooling. Further, we ask and answer how our categories and observations illuminate the issues involved in a way that enhances both individual reflection and shared communication between and among educators and the communities in which they work.

We conclude, not surprisingly, that our work is helpful, but not enough. A fuller treatment of the moral contours of the education of a democratic public requires: (1) open and continuing consideration of the meaning of the moral vis-à-vis democratic social arrangements, and (2) a language of schooling that is not so clearly bifurcated between academic and moral. Continued attention to these issues accompanies the premise with which we began—that whatever the moral is, however it is construed, the moral matters in American schooling.

1

The Moral Resurgent

Shortly after becoming President, George W. Bush was calling for character education in our schools. In an April talk at Central Connecticut State University, the President asserted, "Education is not complete unless we're willing to teach our children not only how to read and write but the difference between right and wrong" (Bush, 2001, para. 46). The President's statement is emblematic of the trend we highlight here: Over the past two decades, there has been an increasing effort to make the moral visible in American schools. Of course, not all will agree on just what it means to know "the difference between right and wrong." Still, this disagreement should not obscure shared interest in moral matters.

While the President uses his bully pulpit to advance the need for character education, other signs confirm this shared interest. The American public expresses its strong support for teaching values in school (Rose & Gallup, 2003). University professors call for "moral leadership" (Sergiovanni, 1992) and urge school administrators to "put love at the center of the American educational vision" (Hoyle & Slater, 2001, p. 790). Educational researchers examine the effectiveness of various approaches to moral education (Solomon, Watson, & Battistich, 2001) and conduct observational and ethnographic studies of the "moral life of schools" (e.g., Jackson, Boostrom, & Hansen, 1993; Noblit & Dempsey, 1996; Simon, 2001). School reform leaders remind us of "the moral obligation of teachers to ensure equitable access to and engagement in the best possible K–12 education for all children and youths" (Goodlad, 1994, p. 87), and educational organizations plan conferences around themes that are explicitly moral. In short, *moral* and *schooling* are often appearing in the same sentence.

A closer look at the context of the President's statement qualifies our claim. At Central Connecticut, President Bush spent 15 minutes specifying his plan for "accountability as the cornerstone of educational reform" and just 1 minute focusing on character education. He used dozens of sentences to specify the particulars of testing and its consequences and just one sentence to articulate fairness as a goal of his plan. This, too, is emblematic of the point we make in this chapter. While there is a resurgent interest in the moral dimensions of schooling, this interest nonetheless pales in comparison to the rhetoric and research that renders the moral elements of education invisible. As a survey of newspaper reports and educational journals will confirm, practitioners, researchers, and theorists tend to focus on the factual, scientific aspects of teaching and learning, ignoring or sidestepping questions of value and purpose. And for reasons that we explore in Chapter 2, educators tend to mask the moral contours of their work even when they recognize them. We refer to this dominant rhetoric and research as the domain of the "moral invisible."

In this chapter we set the context for our work by documenting the increasing attention given in recent years to the moral dimension in schooling, increasing attention that has, perhaps ironically, taken shape against the backdrop of a dominant discourse of standards and testing. Our focus here, and throughout this work, is on the domain of the "moral visible," on the work of those who persist in identifying and exploring the moral dimensions of schooling.

Our intention is not to write a history of moral education in the public schools, a task that has been ably done by B. Edward McClellan in his *Moral Education in America* (1999). Rather, our attention is focused on the last two decades of growing interest in all aspects of schooling as moral. Our concern with the moral is broader than the terrain traditionally associated with moral education, as indicated by the vignettes in the Introduction, and narrower in time than the history of American schooling.

We start with the publication of *A Nation at Risk* in 1983, since educational commentators commonly assert that this document initiated the academic accountability movement now dominating the educational landscape. This document prompted interest in the moral even as it obscured it, and we demonstrate that. We highlight "character education" as the most public indicator of the moral resurgent. Following that discussion, we survey the literature of schooling in recent years that has contributed to a broader theoretical understanding of schooling's moral dimensions. The chapter ends with an array of examples that demonstrate broadening moral concerns in educational practice.

THE RISE OF ACADEMIC ACCOUNTABILITY

In a very real way, *A Nation at Risk* initiated the current emphasis on academic accountability. Its authors, the National Commission for Excellence in Education (NCEE, 1983), argued that America had "lost sight of the basic purposes of schooling, and of the high expectations and disciplined effort needed to attain them" (para. 3). The effect of this blindness was "a rising tide of mediocrity" that was putting "American prosperity, security, and civility" at risk (para. 1).

Note that prosperity was listed first in order of importance, a consideration that seems to shape the report's conclusions. The most publicized findings highlighted the "knowledge, learning, information, and skilled intelligence [that] are the raw materials of international commerce" (para. 7). The recommendations in the report focused on academic content, standards and expectations, instructional time, leadership, and fiscal support.

These recommendations have powered a 20-year agenda of school reform extending across the terms of both Republican and Democratic presidents and several shifts in the congressional balance of power. This agenda has been dominated by the efforts of states to articulate high standards of knowledge and achievement and to implement high-stakes testing of students, most recently under the specter of No Child Left Behind. IBM Chairman and CEO Louis Gerstner captured the tone of accountability for results when he told the National Governors Association in 1995 that our schools require "a fundamental, bone-jarring, full-fledged, 100 percent revolution that discards the old and replaces it with a totally new performance-driven system." Gerstner continued, "Until we're prepared to penalize students, teachers and administrators for lack of performance, the system will fail." The solution is for a governor to act like a corporate chief and "confront and expel the people and the organizations that are throwing up roadblocks to the changes you consider critical" (quoted in Pierce, 1995, p. A28).

To many standards advocates, the suggestion that children and profits are equivalent is questionable, if not offensive. Nonetheless, most do accept Gerstner's emphasis on personal academic achievement, achievement that is of the very highest quality for all students. Academic excellence for all becomes the means to eliminate the socioeconomic inequalities of U.S. society. From this equity-oriented interpretation of high standards, the only question left for serious debate is what counts as high performance for children at each developmental stage. Such decisions are to be left to the individual states, but the federal No Child Left Behind legislation of 2001 requires each state to demonstrate steady, yearly progress—for all its demographic groups of students—until by 2013–2014 every student achieves at grade level in reading and mathematics.

The authors of *A Nation at Risk* (NCEE, 1983) anticipated the attempt to use high standards to address social inequalities: "All, regardless of race or class or economic status, are entitled to a fair chance and to the tools for developing . . . the mature and informed judgment needed to secure gainful employment." However, their concern extended

> well beyond matters such as industry and commerce. It also includes the *intellectual, moral, and spiritual strengths* of our people that knit together the very fabric of our society. . . . A high level of shared education is essential to a free, democratic society and to the fostering of a common culture especially in a country that prides itself on pluralism and individual freedom. (para. 8; emphasis added)

Business interests and the economic well-being of students are not the only interests; intellectual, moral, spiritual, and civic concerns also matter.

In the section on recommendations, the authors of *A Nation at Risk* (NCEE,1983) are explicit about values when they address parents.   *Parents*

> You bear a responsibility to participate actively in your child's education. You should encourage more diligent study and discourage satisfaction with mediocrity and the attitude that says "let it slide;" . . . and be an active participant in the work of the schools. . . . Finally, help your children understand that excellence in education cannot be achieved without intellectual and moral integrity coupled with hard work and commitment. Children will look to their parents and teachers as models of such virtues. (para. 8)

Here the values and virtues that bind the good society envisaged in *A Nation at Risk* become clearer. A socially, economically, and politically conservative ethos is at work. Integrity, hard work, diligence, discipline, a respect for achievement, and an intolerance for mediocrity are central; they are the virtues that support the drive for prosperity. Teachers model these virtues. Despite—or perhaps because of—this document's focus on academic achievement as it impacts commercial success, a vision of the moral impact and importance of schooling is carefully constructed.

As noted earlier, *A Nation at Risk* is given substantial credit for initiating the current accountability movement. The standards and testing duet that followed in the report's wake has generated an enormous wave of public policy support and what may prove to be an even larger wave of reaction from those directly involved. The opposition to the testing is rooted in a variety of concerns: principals' limited ability to respond to testing demands, students' loss of control over their own education, racial and cultural inequities in resources and results, superficial student learning, technical testing issues, among others (e.g., Cahir, 2001; Canedy, 2003; Henriques, 2003; Medina, 2003; Winerip, 2003a, 2003b, 2003c). These objections are administrative, pedagogical, political, and professional. These objections are also moral.

Many who endorsed—or had only modest reservations about—the testing regimen initiated by *A Nation at Risk* also saw value in the moral themes articulated there. They viewed moral education as important, at least as important as raising academic standards, and, for some, more important in the face of family decline, drug use, violence, and a general lack of civility (e.g., Wynne, 1988).

We turn now to these educators and public intellectuals who fashioned the educational response known as character education. As we highlight character education here, we note that this is the most prominent, but just one of many responses that took shape over the past two decades.

THE EMERGENCE OF CHARACTER EDUCATION

For an article in *Instructor* magazine, Meg Lundstrom (1999) selected the title "Character Makes a Comeback." In that article she noted that the teaching of character that had fallen out of favor is now making an "unprecedented comeback" across the country (p. 25). The learning of old-fashioned values is now more important than ever, Lundstrom said, when youngsters lack respect, bully others, and give in to violent outbursts. Schools have instituted programs that both "provide students with grounding in such values as courage and caring" and "teach them how to solve disputes peacefully" (p. 25).

Despite Lundstrom's contention that "old-fashioned values" constitute the core of teaching character, the character of character education had been a subject of debate. In the early 1990s, the philanthropist Michael Josephson brought together a disparate set of educators interested in character education, and this group endorsed a common approach based around "the six pillars of character": trustworthiness, respect, responsibility, justice, caring, and civic virtue (McClellan, 1999, p. 104). In the character education manifesto authored by Kevin Ryan (1996) and endorsed by educators of widely varying philosophies, character education is about developing virtues, defined as "good habits and dispositions," that help students become responsible and mature adults. The Character Education Partnership offered eleven principles for effective character education (e.g., school as a caring community, parent involvement), intended not to prescribe a single program but to serve as "a guide for educators and community leaders in a school, central office or at the state level" (Schaeffer, 1997). Calls for character education and resources to implement it came from both conservative (Bennett, 1993) and liberal (Greer & Kohl, 1995) locations on the political spectrum.

In a critical review of character education, Alfie Kohn (1997) identified the dominant approach to character education as a "narrow" one generally trying to "fix the kids" through "a collection of exhortations and extrinsic inducements designed to make children work harder and do what they're told" (p. 429). In response, Thomas Lickona (1998), a well-known character educator, contended that Kohn's analysis misrepresented the views of many character educators and entirely ignored the work of the Character Education Partnership. Many character educators, Lickona contended, actually endorsed the "broad" approach to character education that Kohn (1997, p. 437) supports, where the emphasis is not so much on "forming individual characters as on transforming educational structures."

During the 1990s, character education efforts of various types spread quickly and widely over the country (Saks, 1996). However, this movement had taken root a decade earlier when conservative Christians became much more politically active and politicians during the Reagan presidency began to talk quite openly about religion and morality. Public concern grew about teen pregnancy, school violence, and other social ills, and a steady stream of articles appeared in newspapers, magazines, and professional journals about the need for more attention to the moral aspect of schooling (e.g., Wynne, 1982, 1985/1986, 1988; Ryan, 1981, 1986). Early in the decade, writers used the term *moral education* to refer to efforts to make kids good (Ryan, 1981), but by the mid-1980s the term *character education* was increasingly common (Ryan, 1986). Public funding, both state and federal, has enabled a variety of moral education programs to flourish under the broad banner of character education.

BROADENING THE MORAL IN THEORY

While publicity about the moral in schooling focused on the formation of children's character, a number of books appeared during the late 1980s and early to mid-1990s with theses that broadened the scope of schooling's moral impact. Titles included: Michael Apple and James Beane's *Democratic Schools* (1995); Hugh Sockett's *The Moral Base for Teacher Professionalism* (1993); Thomas Sergiovanni's *Moral Leadership* (1992); Nel Noddings's *The Challenge to Care in Schools* (1992); Henry Giroux' *Teachers as Intellectuals* (1988); Philip Jackson, Robert Boostrom, and David Hansen's *The Moral Life of Schools* (1993); David Purpel's *The Moral & Spiritual Crisis in Education* (1989); William Damon's *The Moral Child* (1988); Robert Coles's *The Moral Life of Children* (1986); Jonathan Kozol's *Savage Inequalities* (1991); John Goodlad, Roger Soder, and Kenneth Sirotnik's *The Moral Dimensions of Teaching* (1990); and Ernest Boyer's *The Basic School* (1995). This work came from psychologists, philosophers, administrators, teacher educators, educational reformers, and journalists. Some of these books are about the moral life and/or education of children. Others emphasize the moral aspects of teaching and leadership but also have ramifications for children's experience. Still others have a sociopolitical thrust, raising moral questions about social and political structures. Collectively, these books uncovered moral dimensions of schooling that had been recently neglected.

Ernest Boyer clearly shows the influence of character educators but moves beyond to implicate the structure of the school as a moral medium. In Boyer's proposal for *The Basic School* (1995), a central priority for reforming elementary schools is "a commitment to character," including concern for the ethical dimensions of a child's life. Boyer identified seven basic virtues as central to affirming a commitment to character and made suggestions for how to develop character through the school curriculum, much as character educators often might do. At the same time, however, Boyer argued that character, in the form of virtues, also ought to be developed in service outside the school—service in the home, in religious institutions, and with senior citizens, among other places. Moreover, Boyer recommended that all Basic Schools focus on the development of community, and many of the terms he used to define successful community have a distinctly moral emphasis, such as *purposeful, just, disciplined, caring.*

David Purpel, in *The Moral & Spiritual Crisis in Education* (1989), uses explicitly moral language in his analysis but pays little attention to the moral education of the young. In fact, he believes that the idea of moral (or character) education is redundant, since education itself is "at root a moral endeavor" (p. 31). For example, such routine teaching activities as grading and discipline are moral judgments, and the overall goal of education is to help create a just and loving society—a moral end. To identify how schooling can foster such a society, Purpel examines the interconnections between schooling and the larger social order. His analysis draws on economic, social, and cultural ideas in a way many might see as more characteristic of a political analysis than a moral one. Yet, the overall effect of Purpel's approach is to extend our idea of what constitutes the moral to include not only schooling but also other social institutions. His contention that attending to moral education can actually divert attention from larger moral concerns raises further questions about what is most fundamentally moral.

Democratic Schools (1995), an edited volume by Michael Apple and James Beane, might also seem more oriented toward the political than the moral. Democracy is, as the editors note, "the central tenet of our social and political relations" (p. 4). However, they go on to declare that democracy is the "ethical anchor" by which we orient our thinking and is of special value when "our political ship seems to drift" (pp. 4–5). Like Purpel, Apple and Beane blur the line between the political and the moral. The main body of their book is a series of case studies in which principals and K–12 teachers try to address what specific implications the idea of democracy has for the conduct of classroom teaching and of schooling more generally considered.

Nel Noddings's work, especially *The Challenge to Care in Schools* (1992), extends the moral in yet another way. She explores how a focus on the relational structure of caring can be used to rethink the entire school program, ending the reliance on the academic disciplines as an organizing basis for the school curriculum. Caring, for Noddings, is not a value but an interaction between a carer and a cared-for. This emphasis on relation as the critical moral (and educational) category permeates and drives her entire approach to curriculum design and classroom interaction among teachers and students.

One of the early, and most broadly influential, attempts to enlarge our understanding of teaching as moral is *The Moral Dimensions of Teaching* (1990), edited by John Goodlad and colleagues. Authors of chapters in this volume explored the moral dimension of teaching from such varied perspectives as teacher professionalism, the ethical responsibilities of teaching, accountability, and the practice of teaching itself. In their preface to the volume, the editors lament that discussion about questions of virtue and moral character —concerning institutions as well as individuals—were more central to academic and public discussion several decades ago than in 1990, the year their book was published.

From today's perspective, it is easy to forget how rapidly scholars developed an interest in the moral basis of teaching. This development is reflected dramatically in the way reviews of research have changed. In the third edition of the *Handbook of Research on Teaching* (Wittrock, 1986), only one chapter focused on the moral, and that chapter (Oser, 1986) was centered on the moral education of students. In another chapter on the philosophy of research on teaching, Fenstermacher (1986) observes: "No research on teaching with which I am familiar takes account of issues dealing with good teaching" (p. 40). In the fourth edition of the *Handbook* (Richardson, 2001), a mere 15 years after Fenstermacher's statement, David Hansen's chapter is titled "Teaching as a Moral Activity." Early in that chapter, Hansen (2001b) notes "studies suggest that teaching is inherently a moral activity" and, moreover, that "the literature suggests that teaching is at one and the same time an intellectual and a moral endeavor" (p. 826). His chapter analyzes the varied ways in which the moral is embedded in teaching and by which the moral and the academic are intertwined. In addition to Hansen's chapter, there are two related chapters, one on moral education per se (Solomon et al., 2001) and the other on the idea of caring (Noddings, 2001).

Clearly, research interest in the moral dimensions of teaching and schooling has expanded rapidly in recent years, and educational researchers have proposed a variety of new ways to think about these moral dimensions.

The moral is no longer confined to moral education. In addition, scholars' conceptions about the relationship of the moral and the academic often run counter to the tendency of character educators to see the moral and the academic as separate subjects. In many ways, therefore, recent inquiries are opening up new possibilities for thinking about the moral responsibilities incumbent upon educators.

BROADENING THE MORAL IN PRACTICE

Our effort here is not focused solely on analyzing scholarly inquiries into the moral bases for teaching and schooling. While we are interested in such inquiries and describe a number of them in subsequent chapters, we are deeply interested in the way moral ideas play out in the practice of schooling. The moral domain is a domain of action, as we discuss in Chapter 2; to understand the moral dimensions of schooling in America demands that we look as hard at educational action as we do at educational thought. An amazing range of recent curricular efforts, instructional innovations, legislative fiats, judicial decisions, social developments, and policy initiatives highlight this enormous current interest. Here we list a sampling:

- In 1999, Louisiana became the first state to pass legislation requiring elementary school students to address teachers as "Mr.," "Ms.," "sir," or "ma'am" in an effort to instill courtesy and respect in children (Exstrom, 2000).
- In response to an alarming increase in hate crime among youth, the Southern Poverty Law Center began the Teaching Tolerance project in 1991 as an extension of the Center's legal and educational efforts. Through the support of Center donors, Teaching Tolerance offers free or low-cost resources to educators at all levels.
- Georgia legislation, the Improved Student Learning and Discipline Act of 1999, requires that character education programs in the public schools include 27 character traits, including "respect for the creator" (Jacobson, 1999).
- Schools increasingly are engaged in community-building efforts, ranging from the widespread use of conflict resolution and peer mediation programs to the growing popularity of small schools. "When I don't know the name of every student, the school is too big," asserts Sara Newman, principal of the Brooklyn International School (quoted in "Why Small Schools," 1997, para. 11).
- The dramatic growth of homeschooling in the United States has been fueled, in part, by the desire of parents to have more direct control

over the moral education of their youngsters. One parent commented on her decision to homeschool: "A lot of it is about values. We have a Christian world view, and public schools don't provide that" (quoted in Hart, 2001, p. A1).

- Dennis Denenberg, a retired teacher educator, travels all over the country presenting *Hooray for Heroes*, a one-man show and talk based on a book of the same name that teaches students and educators that "real-life heroes" help all of us become good decision makers (Koenig, 1994).
- When the Chapel Hill, North Carolina, school district required community service (50 hours over 4 years), two high school students filed suit contending that mandatory service entailed involuntary servitude in violation of the Thirteenth Amendment (Portner, 1994). Ultimately, the Supreme Court, without comment, upheld the school district's right to require community service (Jackson, 1997).
- The Supreme Court ruled 6–3 that student-led prayer at football games was unconstitutional, but in his dissent Chief Justice William Rehnquist charged that the majority opinion "bristles with hostility to all things religious in public life" (quoted in Mauro, 2000, para. 8). During the following fall, an observer noted that "students and parents all over the Bible Belt are spontaneously engaging in prayer in the stands" (Anderson, 2000, para. 1).
- Lawsuits have been filed in a dozen states, as school officials challenge spending plans that don't provide fair and adequate funding. A Kansas Supreme Court decision declaring that system unconstitutional has Missouri legislators nervous about the fiscal constraints and responsibilities this may place on them (Wiese, 2005).
- Rabbi Harold Kushner, author of *When Bad Things Happen to Good People*, talked to the 2001 annual meeting of the Association for Supervision and Curriculum Development about the most important of all educational goals: teaching children to be decent people. One key is for teachers to transform classrooms into "sacred places" where every child learns she or he has something unique to offer ("*The Classroom as Sacred Space*," 2001).
- The high-profile report issued by the National Commission on Teaching & America's Future (1996) set a goal not just for having a competent and qualified teacher in every U.S. classroom by 2006, but rather a "competent, *caring* and qualified teacher" (p. 21; emphasis added).
- As part of a reform agenda to increase standards in dress, behavior, and achievement, the Long Beach Unified School District in 1994 became the first large urban public school district to mandate school

uniforms for its elementary and middle schools. In the next 5 years, the crime rate dropped 86% and attendance reached an all-time high on the K–8 school campuses (Zernike, 2002).

- UNESCO, the United Nations Educational, Scientific, and Cultural Organization, has taken steps since September 11, 2001, to assist schools in countries throughout the world in implementing a world-centered curriculum in order to encourage a "culture of peace" (Perkins-Gough, Lindfors, & Ernst, 2002). For the same reason, a fourth-grade teacher in Florida sets up videoconferences between her students and children in other countries (McGoogan, 2002).

These recent developments are each part of the multifaceted, politically complex, and morally rich territory that is contemporary schooling. Before looking in detail at the ideas and efforts of those who strive to make the moral dimensions of schooling visible and explicit, we turn in Chapter 2 to outlining conceptual tools to make sense of the landscape.

2

Constructing the Categories

In the Introduction, we made use of the metaphor of mapping terrain in explaining our task. Our point is not that schooling as a moral endeavor is totally unexplored territory or even that interest in this dimension of schooling is new. From its roots, American schooling has had an explicitly moral aspect and that aspect has generated regular comment. Today, as the discussion in the prior chapter suggests, there is a renewed, substantial, and quite varied interest in educational matters from a moral perspective. Still, the moral contours of schooling remain largely invisible to those navigating its pathways on a daily basis as teachers, students, administrators, parents, policymakers, and researchers; those contours are neither named nor recognized as moral.

Our mapping is intended to make these moral contours visible. In particular, we hope (1) to mark the signs, the common concerns and questions, that guide those who do attend to the moral dimensions of teaching and learning, (2) to enable those who pursue the path toward *students'* moral development to attend as well to those features of the educational landscape related to other dimensions of schooling as moral, and (3) to indicate the ways in which the moral and the academic are correlative features of the topography of schooling. By making the moral contours of schooling visible, as we argued in the Introduction, we hope to create the basis for productive engagement over the role of the moral in schooling.

In this chapter, we offer a set of categories—categories based on possible relations between moral and academic concerns—that we believe are useful in making the moral visible. We begin our articulation of these categories by first examining what might be meant, and what we mean, by the terms *moral* and *academic*. That discussion raises questions about politics, religion, and cultural diversity in relation to the moral in schooling. After acknowledging the power of those concerns, we explain why we chose to develop a category scheme and how we understand the use of these categories in an analysis of this kind. On that foundation, we characterize each of the five categories noted in the Introduction; that is, we specify our claim that the relationship between the academic and the moral in schooling can be understood as SEPARATE, SEQUENTIAL, DOMINANT, TRANSFORMATIVE, or INTEGRATED. We close the chapter with a brief discussion of our personal presuppositions about all of this.

MEANING IN USE: THE MORAL AND THE ACADEMIC

Most readers will assume that the meaning of the moral is controversial. This is partly because the meaning of *moral* is confused with various systems of morality and partly because the meaning of *moral* is itself ambiguous in ways that we discuss below. Readers generally will not assume that the academic is similarly controversial, but we submit that it is just as contentious and as contestable as the moral. When either term is used with reference to schooling, a speaker's meaning cannot be reliably assumed.

Note that throughout this work, we refer to the moral rather than to morality and to the academic rather than to academics. Both *morality* and *academics* have taken-for-granted meanings that we do not intend. *Morality* is often thought to refer to a particular community's code of conduct or set of values. *Academics* suggests the particular basic skills and curricular content linked to successful performance on various standardized tests.

In contrast, we use the moral and the academic as broadly constructed analytic concepts that *include* rather than exclude the variety of contemporary responses to being good and being smart in the context of schooling. For our purposes, the moral encompasses any effort to achieve the right relation with others and the world through action, to (inter)act in ways that make sense out of self and life; the academic involves attempts to create common understanding, to come to know what others know. Specific visions of the right relation and the curricula of common understanding can be either mutually constructed, involuntarily imposed, and/or personally chosen, and they are, of course, always subject to dispute and debate. For us, the moral encompasses the constraints of social mores, the ethical codes of the dominant religious traditions, the virtues of democratic functioning, the demands of social justice, and the primacy of the person's identity and integrity; the academic includes rigorous content standards, curricular scope and sequence, critical thinking, communication skills as codes of power, habits of mind, and great ideas. In brief, the moral is taken to be the domain of what is worth doing and the academic the domain of what is worth knowing. Value is implicated in both terms.

We acknowledge that this broad construction may have the effect of blurring the putative line between the academic and the moral. Substance and procedure are contestable in both. That the two can be regarded as separate, as integrated, and as linked in various ways are all doors we want to leave open as we construct our working definitions. What justifies our doing this? Such an inclusive starting point is suggested by the range of everyday language in use in schools and about schooling.

Students and teachers engage in conversations that count as moral throughout the school day:

> "I am so happy to see Amy and Peter sitting quietly, ready to begin our math lesson."
> "Mrs. Quinn, Brendan is pulling my hair."
> "Boys and girls, this is a wonderful story about friendship, isn't it?"
> "OK, kids, knock it off; sit down and let's get to work."
> "We have a problem. It seems that someone has taken Emily's calculator. Can anyone help us out?"
> "Why did the settlers treat the Indians that way? It doesn't seem fair."
> "Students who plagiarize the work of others will automatically receive a failing grade."
> "Let's all rise and recite together the Pledge of Allegiance."
> "Please show respect for the person who is speaking by listening carefully and then responding."
> "Whose responsibility is it to clean up in the lab?"

In each instance, an implied form of right relation is at stake. Some of the statements commend action-in-relation to teachers, peers, tasks, or others; others note the failure to act consonant with implied relation. In each instance, a sense-making frame of value and response is at work.

Similarly, school handbooks and course guidelines regularly offer moral directives and exhortations, couched in language that may or may not be recognizably moral:

> "Students are expected to act courteously and respect others at all times."
> "We encourage all students to be on time, to complete their work diligently, and treat all school personnel with care."
> "Drug and alcohol use on school grounds will result in immediate expulsion."
> "Our school community will only function well if all members demonstrate our core values of honesty, respect, and responsibility."

Despite the regular use of moral language *in* schools, it is often avoided when debating issues *about* schooling. Rather than *moral language*—that is, language that indicates or calls for right relation through action—we encounter *language about morality*. Consider this small but representative sampling:

> "Whose morals?"
>
> "There hasn't been any morality in school since prayer was banished."
>
> "Kids today need character, and they aren't getting it at home."
>
> "The entire school system is unfair and inequitable. It's just not right that rich kids get better schooling than poor kids."
>
> "Teachers are role models; students learn appropriate behavior from their teachers."
>
> "Actually, students can learn from conflict with each other, but first we should train them in communication and conflict resolution skills so that disagreements can be handled constructively."
>
> "Discipline is the key to effective schooling. Any failure to adhere to the rules must result in consequences."
>
> "Students will flourish in learning communities where they learn to respect one another and themselves."
>
> "Our policy on violence and on drug use is zero tolerance."

Note the shift in terminology. Moral language (the language of relation and action) is replaced by language about morality (a language of judgment with widely varying referents). The moral elicits morals, morality, prayer, character, inequity, right and wrong, role models, appropriate behavior, conflict, communication, conflict resolution, discipline, rules and consequences, community, respect, and zero tolerance, but none of these terms are synonyms for *moral*. Rather, they all mark moral territory in different ways. They sound more or less neutral. They are more or less linked to religious, spiritual, political, or ideological stances. They are more or less hopeful about the prospects for moral progress. They imply more or less external control, greater or lesser personal responsibility.

Scholarly reflection on the moral dimensions in human living, both within and beyond school walls, yields similar tensions. For some, the moral is a matter of constraint on one's liberty; for others, it is the source of liberation. For some, the moral demands certainty; for others, it calls forth ambiguity. For some, the moral is a matter of free will; for others, it is beyond will, even determined. For some, the moral is inextricably linked to religious faith; for others, religious faith impedes moral flourishing. For some, the moral is woven into human nature; for others, human nature makes the moral necessary and difficult. For a very long time, we have thought of the moral as something that resided in individual persons, indeed as a measure of a person; of late, some have thought of the moral as a function of persons in (sociocultural) interaction, in fact, as a quality of that interaction.

For all, the moral is devilishly difficult to pin down. This may be, as Robert Nash suggests in *Real World Ethics* (2002), because there is more than one kind of moral language in operation. Nash describes three: (1) the language of background beliefs (foundational questions about unprovable sources of moral authority), (2) the language of moral character (the intuitions, settings, and narratives that define who we are), and (3) the language of moral principle (the abstractions—rules, principles, ethical theories—that serve as a basis for judging right and wrong). He maintains that we run into rhetorical difficulty with the moral because we confuse various sorts of questions and the terminology we use to answer those questions.

But Nash's distinction, helpful though it is, provides no final answer to the question of what *moral* means. That there are multiple moral languages suggests that there are multiple versions of the moral. There is the version that asks what life is for; there is the version that asks who I am (who we are); and there is the version that asks what I (we) should do. And Nash's analysis is itself caught in a moral philosophical frame that assumes that judgment and meaning are functions of external authority, individual character, and deontological obedience.

In *Bastard Out of Carolina* (1992), Dorothy Allison brings us back to the idea of a sense-making frame of value and response articulated earlier. She recounts a discussion between protagonist Ruth Ann (known as Bone) and her Mama. Bone "got religion" and her various aunts and uncles were speculating about the role of religion in "doing the right thing." Mama, "who almost never went to church, but [who] took God and most issues of faith absolutely seriously," replies: "People don't do right because of the fear of God or love of him. You do the right thing because the world doesn't make sense if you don't. God doesn't have much to do with it" (Allison, 1992, p. 145).

In this brief statement, Allison, through her character Mama, brings Nash's three moral languages together in a way that Nash's own analysis could not. The moral is the domain of human (inter)action. The critical element is not "the right thing" (either as the content of a principle or the consequence-causing act) but "doing right" in a way that "makes sense," constructing the sense of who I am in response to others and the world as it presents itself to me. Thus it is understandable that for some a moral stance seems rooted in religious practice, for their making sense resides there. It is understandable that for some a moral stance seems rooted in a political vision or in ideological commitments, for their making sense resides there. It is understandable that for some a moral stance seems rooted in a spiritual sensibility, for their making sense resides there. But for all—for teachers and students in schools and for those who talk about schooling—the moral is about making sense of our lives through interaction. It is the domain of what is worth doing.

This is the meaning of *moral* with which we begin this project of survey and analysis. We offer a meaning—tentative and hypothetical—that allows us to begin without excluding any of those potential exemplars of the moral as it appears with regard to schooling.

If the moral is the domain of what's worth doing, what meaning of *academic* can be hypothesized that would similarly include the range of possibilities present in the contemporary landscape of schooling? We developed a view of the meaning of *moral* by looking first at the languages that operate in the domain. What are the languages that operate with respect to things academic?

We start with the different languages employed by those who are the primary participants in the process of schooling, students and teachers. When speaking *about* their work, teachers speak of objectives, of lessons, of strategies, of assessment, of standards, of learning, of skills, of concepts, and so on. When speaking *about* their work, students speak of reading the chapter, of passing the test, of completing the project, of writing papers, of going to recess, of moving on to fifth grade, of graduating, and so forth. This listing suggests that the academic is a coordinated process involving goals, strategies, and achievement or failure. That characterization of the academic, though not wrong, seems incomplete. What is the language used by teachers and students *in* their work? Is it any different? Any more revealing of what academic means?

"What do you mean, Joanie, when you say that bats are our friends?"

"Mr. Thomas, do I start my name with a big letter or a small one?"

"If I have two pencils and you have two pencils, how many do we have all together?"

"Please copy your homework from the side board."

"Mrs. Martin, we all read about Thomas Jefferson but we're confused. How he could say that 'all men are created equal' and still own slaves?"

"Now that we've talked about what a democracy is, what difference do you think it would make if the people in our country never went to vote?"

"Does everybody understand what happened when you heated the water? Did the sugar go away?"

"You will complete your research paper in stages; first, the investigation and notetaking, then the outline, then the rough draft, then the final draft."

"Do we have to know the names of all the characters in *Romeo and Juliet* for the test?"

Some of the statements and questions above speak to processes of teaching and learning that we routinely characterize as academic. Still, something more is evident, even primary. It is the pursuit of common understanding. In many cases in school, the student is led to re-create the teacher's understanding; in other cases, the creation of common understanding is a mutual effort. Both the process of the academic pursuit and the nature of the understanding sought are contestable and are in fact widely contested today by school reformers, researchers, and policymakers.

> "Standards-based education will ensure that every child will have the tools to succeed in the 21st century."
>
> "Let's begin our planning for instruction by identifying the 'big ideas,' the 'enduring understandings' we want our students to make their own."
>
> "Drill and practice of basic skills remain the cornerstone of effective education."
>
> "'Habits of mind' ought to be our focus in schooling. If young people develop appropriate habits of mind, knowledge of specific facts and ideas will follow."
>
> "There is 'core knowledge,' a set of references, facts, and skills that all must have to participate in a democratic society."
>
> "Education is for liberation, for freeing human beings to think and act critically in the world. Such an education begins with and works through the experience of the student."

Here again we see suggested processes of goals, strategies, and achievement. In each case, particular goals imply specific strategies and indicators of success. The academic covers a broad territory from basic skills through core knowledge to enduring understandings and habits of mind. For some, the boundaries of the academic are stretched almost beyond recognition to images of liberation. In each case, as in the language of teachers and students in schools, the academic is about the creation of some common understanding and the processes that get us there. It is about coming to know what others know. It is the domain of what's worth knowing.

Thus we begin our effort to make the moral visible in American schooling by sketching the outlines of both central educational domains. The moral—interaction seeking the right relation—will become recognizable against the background of the academic. The academic is the creation of common understanding and the processes that lead us there. We use both *moral* and *academic* here in a deconstructive temper; that is, we acknowledge the power of these terms—as typically used and putatively understood with reference to schooling—but also use them in analysis in such a way that their meaning and usefulness will be called into question.

Note that *academic* and *moral* as we have set out their meanings are not opposites, although they are sometimes used that way. This may be because they are associated with other pairs of supposedly binary terms: *cognitive* and *affective, intellectual* (reason) and *spiritual* (revelation), *science* and *religion, thought* and *action, mind* and *body, fact* and *value*. These other pairs of terms have their roots and particular usefulness in discourses—psychological, philosophical, theological—that are not specific to schooling. We will not make use of these related distinctions here. Rather we focus on *academic* and *moral* because they are terms that can be generated directly out of an educational intention. Education is about doing, making sense, shared understanding, and a sense of progress or development. We make no claims initially about whether and how the academic and the moral are related in the process of contemporary schooling. Nor do we claim that they are distinct domains. To determine the nature of the domains and their relationship is the task of our analysis.

WHY THE MORAL RAISES A RED FLAG

We asserted earlier that both *academic* and *moral* are contestable concepts. *Academic* not only refers to the traditional school subjects; it also prompts talk of habits of mind, big ideas, codes of power, and even human liberation. *Moral* not only refers to the Ten Commandments; it also generates thinking about social justice, the nature of community, systems of values, and the power of politics.

However, the use of the term *moral* in relation to schooling raises a red flag that typically is not engendered when the term *academic* is employed. What is and is not at stake? Why is it that the presence of the academic is taken for granted while the presence of the moral is suspect? One can make a reasonable historical case that the moral was the controlling interest in the creation and development of schooling from the Puritans' Satan Deluder Acts, to Mann's common school, to the proliferation of parochial schools (Roman Catholic in the early part of the 20th century and conservative Christian in the latter part of the same century), to the popularity of homeschooling in recent years.

Why, then, do we hesitate to speak directly and respond forthrightly to the moral contours of any educational endeavor? Three related factors seem significant. All three have roots in the American experience of diversity and in the peculiarly American tension between individual liberty and social control. All three also reflect an abiding respect for parental prerogatives in the moral domain. The first is a fear of values indoctrination and of the controversies that accompany this danger. The second is a respect for the differentiation between church and state. The third is a recognition that both cultural diversity and national identity are at stake in schools as public, democratic institutions. We consider each factor briefly.

The Danger of Indoctrination

An American culture built on an Enlightenment heritage and a capitalist economic vision relies on individual autonomy and personal responsibility. Indoctrination, teaching in such a way as to ensure a partisan or sectarian point of view, undercuts both autonomy and responsibility. In order to minimize the possibility of indoctrination, educators often go to the extreme of eliminating anything that might be construed as partisan or sectarian. This is based in part on another legacy from the Enlightenment: a fact–value split in our "folk (epistemological) theory."

The "man on the street" believes that there are facts and there are values. The facts are public, demonstrable, and capable of being shared by all; the values are private, personally determined, and individually held. Even those who believe that their values are certain and given by divine revelation (as in the case of the Judeo-Christian revelation of the Ten Commandments) tend to make use, in informal conversation, of a fact–value distinction. Efforts to appeal to democratic values or commonly held values typically do not overcome this firmly and uncritically held view. Facts are academic; values are moral. Schools deal in facts, not values. Therefore, the academic is in; the moral is out.

Our folk epistemological theory distinguishing fact and value is loosely linked to a similarly simplistic view of the political as partisan. Politics may be broadly understood as the art of the possible, but that is not how we usually think about it. When someone refers to politics, most assume the reference is to partisan conflict. We think of Republicans and Democrats, about conservatives and liberals, about right wing and left wing. This kind of politics is thought to be about value-laden judgments and about winning others over to one's own point of view. Although we have come to understand that "the personal is political," that interest-group conflict is enacted in schooling, and that "facts" embody perspectives—all insights that point to schooling as a thoroughly political activity—we are loath to open any door to indoctrination by those who act in an obviously partisan manner.

Just as we take for granted the need to safeguard our own moral and political autonomy, so, too, do we guard our religious autonomy. Most would agree with the "new consensus" reached by education groups led by the First Amendment Center at the University of Virginia that "religion must be taught objectively or neutrally; it must be the purpose of public schools to educate students about a variety of religious traditions, not to indoctrinate them into any particular tradition" (Haynes, 1998, p. 6). Nonetheless, educators have responded in the extreme, avoiding the issue and choosing to teach as if religion were unimportant if not nonexistent. A fear of indoctrination and a fear of controversy often lead to a narrower view of what schooling can tackle or accomplish. This will be discussed further in the next section.

The moral raises a red flag in part because the moral—and its political and religious variants—raises the specter of indoctrination. There is no more inherent controversy about moral matters than about academic matters. Both are controversial, as the lively contemporary debate between standards advocates and inquiry advocates attests. But the academic usually is not associated with indoctrination, whereas the moral often is.

The Uncertain Relation of Church and State

Another equally potent source of concern about introducing moral language and moral deliberation into public schooling is the difficult relationship between church and state, especially after *Engel v. Vitale* (1962). The Supreme Court's decision to disallow organized, compulsory prayer in public schools has been viewed by many as a decision to open the schools to disorder and immorality. Despite the Court's clear statement permitting the academic study of religion in *Engel* and in *Abington v. Schempp* (1963), and despite subsequent Court decisions allowing voluntary, student-organized prayer in specific circumstances, some people are concerned that less prayer in schools has resulted in widespread misbehavior, lowered achievement, diminished respect, and increasing violence.

The myriad fears associated with *Engel* and the long line of divisive Court decisions over the past 40 years have impaired our ability to engage in a reasoned discussion of the moral in relation to schooling, at least public schooling. Religious issues of emotion and commitment intrude precisely because for many the moral does implicate religious faith and practice. That this is so is not surprising; what is noteworthy, if not surprising, is how much trouble we have addressing the religious dimensions of the academic. The religious dimensions of academic subjects only rarely register on the public radar. Even when religious matters do receive academic attention (e.g., the study of John Milton's poetry or the Puritans' political practices), their nature *as religious* is often obscured. This is so despite the Supreme Court's explicit attention to academic and religious links in *Abington*.

If *Abington* made it clear that teaching about religion as part of a secular program of education was permissible and perhaps even desirable, *Epperson v. Arkansas* (1968) made it just as clear that teaching about secular ways of understanding such as evolution could not be banned. Moreover, in *Edwards v. Aguillard* (1987), the Court stipulated that a state could not require a "balanced approach" to creation science and evolution when the requirement's purpose was religious. Behind all three decisions—as well as the more recent Ten Commandments decisions (*McCreary County v. ACLU of Kentucky* [2005]; *VanOrden v. Perry* [2005]—is the notion of secular intent. When the intent of a policy is at least partly secular (i.e., academic), the policy is permissible. Religious intent does not defeat a policy, but *solely* religious intent does so.

The Establishment Clause of the First Amendment requires that the state adopt a stance of neutrality toward religion in general and among various religious sects. Neutrality has long been interpreted as separation, borrowed perhaps from Jefferson's phrase about the "wall of separation" between church and state. But such an interpretation of neutrality is simplistic. The key to neutrality is not separation but critical consideration. One is neutral when *any* interesting and important worldview is open for consideration and all are subject to the same generous but critical consideration.

In 1988, a broad coalition of 17 major religious and educational organizations issued "Religion in the Public School Curriculum: Questions and Answers." That statement articulating a "new consensus" about the appropriate place of religion in schooling is rooted in an understanding of neutrality as careful, critical consideration (Nord & Haynes, 1998). While religious groups and educational leaders agreed to this view almost two decades ago, its tenets have not been widely incorporated into teaching practice. This is partly because of the taken-for-granted view of church and state (i.e., public school) as separated by a wall, partly because of the continuing fears of indoctrination discussed above, and partly because teachers are themselves not prepared to teach about religion in knowledgeable and morally neutral ways. Because the moral is held hostage by its links to religious belief and practice, any consideration of the moral in public school settings is presumed to breach the church–state wall. To many, such a breach seems impermissible.

Cultural Diversity and National Identity

Fear of indoctrination is rooted in a respect for individual freedom of choice and action. Maintaining a wall of separation between church and state is grounded in a desire to protect persons and groups from government interference and to preserve public space from the control of particular groups. The third influence shaping our hesitance to speak the language of the moral in public school settings stems from a similarly complex challenge: the fact of cultural diversity in the face of a need for national identity. A focus on diversity raises the specter of moral relativism under the guise of group rights.

An emphasis on national identity opens the door to an imposition of the beliefs and practices of the dominant culture.

Multicultural education is the term used to designate efforts to take cultural diversity seriously in school. Many multiculturalists want to expand the idea of what it means to be an American and are inclined to think about cultural diversity within the context of a broad set of common values. Other proponents of multicultural education fear that a focus on common values inevitably privileges *dominant* values. Moreover, multiculturalists are associated in the public eye with those who practice identity politics; that is, with those who argue that cultural markers (including race and ethnicity, but also class, gender, sexual orientation, etc.) are elemental to persons' and groups' identity and ought to be prioritized, preserved, and respected.

Prioritizing cultural diversity opens the door to varied cultural mores. One might think that such openness would lead to direct, comparative discussion of the moral. However, the American tendency toward tolerance tends to put culturally based behaviors beyond moral judgment and even foster "political correctness." In its simple-minded caricature, one who is politically correct withholds all judgment and is critical of those who make any moral judgments. Moral relativism is implied; moral silence is the norm.

While some support multicultural education as a fitting response to the fact of cultural diversity, others fear that "the disuniting of America"—to use Arthur Schlesinger Jr.'s phrase—may result from highlighting such diversity. Schlesinger (1998) asserts:

> Those intrepid Europeans who had torn up their roots to brave the wild Atlantic *wanted* to forget a horrid past and to embrace a hopeful future. They *yearned* to become Americans. Their goals were escape, deliverance, assimilation. They saw America as a transforming nation, banishing dismal memories and developing a unique national character based on common political ideals and shared experiences. The point of America was not to preserve old cultures, but to produce a new *American* culture. (p. 17; emphasis in original)

The "eruption of ethnicity," Schlesinger's characterization of the cultural diversity movement, has had positive consequences in calling Americans back to the universal application of their own principles, but Schlesinger also sees destructive consequences in construing America as a nation of groups, not of individuals.

Schlesinger and others may well be right that there has been an identifiable American identity and that this sense of common identity has been both intentional and effective. Yet this historical "fact" does not necessarily dictate that what has been the national identity can or should ground common efforts *now*. To appeal to assimilation, some past sense of identity, is to raise the threat of cultural imposition. Ironically, both a focus on diversity and an emphasis on national identity have the potential to open up the moral conversation by highlighting beliefs, values, and cultural practices. Yet the backlash in response to each (the cry of "politically correct" and accusation of "cultural imposition") leads to masking the moral.

UNCOVERING THE MORAL

Despite our fears of indoctrination, despite our respect for a church–state division, despite our competing desires for cultural diversity and national identity, the moral dimensions of educating the next generation remain. We turn here to uncovering those dimensions of American schooling.

Today's "moral revival" is the predictable result of the events of the past 40 years. When the Supreme Court ruled that state-sponsored prayer in public schools was unconstitutional, educators responded by rendering all religious references suspect. When that happened, many citizens (including parents and teachers) feared that the moral exited schools as well. At about the same time, parallel movements for civil rights and a new wave of immigration spotlighted cultural diversity, bringing different mores to school communities. Just as educators were downplaying elements of "traditional moral inculcation" in favor of a focus on "rigorous" academic programs, values and practices of nondominant cultures entered to complicate the picture. Some educators tried to bring the moral back in a neutral form through values clarification or instruction in moral reasoning or democratic community building, usually with limited success. The truth is that nobody ever removed the moral from schools; it could not be done. The moral was just covered up, obscured from view, couched in the language of classroom management and discipline, in the structure of teaching strategies like cooperative learning or learning communities, or in the practices of standardized testing. The moral contours of schooling have been rendered invisible.

Here we uncover those moral contours, as others have been trying to do for the past two decades, and replace the moral alongside the academic. The framework we offer is grounded in the reality of schooling and its purposes—academic and moral—not in moral philosophy or in social psychology or in political theory or in religious sectarianism, though all of these may be relevant to a full consideration of the issues. We employ the moral and the academic as conceptual anchors for a category system that will allow survey and analysis of the contemporary terrain. Both survey and analysis are intended to support constructive engagement across religious, political, and ideological lines around the questions and issues prompted when the moral is made visible.

CONSTRUCTING THE CATEGORIES

We begin our survey of the contemporary terrain where the moral and schooling overlap by stating three dimensions of concern and follow that by delineating five categories of action and articulation, that is, five typical responses
by educators when they realize that the moral and schooling go together.
This final statement of categories is more straightforward than was the process of their creation. The three dimensions are analytic constructs that we
identified as we tried to categorize various available programs, policy statements, school designs, research reports, curriculum proposals, and theoretical essays. We proposed categories, categorized educational efforts, ran
into pitfalls, reworked the logic of the categories, altered the categories,
recategorized, and so on, working back and forth until the categories took
final shape and the dimensions that differentiated the various categories were
clear.

It is important to acknowledge that the programs and views discussed
in the central part of this book existed prior to the creation of our categories. The educators who authored these efforts never categorized their own
approaches in this way and, in fact, only rarely articulated any sense that
there might be alternative ways of living out the moral/schooling overlap.
This is precisely our proximate purpose: to lay bare some clear differences
between and among approaches to moral/schooling and to articulate the
assumptions, implicit though they may be, that underlay these efforts. Un-
articulated assumptions block clear communication. Under conditions of
racial, ethnic, religious, and political diversity, effective communication—
about both academic and moral dimensions of schooling—is complicated but
crucial if we are to achieve our ultimate goal; that is, if we are to reclaim
schooling as a moral endeavor.

Let us make clear that our categorizing does not match the usual ways
of thinking about the moral in schooling. For example, political ideology is
not an organizing principle for our categorizing. Neither is religious belief,
faith stance, or moral source. Neither is race, class, or gender. In fact, we
view this as a strength of our way of making sense of present moral/school-
ing efforts. Persons across the contemporary political spectrum, across faith
lines, across moral philosophies, and across cultural categories actually share
a similar range of responses to the moral/schooling challenge. And we hope
our set of categories will facilitate communication about the moral in schooling among those who often end up in warring camps.

Neither do our categories differentiate those whose primary interest is
moral education from those who are more broadly interested in the moral
dimensions of schooling. As you will see, programs explicitly devoted to students' moral development are grouped with research that blurs the bound-

aries of the moral and the academic and with instructional prescriptions that view every aspect of teaching and learning as moral.

What distinguishes the five types of responses we have discerned? To answer that, we focus on the relationship between what is, in ordinary language, referred to as "the academic" and what is referred to as "the moral." In daily parlance, the academic identifies those elements of educational practice and product linked to knowledge and skill, and the moral identifies those elements of educational practice and product linked to right action and the good. As discussed above, we have chosen to rely on still broader meanings as we begin this project. The academic involves the creation of common understanding; the moral seeks the right relation, doing "the right thing because the world doesn't make sense if you don't." Whether this distinction can be (or ever is) actualized is a complex educational philosophical question and one we will not address at this juncture. What we do know is that the distinction is firmly lodged in our folk theory of education, and we will rely on it initially to make sense of the various efforts to articulate the moral dimensions of schooling. We turn then to the three dimensions of concern that distinguish our categories, casting these dimensions as questions:

3 dimensions that distinguish categories.

First, what is the *degree of connection* between the academic and the moral in the educational effort or view?   *tight or loose*

Second, what is the *nature of the relationship*, if any, between the academic and the moral in the educational effort or view? *linking or blending*

Third, which of the elements—the academic or the moral—is the *moving force* in the effort or view?

The observant reader will notice immediately that these dimensions, while distinguishable, are not discrete.

The connection between the academic and the moral can be tight, loose, or nonexistent, that is, a continuum. When there is a relationship between the two, that connection may be a linking or a blending. In both types of connection, one element may obscure or alter the other. One appears to move or drive the relationship, to motivate action, to guide decisions; the other appears less important, more malleable.

These questions enable us to place contemporary discussions of *moral/education* into one of five categories (Table 2.1):

Separate

In this approach, schooling is viewed as the sum of distinguishable academic and moral goals, practices, and results. Neither focus takes precedence over the other. Each operates in an important but independent manner. It is

Table 2.1. The Categories

Category	Defined	Degree of Connection Between Academic and Moral	Nature of Relationship Between Academic and Moral	Moving Force (academic or moral as key to action)	Exemplar
SEPARATE	No interface between moral and academic	None	Discrete domains	Independent	Edward Wynne's *Character Education*
SEQUENTIAL	Moral precedes academic or vice versa	Loose	Linked sequentially	Moral when moral precedes academic; academic when academic precedes moral	Boys Town Program (moral moving force) Adler's *Paideia Proposal* (academic moving force)
DOMINANT	Moral dominates academic or vice versa	Loose	Linked substantively	Moral when moral dominates academic; academic when academic dominates moral	Lancaster Catholic High School (moral moving force) E. D. Hirsch's Core Knowledge Project (academic moving force)
TRANSFORMATIVE	Moral transforms academic or vice versa	Tight	Blended sequentially and substantively	Moral when moral transforms academic; academic when academic transforms moral	Nel Noddings's Centers of Care (moral moving force) Ted Sizer's Coalition of Essential Schools (academic moving force)
INTEGRATED	Moral and academic transform each other	Tight	Blended substantively	Dialectical	Central Park East Secondary School

possible for an academically proficient student to be morally lacking and vice versa. It is also possible for teachers and schools to function in a morally praiseworthy manner but to be academically inept. Much of what goes by the rubric of "character education" belongs in this category. So do many service learning programs. Recent attention to educators' professional ethics is also a variant of this tendency to separate the teachers' pedagogical performance from the ethical issues that may intrude.

Sequential

This stance also acknowledges that educational efforts require attention to both the moral and the academic, but here these two domains, though distinguishable, are related to one another in a sequential way. That is, attention to one precedes and is instrumental to attention to the other. This view has two variants.

The more common is MORAL FIRST. The moral is viewed as the precondition or prerequisite for the academic. There is a link between the two in that without students' moral development, academic success is impossible. The moral comes first in order of action but is both instrumental to and separate from academic purposes and projects. Once some level of moral order and/or moral development is achieved, full attention can be paid to the demands of the academic. Joseph Gauld's Hyde School represents this perspective, as does the Boys Town Model.

Conceptually possible, but not prevalent in contemporary discussion, is ACADEMIC FIRST. Mortimer Adler's *Paideia Proposal* (1982) is the best exemplar of this type of thinking we were able to identify. Some educational critics articulate positions that seem to fit this subcategory, suggesting that careful attention to academic matters makes moral ends possible. However, they stray from a sequential view because the emphasis on the academic does not simply precede and facilitate an emphasis on the moral. Rather, the academic either dominates the educational space, making specific attention to the moral unnecessary, or becomes part of an educational vision that explicitly integrates the academic and the moral (see below).

Dominant

The moral and the academic constitute distinguishable sets of concerns, both relevant to education but clearly not occupying equal educational space or demanding equal attention. The dominant element is the focus of theoretical and practical effort; the dominated element, though not dispensable, calls forth no particular effort, no careful examination. Views in this category can be differentiated from SEPARATE views by virtue of the imbalance of importance between the two categories and the relative dependence of one on the other; DOMINANT views can be differentiated from SEQUENTIAL views in that the elements are not linked instrumentally but subordinated one to the other. DOMINANT views come in two variants.

The first is MORAL DOMINANT. That which is moral matters more than that which is academic. The constant here is the dominance of moral concerns and the desire to state those concerns clearly and to maintain their priority over academic demands. The dominance can be so complete that academic concerns are actually subsumed into moral ones. Many parochial schools, some critical theorists, and educators who focus on multicultural awareness, though not usually seen as obvious allies, take a similarly MORAL DOMINANT approach. As we shall see, the nature of the moral expands in this category to incorporate power relations (sometimes relegated to the political domain) and interpersonal understanding (sometimes relegated to the cultural domain) as well as religiously grounded systems of morality.

The second variant is ACADEMIC DOMINANT. In the realm of educational action, that which is academic matters more than that which is moral. Educators whose views fit this subcategory remain persistently focused on the academic goals and processes of schooling. The moral matters, even to the extent of providing justification for an academic focus, but the academic so commands center stage that the moral can get lost in the shadows. Or perhaps it is more accurate to suggest that the academic takes up so much space that it envelops moral considerations. E. D. Hirsch and Marva Collins are educators whose ACADEMIC DOMINANT approach is exemplified in a wide range of schools, inner city as well as privileged suburban and private settings.

Transformative

Positions, programs, and practices that can be categorized as TRANSFORMATIVE are marked by a significant melding or blending between the academic and the moral, but it is a blending that moves in one direction only, initiated by one element, imposed on the other. Either the moral or the academic can transform; either can be transformed. Thus we describe two variants of this category, the MORAL TRANSFORMATIVE and the ACADEMIC TRANSFORMATIVE.

In the MORAL TRANSFORMATIVE, the moral dimension is distinguishable from the academic, acting as a kind of leaven on the academic, altering its substance in clear and meaningful ways. While academic concerns matter, moral concerns matter more because they reshape the academic, making it what it ought to be. Thus the moral is the moving force, the boundary between the two is blurred, and the academic as a domain—that is, what counts as academic—is transformed. Nel Noddings's work on the caring curriculum is a premier example of this kind of approach.

The ACADEMIC TRANSFORMATIVE subcategory represents the same kind of transformation described above but with the domains switched; apparently, the academic can shape the parameters of the moral. This view is far less common, and we offer just one example—the work of Ted Sizer. Sizer's written explorations over the past 25 years express a view in which proper attention to the academic not only makes the moral possible but also makes the moral what it is and ought to be.

Integrated

In this approach, teaching and learning do not allow us to distinguish that which is moral from that which is academic except for purposes of analysis. Academic purposes have moral import; moral standards guide even activities that are clearly academic. Student–teacher relationships are utterly moral; they are also a critical piece in the puzzle of effective instruction. Curricula incorporate facts about the world, perspectives on those facts, and values that shape those perspectives. Classrooms are value-laden environments for learning. Lesson plans include this and not that. When push comes to shove, it is difficult to say that a particular element is moral but not academic or vice versa. The blending is bidirectional. The relationship between the academic and the moral is dialectical. In truth, the academic and moral elements are not really distinguishable. Debbie Meier and the staff of the Coalition of Essential Schools' Central Park East Secondary School and Landon Beyer and his students' democratic classrooms have developed programs that make it difficult to distinguish the academic and the moral. Philip Jackson, Robert Boostrom, and David Hansen, along with a number of other researchers and educational theorists, offer both descriptive and prescriptive analyses exemplifying this approach.

These are not five categories that can be tracked across a single line. In some sense, the first category, SEPARATE, might be seen as the opposite of the last category, INTEGRATED, but the categories in between do not fall neatly along a continuum. Both SEQUENTIAL and DOMINANT suggest separation more than integration, but the relationship between the moral and the academic is quite different in these two categories, and both categories are complicated by the fact that either element, the moral or the academic, can act as motive or moving force. TRANSFORMATIVE suggests integration more than separation but lacks the mutual effect assumed in INTEGRATED. And again, this category is complicated by two variants, one guided by moral concerns, the other by academic concerns. Clearly, today's calls for moral/schooling simply are not bounded by intellectual elegance or simplistic categorizing.

At this point, we remind the reader of a concern articulated in Chapter 1—that much of contemporary discussion about, research in, and theorizing on educational practice is cast in terms that never hint at the presence or importance of the moral. This is an oddly ahistorical view, given the clearly articulated concern with the moral goals of schooling from the Puritans through Horace Mann to today. It is a scientific, some might say positivistic, view, utilizing the kind of language that does not explicitly enable the moral dimensions of teaching and learning to be perceived. It also represents the assumption, not widely acknowledged consciously but nonetheless present in our language and our practice, that education is a matter of the head, not of the heart or spirit or soul. In what follows, we attend to those who *do* acknowledge the role of the heart, spirit, or soul in education, while admitting that much of what passes as educational discourse does not. We (re)search this terrain, now being mapped out by persons of differing cultural, political, and religious positions, looking for clues about how educators can and must respond if moral/schooling is not to become an oxymoron.

The survey that we undertake here will not be exhaustive. The good news is that many educators of goodwill have begun to theorize and practice moral/schooling over the past two decades; there are more examples than we can possibly characterize or categorize. We offer a sampling that we hope will reveal a pattern, but our sampling is not representative in terms of prevalence of views. Were we to sample based on frequency of incidence, character education efforts would dominate the landscape. Rather we sought out the range of possible responses at all levels of schooling. We looked for proposals and programs that were influential, that were distinctive, that represented ideological diversity, that gave voice to both religious and secular positions, that were the work of culturally diverse educators. We gave preference to exemplars that offered both proposal and program; that is, we looked not only for provocative ideas but also for their instantiation in the practice of schooling.

We acknowledge that there are proposals and programs that might be described as "eclectic," at least when considered vis-à-vis our categories. The state of Wisconsin's "Citizenship Initiative" and Thomas Lickona's "Center for the 4th and 5th R" are two such efforts that integrate the academic and the moral when practical and keep them separate when that works. We will describe those two examples briefly in Chapter 8 after the categories have become delineated. Only then will it make much sense to acknowledge their "eclecticism." For now, we recognize that in the next five chapters we highlight only examples of thinking and practice that seem to represent a distinctive way of thinking about the moral/academic relation.

We also note at the outset the perils of suggesting any taxonomy, any category system, for educational action. The "tyranny of categories" is well known; categories can be constructed purely as a heuristic device but fast become seemingly metaphysical realities. We seek to avoid that peril here by insisting from the start that our categories are not containers but characterizations. They are akin to Max Weber's (1949) ideal types, a mental construct that is analytic, not normative. We admit readily that our categories, our "types" of approaches, are conceptually pure and not found in reality in a similarly pure sense. We claim only that the kinds of thinking we outline conceptually are present in both discourse and action in the realm of contemporary schooling, and we use the exemplars to demonstrate that presence.

In other words, we use our categories in order to expose some features of actual responses to an existential educational challenge. We recognize that SEPARATE, SEQUENTIAL, DOMINANT, TRANSFORMATIVE, and INTEGRATED constitute one, admittedly limited, way of thinking about educational purposes. Indeed, *the moral* and *the academic* are themselves heuristic characterizations of human educational experience, not categories of existence. And so we proceed, but with caution, to make sense of contemporary efforts to see the moral in schooling and to see schooling as moral.

WHERE WE BEGAN

Given our earlier discussion about values, indoctrination, culture, perspective, and neutrality, it seems important that we clarify our own presuppositions about moral/schooling. This project grew out of our shared perception that schooling would be better—more effective, more focused, more educative, more true to its role in a democratic society—if its moral dimensions were clear, acknowledged, and available for scrutiny and reconstruction. We began our exploration here with significant sympathy for the understanding that the moral and the academic both matter. As educational theorists, we have found it difficult to separate the moral and the academic in conceptualizing the practice of teaching. That is, we leaned toward a view of the two dimensions as integrated in the practice of teaching. But we also began with a healthy skepticism, caused in part by linguistic constraints, about the "cash value" of an integrated view when seeking and offering practical guidance for teachers. The distinct terms *moral* and *academic* exist because they have served some purpose in the past. We ask what practical purpose they can continue to serve.

It is also important to acknowledge that we have been guided by a preference for democratic schooling, a preference that has at once moral and academic dimensions. We believe that schooling as an institution ought to be organized, insofar as possible, democratically. This does not mean that students have the same voice as teachers in instructional matters or in matters of conduct. Teachers have legitimate authority based on knowledge, expertise, judgment, and life experience that students cannot approximate. What it does mean is that every aspect of schooling—from student–teacher interactions and school behavior policies through school board deliberations and state funding decisions—ought to be reexamined for the possibility of extending its democratic operation. As John Dewey maintained more than a century ago, only students who experience democratic functioning will learn to function democratically. There is no better place than school—children's first, most pervasive public forum—for that to occur.

Finally, we began with a presumption of goodwill on the part of all who have put forward views of moral education and descriptions of the moral contours of teaching and learning. Starting with what Peter Elbow (1986) refers to as "methodological belief" (rather than "methodological doubt"), we present various views as valuable in their own terms, convinced that each of the approaches expressed by our categories has some substantive insight to offer to the broader public engagement regarding moral/schooling.

Each of the next five chapters focuses on one of the five categories. All five chapters have roughly the same structure. Each begins with some greater explication of the category than already provided and lists the exemplars to be described in the chapter. Each of the category exemplars is featured in a separate case in order to preserve the integrity of the program or proposal as offered. Descriptive cases typically are followed by a general discussion of the assumptions made by those who take that particular type of approach. As part of that general discussion, we consider the possibilities and dangers that seem common to approaches of that type. We turn now to concrete cases.

3

The SEPARATE Category

[handwritten margin note: character educ. service learning ethics of teaching]

In everyday conversation, we frequently speak of academic ability and moral character in a way that presumes these two endeavors are independent of each other. Apparently, a person can achieve academic excellence without any corresponding improvement in moral status or be academically unsuccessful but still good. We see no contradiction in characterizing a person as both bright and ruthless or as simple but good-hearted.

In this chapter, we identify three clusters of approaches to making the moral visible in schools—character education, service learning, and the ethics of teaching—that represent this disconnect and consider each in turn. We begin with a brief discussion of the three clusters in general and then provide specific programmatic examples.

"Character education" is, as noted in Chapter 1, an expression with both a broad and narrow focus in contemporary parlance. Broadly speaking, it suggests any contemporary effort at children's moral development (Lickona, 1991). More commonly and more narrowly, however, character education evokes the development of the individual child's character, typically through the inculcation of traditional (and fixed) moral values. Traditional values are expressed in behavioral form as virtues, and virtues are often taught through direct instruction. In fact, character education is sometimes taught as if it were a school subject in its own right. Allen Academy and the Heartwood Institute are offered as programmatic exemplars. The description of these two is preceded by a discussion of the thinking of two well-known advocates of character education narrowly construed: Edward Wynne and William Bennett.

Service learning is another morally motivated educational initiative that typically divides the academic from the moral. A widely accepted definition suggests that "service learning emerges from helping others and reflecting on how you and they benefited from doing so" (Howe, 1997, p. iv). In this way of thinking, the moral is the central element in service learning, and direct experience is the starting point for personal reflection. That is, service plus reflection results in learning of a moral kind.

In truth, this kind of experiential learning theory seems potentially powerful for both moral and academic goals. Indeed, some (e.g., Carter, 1997) argue that service learning is a useful way to regenerate the traditional academic curriculum by connecting school learning to the real world, by fostering interdisciplinary study, and by making abstract ideas more concrete. While not all proponents of service learning have a narrowly moral intent, it is the case that specific efforts to implement service learning commonly disconnect moral goals and experiences from academic ones (Coles, 1994; Williams, 1991). The examples we describe—the Maryland Service Learning requirement, St. Mark's Elementary School, and the Early Adolescent Helpers Program—illustrate the ways in which the moral and the academic tend to be separate, regardless of the intentions of service learning proponents.

Service learning and character education typically appeal to persons with different political leanings. Most versions of character education express goals in terms of a conservative set of virtues that stress the personal uprightness and integrity of the individual. Service learning evokes liberal associations. To be of service to others shifts the focus away from the development of individual character toward a sense of communal responsibility, a liberal but not critical stance.

The third and last "movement" included in this chapter studiously avoids association with any particular political orientation. Nor is its focus the development of students. Still, it is an effort to bring the moral dimensions of schooling to light. The term *ethics of teaching* refers to teachers' reflective consideration of the moral quality of their actions toward students as well as toward other teachers and, in some cases, toward the subject matter itself. We first characterize this cluster of efforts in general, particularly the tendency to view ethical considerations as an overlay on the academic aspects of teaching. We then describe two examples of this trend: Ken Strike and Jonas Soltis's long-lived and best-selling text *The Ethics of Teaching* (1985) and what might be characterized as the "standard approach" to teaching methods in teacher preparation programs. As both our general discussion and our exemplars suggest, the ethics of teaching can be, and usually is, considered apart from a teacher's attempts to create understanding.

We have not included any of the contemporary standards-based efforts to reform schools. In Chapter 1, we distinguished between efforts to make the moral visible in schooling and those that render the moral invisible. Our focus is on the former, on the full range of programs and proposals that make the moral visible. While the contemporary standards movement is a complex phenomenon driven by a range of motivations, its internal logic and public language are appropriately viewed as moral invisible. Therefore, the standards-based movement is not treated here.

[handwritten margin notes: Wynn: observable conduct / Bennett: character traits]

MAKING THE CASE FOR CHARACTER EDUCATION

The contemporary interest in character education that began in the late 1980s and bloomed all through the 1990s was preceded by a decade of articles and other writing on this topic. Perhaps the earliest and strongest proponent of character education was Edward Wynne, a professor of education at the University of Illinois at Chicago. Writing on the eve of *A Nation at Risk*, Wynne (1982) argued that we should stop dwelling on character education as entailing particular ideas and beliefs and focus instead on observable conduct. "Do students," he asked, "tell the truth under temptation, avoid vandalism, display tact and courtesy, practice generosity and charity, follow directions, attend school regularly, and come to class on time? If so, they are displaying good character" (p. 187).

At the same time, Wynne did express interest in academics. In a "For Character" school recognition program that he helped operate in Chicago in the 1980s, schools were rewarded when "students demonstrate high levels of positive conduct and academic effort" (Wynne, 1988, p. 425). However, the kinds of student conduct to be rewarded were linked only indirectly to academics, for example, being crossing guards, tutoring peers, raising funds for the school or community, participating in academic group projects and team competitions. The "academic" component in the school recognition program stressed personal effort and service to others rather than academic learning. Wynne, in fact, did not believe that conduct indicative of good character required that a student excel at academics. "All the student has to do is make a genuine effort" (p. 426). At times, Wynne implied that his vision of the academic was derived from his view of character, but he was quite insistent that schools give equal priority to character and academics. Under this condition of equal attention, "students have opportunities to succeed in either or both areas" (p. 426).

While Wynne worked hard to foster character education in the elementary and secondary schools, the person now most associated in the public's mind with character education is William J. Bennett. In contrast to Wynne's emphasis on observable conduct, Bennett stressed character traits. Originally the Secretary of Education during the Reagan presidency, Bennett published *The Book of Virtues* in 1993. He compiled dozens of stories from literature and history; each story was grouped with a virtue such as self-discipline, courage, perseverance, or faith. Although Bennett's book initially received a dismissive review in the *New York Times*, by 1994 *The Book of Virtues* was in its 14th printing and had sold over a million copies, and Bennett had become a "virtuecrat" (Fineman, 1994).

For Bennett, the moral and the academic are quite distinct domains, each separately worthy of attention. Prior to the publication of *The Book of Virtues*, Bennett was best known for his advocacy of a strongly academic curriculum. While he was Secretary of Education in the late 1980s, he had issued his vision of a strictly academic curriculum, a rigorous program of study called "James Madison High School."

More recently, however, Bennett has focused on character education, making the case for instilling the young with specific character traits. "Life is a moral endeavor," according to Bennett (1995). "Moral education," he continues, "must involve following rules of good behavior. It must involve developing good habits, which come only through repeated practice" (p. 12). The key is to raise our children *as moral and spiritual beings* by offering them unequivocal, reliable standards of right and wrong, noble and base, just and unjust" (p. 12; emphasis in original). Bennett (1993) believes this firm and clear approach is possible because most Americans "share a respect for certain fundamental traits of character: honesty, compassion, courage, and perseverance."

Determining the nature of such traits can be more difficult than Bennett seems to suggest. In examining two practical efforts to enact character education, we shall see that character educators do not always agree on the specific virtues and values to be highlighted. However, they do share Wynne's and Bennett's aversion to ethical relativism, as well as their commitment to helping students acquire a clear sense of right and wrong.

Allen Academy

An 1899-era brick schoolhouse in Dayton, Ohio, was renamed in 1989 as Allen Classical/Traditional Academy. This elementary school was to offer "a classical education in literature, the arts, and music" (Bernardo & Neal, 1997, p. 35). When named principal in early 1989, Rodolfo (Rudy) Bernardo became the third principal during that school year. Test scores were low, discipline problems common, and teachers' attendance the lowest in the school district. Principal Bernardo vividly remembers how excited he was to be a first-time principal able to focus on developing a curriculum focused on classical education and how chagrined he was that "before the school day had even begun, students were lined up in the office to be disciplined" (Bernardo & Neal, 1997, p. 34).

Bernardo's hard-line disciplinary approach galvanized a number of parents to organize and claim that their children were being treated unfairly. In response to this crisis, Bernardo appointed a committee of six teachers, two parents, and two students and charged this group with "assessing the problems which undermined the school" (Bernardo & Neal, 1997, p. 34). The committee recommended, and the Allen faculty approved, a mission statement that called for "development of the Allen Family so that all may become responsible, productive, well-informed citizens, fulfilled socially, intellectually, and morally through experiences of classical literature and character education" (p. 35).

At this point, the faculty anticipated that there would be a connection between the moral and the academic at Allen Academy, a connection embedded in children's literature. However, while the teachers did establish four major themes for character-based literature (being the best that I can be, making friends through books, remember when, and it's a small world), and did select grade-level books for each theme, Bernardo and his staff saw a more immediate need for infusing "a schoolwide ethos that put into action the understandings that were emerging from the literature study" (Bernardo & Neal, 1997, p. 36). Apparently, Bernardo's major hope for character education programming was that it reawaken awareness of America's traditional values, which he felt were "very important to a democratic society, but that somehow, somewhere along the line, were relegated to the background" (quoted in DeBrosse, 1993a, p. 6A).

The resulting character education effort never did draw on children's literature but instead involved a free-standing character education program with three parts: a discipline plan, school uniforms, and a "Word of the Week" program. The moral and the academic at Allen evolved separately, despite the staff's professed desire to develop relationships between the two.

There was broad agreement among the faculty that "children need to live in a moral climate if they are to mature into responsible, trustworthy adults . . . . They need to understand that school rules, like societal rules, are instituted to ensure 'a safe, caring, and orderly environment' (Allen Academy, 1996)" (Bernardo & Neal, 1997, p. 36). The code of conduct developed by the faculty had both general rules (e.g., students must speak respectfully) and specific lunchroom rules (e.g., students will stay in their seats). Consequences for disobeying rules were made clear, and any violation by a student was to be handled by the teacher who observed the infraction. Similarly, a student following the code of conduct was to be praised by any teacher who witnessed that action.

The code of conduct was viewed as one part of teaching children virtuous ways of behaving. School uniforms were another part intended to help children "to learn a standard of dress, to look past external appearances, and to achieve a sense of belonging" (Bernardo & Neal, 1997, p. 36).

The faculty also decided to introduce students to one character trait each week, a plan that became known as the "Word of the Week" program. Thirty-six character traits, 18 pairs of related terms, were identified through faculty discussion and by consultation with church and community groups. Related traits were taught back-to-back for 2 consecutive weeks; the school year, for example, began with the teaching of "punctuality" and "promptness" over a 2-week period.

The "Word of the Week" approach essentially involved making character education a school subject, separate from the regular academic curriculum. Each Monday morning Principal Bernardo announced the character trait for that week over the public address system. From Tuesday through Thursday, during homeroom period, teachers spent 5 to 10 minutes discussing the trait or reading an illustrative story. On Friday, the word for that week was featured either in a 10-minute assembly in the auditorium or in a videotape that was broadcast to all Allen classrooms. During the school year, each homeroom was responsible for presenting one schoolwide assembly and for creating one video. When possible, the character trait for the week was to be worked into other curriculum areas.

As with the schoolwide discipline plan, all teachers were expected to assume responsibility for reinforcing the character traits in the "Word of the Week" program. Should a teacher notice a child from another classroom performing a deed consistent with the current "Word of the Week," that teacher was to praise the child. This child, moreover, would be given a ticket that could be used at the "incentive store" to buy pencils, toys, or other items. At Allen, this heavy reliance on identifying and rewarding good behavior became an end in itself.

Academic study nonetheless remained an important goal at Allen Academy. In later descriptions of his work, Bernardo notes that student test scores rose dramatically between 1989 and 1995 (Bernardo & Neal, 1997). However, this increase in student achievement seems to have been more a fortuitous outcome than a planned consequence of the character education program at Allen. The motivating force behind the character education program was the promotion of basic virtues and the improvement of classroom discipline. In addition, the higher test scores at Allen may have resulted from attention to test-taking strategies and to additional instructional time that apparently was an unplanned by-product of improved classroom discipline (Scott, 1992).

Why was the divide between character education and academic study at Allen so clear despite the early commitment to integration through the study of literature? It may have been Principal Bernardo's focus on the character traits themselves. Perhaps his passion for character traits helps explain his very direct method. One journalist who observed him working with Pittsburgh teachers described Bernardo as "a revivalist preacher exhorting his flock," while believing that "good character can be taught to children . . . by the simple repetition and discussion of certain words and 'traits'" (Carpenter, 1999).

The effects of the character education curriculum at Allen Academy were evident in the behavior of the students. Visitors to the school noted how polite the students were, parents commented how the school no longer had out-of-control kids, and teachers at Allen Academy not only saw less aggressiveness among students but also a growing sense of students' caring for one another (DeBrosse, 1993b). When Bernardo resigned in 1996 to take a position in another district, Allen Academy parents were deeply upset (Kline, 1996), a dramatic turnaround from 7 years earlier, when parents had banded together to protest the suspensions by beginning Principal Bernardo.

Heartwood Institute   *"liberal"; literature based*

The Allen Academy approach to character education is based on traditional, conservative virtues and direct instruction, but character education can also have a more liberal value orientation—or be what Alex Molnar (1997) refers to as "expansive" rather than "traditional" (p. x). One such effort is Heartwood Institute's "An Ethics Curriculum for Children." Created in the 1980s in Pittsburgh and piloted in the Pittsburgh city schools, the Heartwood Institute approach to learning character through children's literature has been tried by more than 2,000 schools in 40 states (Heartwood Institute, 2004).

The Heartwood character education curriculum, read-aloud and literature-based, is identified by its developers as multicultural in orientation. It offers ethical content for elementary school grounded in seven virtues, each of which is called an attribute of character. To the attributes of *Turn* courage, loyalty, respect, and honesty, which are commonly used in many character education programs, Heartwood adds three attributes that might suggest a liberal orientation: hope, love, and justice.

While no simple relationship can be drawn between these particular character attributes and either a conservative or a liberal orientation, the developers of the Heartwood ethics curriculum make it clear that they want to broaden the perspectives of children. One criterion for selecting stories is that they not promote stereotypes on issues related to gender, age, or race, among others. Recommended stories come from around the world, and teachers are encouraged to have children place pins onto a world map to mark the settings of Heartwood stories. As the year progresses, children will see "pins all over the map, illustrating the fact that people all over the world value and practice the seven attributes" (Heartwood Institute, 2001a).

The Heartwood Institute also uses its website to list such ethical codes as the values of the Boy Scouts, the eight Confucian virtues, the 13 core values of the YMCA, and the seven principles of Kwanzaa. While noting that the listing of a code does not entail endorsement, the Heartwood Institute program developers also are clear that children should see character development in a multicultural context.

Despite the relatively unusual focus on liberal values, the Heartwood Institute's effort is very similar to Allen Academy (and the Wake County case cited in the Introduction) in that character education is conceived as largely separate from academic study. The Heartwood Institute (2001b), for example, endorses a particular lesson plan format called the "Heartwood Lesson." For each lesson, the teacher is to focus on a single character attribute, discuss that attribute, read a story related to the selected attribute, discuss with students how the story's characters exhibit that attribute, and engage in an activity that gives students a sense of what it would mean to act on the attribute.

The Heartwood pattern, as with Allen Academy, is to focus on one character attribute at a time. Heartwood draws on children's literature, but each story is included in the Heartwood curriculum in order to develop a specific character attribute. Heartwood's creators do recommend that Heartwood lessons be infused in the various subject areas, but the prescriptive nature of the recommended Heartwood lesson plan does not foster—and even inhibits—such integration. The Heartwood Institute (2001a) seems to recognize this discrepancy between their recommended plan and an integrated approach by noting that after a teacher becomes familiar with teaching the Heartwood attributes, "she will see frequent opportunities to highlight them in lessons and activities throughout the day, reducing her reliance on the Heartwood materials." However, even when using a less structured teaching style, a teacher can easily separate the teaching of an attribute from academic study, especially if the recommended Heartwood lesson plan continues to be employed.

Narrowly construed, character education is focused on the development of the character of individual students and based on the assumption that character can be developed through didactic instruction related to specified virtues. We turn now to service learning, a program that situates individual moral development in the context of community action.

SERVICE LEARNING

Like character education, service learning suffers from some identity confusion. The most outspoken advocates of service learning claim that it is "a teaching method that combines meaningful service to the community with curriculum-based learning" (Maryland Student Service Alliance, n.d.). This suggests a two-pronged purpose grounded in both civic and academic renewal. The National Service-Learning Clearinghouse (2005), an online resource center, defines service learning as "a teaching and learning strategy that integrates meaningful community service with instruction and reflection to enrich the learning experience, teach civic responsibility, and strengthen communities" (para. 1). In each of these definitions, a possible link is suggested between service and academic goals. And in both definitions, service learning is distinguished from community service, volunteerism, and work–study by its explicit connection to civic understanding and by the use of reflection to make the connection between action and civic understanding.

State of Maryland Service Requirement

The state of Maryland has what is likely the largest-scale, longest-lived, and most documented program of required service learning. Implemented in 1993, the program requires that students accumulate 75 hours of service learning experience to be eligible for graduation. The hours may be spent in direct service, indirect service, or advocacy. There is some stated expectation, noted in the first definition above, that service will have a direct academic link. However, as some commentators have noted (Galley, 2003) and is indicated by a review of Maryland's award-winning program descriptions (Maryland Student Service Alliance, n.d.), the classroom link is typically indirect. In the specific case of the Maryland program, it appears that claims of academic impact were incorporated to garner political support for a program that was proposed to serve civic and moral goals separate from the academic curriculum (Goldsmith, 1995; Townsend, 1992).

Since Maryland put its requirement into effect, major school districts (but no other states) have followed suit. Washington, D.C., Atlanta, Chicago, and Philadelphia all have service learning mandates based on rationales similar to that of Atlanta. The Atlanta program focuses on students' "responsibility to help others" (Westheimer & Kahne, 2000, p. 52), without reference to academic purposes.

There *are* service learning efforts that fully integrate academic goals and moral goals, that select and design service activities that will enable student mastery of academic content (see, e.g., Goldsmith, 1995). But these programs are exceptions. In Maryland and elsewhere, service learning can be distinguished from community service not by any link to academic mastery but by use of particular classroom strategies, especially reflection. We turn now to two examples of service learning in which the moral dimensions are valued independent of and separate from any academic outcomes.

St. Mark's Elementary School

Located in a large midwestern city, St. Mark's Elementary School serves a low-income area that is also predominantly African American. All but 1 of the 294 students at St. Mark's are African American, and 21 of the 33 staff members are also African American. Only 11 of the 33 faculty members are Catholic, and less than 30% of the students at St. Mark's are Catholic.

St. Mark's functions ecumenically. Each month the school community celebrates either a Mass by a local Catholic priest or a non-Eucharistic liturgy led by a nonordained Catholic or a local non-Catholic pastor. When asked about community service, one teacher at St. Mark's observed, "faith shows itself in action" (quoted in O'Keefe, 1997, p. 57), although many of the specific service activities at St. Mark's could be conducted in a public school.

Some service activities at St. Mark's are aimed at fostering community within the school. In the "Agape" program, for example, students get "tickets" when they violate the school's code of conduct; they then devise a plan, along with the teacher and the school social worker, to regain self-control and to provide restitution, if appropriate, for disrupting the school community. A second program, the "Put-Up Club," is used in disorderly classrooms. A student is invited to "put up" someone by devising and performing some act of kindness for that person. This service to the school community parallels some character education efforts (O'Keefe, 1997).

Along with attempting to build a school community, members of St. Mark's School also stress connections to the larger community. Every child is individually responsible for an ongoing service activity such as visiting the sick or elderly. In addition, each classroom of youngsters conducts a monthly community service project. One widely used class project engages students in collecting canned food, stocking these items in the parish food pantry, and helping out with distribution of this food to the needy. Meals on Wheels is another common class service project; students learn about this program, reflect on its importance, and also create seasonal decorations for food trays. Examples of other class projects include making paper dolls for children in the local hospital and participating in periodic cleanup campaigns in the neighborhood. Occasionally, the entire school becomes involved in a service activity. After failing to get the city to demolish several abandoned crack houses next to St. Mark's, the principal organized a hand-in-hand prayer circle of students and teachers around these houses. She invited the media; within days the buildings were gone (O'Keefe, 1997).

This last project differs from other out-of-school projects conducted at St. Mark's School. Most community-based projects at St. Mark's can be described as ameliorative efforts in which the goal is to make the life of the elderly easier, to help the sick regain their health, or to lessen the suffering of the poor. Mobilizing the St. Mark's community to protest the presence of crack houses, however, suggests a more activist stance, an unwillingness to accept present social conditions and a desire to seek redress of one such condition.

At St. Mark's all service learning efforts—those inside the classroom and the school as well as those in the broader community—are separated from the realm of academic study. There is some evidence that the results and meaning of various projects were discussed in the classroom, but any such discussions were disconnected from the ongoing academic curriculum. The belief that "faith shows itself in action" is viewed as adequate grounding for community service at St. Mark's Elementary School.

The Early Adolescents Helper Program

Among those who have advocated service learning the longest, it is the classroom strategies of training and reflection—not a particular link to the regular academic curriculum—that differentiate service learning from community service. Community service is exemplified in the Christmas-time visit to a nursing home or a holiday meal service; service learning "gives youngsters the opportunity to take on helping roles over a period of time and enables them to prepare for and reflect on their experiences—in other words, to learn from them" (Harrington, 1992). Educators at the Early Adolescents Helper Program focused on the developmental value of service learning experiences for middle school students; these youngsters develop a sense of feeling useful, needed, and important.

The Early Adolescents Helper Program was a network of service learning programs in middle schools in the eastern United States that began in the early 1980s in recognition of middle school students' developmental need for connection and meaning. (See also Carnegie Council on Adolescent Development, *Turning Points*, 1989.) This network has continued to grow over the past two decades and became the National Helpers Network and, more recently, Young Citizens. Founder Joan Schine remained active as an advocate for service learning throughout that time, organizing programs and publishing reports, scholarly reviews, and curriculum materials related to service learning (Schine, 1997; Schine & Harrington, 1982).

Students serve as individual care volunteers in a nursing home, as tutors for younger elementary students, as big brothers and big sisters to younger children, as play coordinators in a Head Start center, as homework helpers after school, as counselor aides in Boys and Girls Clubs, and even as assistants in a veterinary office. Sometimes the service learning occurs during the school day; sometimes it occurs after school or on weekends. In all cases, the service is direct, placing students in regular (usually weekly) contact with those whom they serve. This is not surprising, given the focus for early adolescents on connection and relationship.

Students participating in the Helper Program and successor programs experience the preparation–action–reflection formula recommended by the

Maryland Student Service Alliance. A weekly seminar is part of any placement. Early seminars are designed to provide training through role-playing,
simulation, and discussion; later seminars involve oral and written reflection and problem solving. Trained adults prepare students and help them to
process their experience.

Joan Schine's work in service learning represents a clear concern with
students' individual growth for their own sake as well as for the betterment
of the community. While she acknowledges the likelihood that academic
performance will improve as their capacity for connection and responsibility improves, her motivation is moral rather than academic. The academic
matters, but service learning is rooted in moral matters.

"code g ethics have limitations"

THE ETHICS OF TEACHING

Our examples of separating moral concerns from academic ones have thus
far been drawn from character education and service learning, both instances
of educators trying to foster desirable behavior or beliefs on the part of students. The teacher also can be the object of attention. And, in fact, there has
been renewed interest, as in other professions, in professional ethics. The
ethics of teaching is based in "those norms, values, and principles that should
govern the professional conduct of teachers" and other education professionals (Strike & Ternasky, 1993, p. 2). A wide variety of interesting questions
are pertinent to professional ethics, ranging from "Ought the teacher ever
punish a group of children for the misbehavior of one child?" to "What constitutes fairness in grading?" to "Where does the private behavior of a teacher
start and the professional domain for which the teacher is publicly accountable end?"

These and other questions about the proper professional behavior of a
teacher have long been at least indirectly addressed by codes of ethics, codes
that are composed of general statements. The Code of Ethics of the National
Education Association (NEA), for example, contains 16 general statements
grouped under two general principles: "commitment to the student" and
"commitment to the profession" (National Education Association, 1975).
Statements in the NEA Code are introduced by the terms *shall* and *shall not*,
suggesting that the ethics of teaching concerns issues of clearly determinable
right and wrong teacher behavior.

However, codes of ethics do have significant limitations in guiding professional action. First, they are stated generally to convey what is obviously
egregious behavior (e.g., "shall not intentionally expose the student to em-
barrassment") and, as a result, simply provide a kind of frame around the
outer limits of teacher behavior. Codes of ethics do not tell professional edu-

cators much about what to do in everyday instructional circumstances. Second, issues identified as "ethical" occur in an intermittent way when pressing difficulties or dilemmas arise about what the teacher ought to do in his or her relationships with students or colleagues (Hansen, 2001b). That is, teachers only think of ethical as a descriptor for those circumstances that are especially problematic in an obviously moral way. The net effect of these two limitations is that codes of ethics can be viewed as irrelevant to a teacher's "real work" in instruction. The moral (the ethical teacher) and the academic (the effective teacher) become separated in practice. One can apparently be ethical without being effective and vice versa.

In the ethics-of-teaching approach, the moral elements of teachers' practice can be disconnected from the academic substance of teachers' work in other ways as well. Even those NEA Code items that refer to academic concerns (related to "independent action in learning," "varying points of view," and "suppress or distort subject matter") are more about the process of student learning than they are about its substance. A teacher can be judged an ethical teacher without inquiring too closely into the academic quality of his or her work. The ethical teacher will be the one who treats students with respect for their points of view and regard for due process. The ethical teacher will not discriminate unfairly. The ethical teacher will not deliberately suppress or distort subject matter relevant to the student's progress.

But what do these ethical limits offer in the academic affirmative? Does our hypothetical ethical educator work "to stimulate the spirit of inquiry, the acquisition of knowledge and understanding, and the thoughtful formulation of worthy goals," as stated in the NEA's Principle of Commitment to the Student, just prior to the listing of the eight "shall nots"? In this principle, the NEA offers a basis for a substantive integration of the moral and the academic in a teacher's work, but a code-of-ethics approach typically does not use this kind of formulation as its starting point.

In most states, teacher certification standards require limited training in ethics. While selected preparation programs do have a substantial course or experiential requirement, it is more common for future teachers to encounter ethical issues—if they encounter them at all—as an isolated element in a Methods course or as a self-contained unit in Social Foundations coursework. Below, we examine a text designed for this latter purpose, followed by a look at the ethics component of a typical Methods course.

As we shall see, preparation in the ethics of teaching tends to be analytic rather than communicative and constructive. This tendency toward analysis is a strength, offering future teachers skills they often have not acquired elsewhere in their preparation. But this approach leads to a separation of the moral from the academic in two ways: first, because the effective teacher and the ethical teacher are not treated in tandem, and second, because the moral dimensions of academic content are viewed as procedural rather than substantive.

Strike and Soltis

First published in 1985 as part of a series of case-based texts in teacher education, *The Ethics of Teaching* is now in its fourth edition. Kenneth Strike and Jonas Soltis collaborated on this slim volume that combines theoretical speculation about the "nature of ethical inquiry" with demonstration cases and methodological reflection and with concrete cases and disputes for student inquiry. A statement of the NEA Code of Ethics sits prominently in the text's opening pages, and an excerpt from the Code serves as an epigram for each substantive chapter. "A Note to the Instructor" offers pedagogical suggestions for how to use the book's various chapters. The authors also offer tips for implementing a case method of instruction, describing their work as "a versatile pedagogical tool useful in getting students to think about and be more sensitive to the ethics of educating" (Strike & Soltis, 1985, p. xii).

The book begins with a preliminary consideration of the nature of ethical inquiry. The authors presage their method by starting with a case for consideration and using that case to illustrate the two most common theories of ethical deliberation: consequentialist theories and nonconsequentialist theories. Rather than make a claim that one is to be preferred over the other, Strike and Soltis juxtapose the discussion of the two to do two things:

- Highlight the strengths and weaknesses of each approach
- Model a kind of dialectic consideration they will later call "reflective equilibrium."

The text proceeds with a similar structure through three chapters that constitute what the authors view as the central "ethical dilemmas of teaching": punishment and due process, intellectual freedom, and equal treatment of students. Each chapter begins with the relevant excerpt from the NEA Code of Ethics and consists of a case, some initial discussion, conceptual analysis, and reflections on method. The three concept-oriented chapters are followed by what is the conceptual heart of the book: a chapter outlining the notion of reflective equilibrium.

Strike and Soltis favor objective moral reasoning to defend against relativism. They are concerned about the structure of moral argument and the status of factual and normative premises. They point out that the admitted ambiguity of moral deliberation is not necessarily a bar to rational conclusions. That something is presently unknown does not mean that it is in principle unknowable. Careful inquiry can lead to new answers in ethics as it does in other fields. Objective moral reasoning can and should be pursued.

The last two chapters of the book consist of provocative cases and disputes that will allow future teachers opportunities for the kind of analysis and reflection that Strike and Soltis have outlined. Dilemmas include, among others, a teacher who is asked to lie about a due process issue (p. 82), a teacher who must make a call on plagiarism complicated by the use of technology (p. 85), a teacher who crosses the line between instructor and friend (p. 86), a teacher facing parental complaints over values clarification (p. 94), an issue over individual difference and equality of opportunity (p. 98), an issue about the use of behavior modification (p. 102), and an issue regarding sex education (p. 105). Some of these dilemmas are loosely linked to academic subject matter; many are not at all so linked.

What determines our placement of the ethics of teaching as SEPARATE is that the thinking about the dilemmas is largely isolated (in language and in time) from the thinking about what one does as a teacher to plan instruction. Ethical dilemmas arise in distinctive, distinguishable moments and are deliberated using a distinctive ethical method. A teacher's moral responsibilities are treated independent of his or her academic responsibilities.

A Methods Module

While Strike and Soltis offer a focused, well-reasoned treatment of the ethics of teaching, most future teachers get far less. Imagine a typical undergraduate course in the Methods of Teaching Science (reconstructed from sample syllabi readily accessible on the Internet). The 14-week syllabus lists the following topics for consideration: cooperative learning; science teaching resources; integrated science projects; inquiry-oriented teaching; planning for effective instruction; the modeling method, learning cycles, and modeling cycles; problem-based learning; use of demonstrations and student laboratory work; personal and physical safety in the class, lab, and storeroom; legal considerations of science teaching; lesson study project; structured problem solving, assessing, scoring, and evaluating; test and rubric construction; *student cheating and teacher ethics*; classroom management; students with disabilities; graphic organizers in science teaching.

Note that teacher ethics is part of one class session, apparently at the tail end of a cluster of topics linked to assessment and prompted by the ethical issue of cheating on evaluations. Further investigation reveals that the lesson focus is broader than student cheating, however. The syllabus makes that clear in its statement of objectives for the cheating/ethics lesson:

At the conclusion of this lesson the student should be able to: distinguish between ethics and morals; identify at least two sources of professional teaching ethics; name the general areas to which professional teaching ethics apply; identify and explain the three main elements of a code of professional conduct (concern for the student, concern for the public, and concern for teaching as a profession); explain the meaning of and rationale for the various NEA principles; explain the basis of student character development; explain a number of ways to minimize cheating behaviors.

This single lesson is set within a Special Methods course and taught by an instructor with no expertise in ethical theory and, perhaps, little interest. The course reading list gives no hint that students and instructor consult the kind of text that Strike and Soltis offer, nor can we imagine how there might be time to do so were there an inclination. The NEA Code of Ethics, despite its generality and limitations, seems to be the only resource utilized. The stated objectives suggest that the goal is a rudimentary awareness that ethics matter; the caliber of ethical reasoning does not seem to be an issue. And the position of the topic late in a long list of other course topics suggests that the ethics of teaching is considered separate from any substantive understanding of the planning, instruction, and assessment that is the teacher's primary work.

There are other moral considerations in the overall course objectives, borrowed as they are from the National Science Teachers Association (1996) standards. There is reference to the "values, beliefs and assumptions inherent to the creation of scientific knowledge within the scientific community, and contrast science to other ways of knowing." There is a call to "create a community of diverse student learners who can construct meaning from science experiences and possess a disposition for further inquiry and learning." There is a focus on "interactions with students that promote learning and achievement." There is a mandate to "design and manage safe and supportive learning environments reflecting high expectations for the success of all students." Each of these is arguably moral as well as academic; that is, each is concerned with what's worth doing as well as what's worth knowing. But in the hypothetical course represented here, these moral matters are not represented as moral. Only one narrow wedge of the course is represented as moral, and that piece is kept separate from the academic part of the pie.

POSSIBILITIES AND DANGERS

Perhaps the greatest contribution of those contemporary educators who fall within the tradition of separating the moral from the academic is that their efforts have led to the moral arena receiving renewed emphasis in the elementary and secondary schools and, to some extent, in teacher education. During the 1980s Edward Wynne, Kevin Ryan, William Bennett, and others articulated a vision of schooling that gave central attention to the moral dimension. The mid-1980s also marked the appearance of the first edition of Kenneth Strike and Jonas Soltis's *The Ethics of Teaching*. A wide variety of character education and service learning programs appeared on the educational scene in the 1990s. All this advocacy and practical curriculum work renewed the interest, among the public and educators, in the moral dimension of teaching at precisely the time that the contemporary movement for academic accountability was gaining momentum.

In addition to renewing attention to the moral in schooling, the SEPARATE approaches described in this chapter have a practical advantage; they are relatively easy to implement in school settings. This ease of implementation results from two conditions: (1) separating the moral from the academic means that any newly initiated moral program does not challenge the structure or content of academic programs already in place, and (2) most efforts at character education, service learning, and ethical training are clearly focused and narrow in scope and outline concrete steps for action.

While several of the categories introduced in subsequent chapters contain approaches that challenge or transform conventional formulations of the academic curriculum, approaches in the SEPARATE category tend to accept status quo versions of the academic. For example, proponents of character education and service learning acknowledge and frequently embrace academic accountability, but they emphasize that such accountability is only one element of good schooling. How the academic is to be conceived is not their concern. Thus, while they do have to convince their constituents that the proposed program is worth the time, they do not awake "sleeping giants" by calling for the rethinking of the existing academic curriculum.

The implementation of character education, service learning, or ethical training is also facilitated by the tendency of these programs to be clearly specified and narrowly focused. For example, the Heartwood lesson plan guides and coaches the teacher on how to introduce the selected virtue, read the story, discuss the way(s) the story's characters exemplify that virtue, and identify an activity to help students visualize how they might act on the selected virtue. Allen Academy's "Word of the Week" program developed a similar level of specificity, following a structure that was implemented schoolwide. The Early Adolescent Helper Program targets direct service, especially with younger students and senior citizens, and provides protocols for both preparing for this service and reflecting about its results. Strike and Soltis supply both a method and cases to help future teachers hone their abilities at ethical deliberation.

Specificity, however, is a double-edged sword and can lead to problems. Two dangers merit consideration: the risk of oversimplification and the risk of indoctrination. These two dangers may be interconnected.

Concrete and straightforward approaches to the ethics of teaching, character education, and service learning can also lead to oversimplification of moral situations. We have already noted how using a code of ethics as a basis for teachers' moral judgment narrows the field of moral deliberation. Ethical situations often do not readily fit under a specific point in such codes as that endorsed by the NEA. Strike and Ternasky (1993) describe the NEA Code of Ethics as "platitudinous and perfunctory" (p. 2). While the Strike and Soltis text does not oversimplify moral judgment, it does tend to circumscribe a limited set of potential moral issues. And the practice of inserting a brief discussion of the NEA Code of Ethics into an already full Methods course does seem simplistic.

An analogous form of oversimplification can arise when character education programs are grounded in an array of virtues, especially when these virtues are taught one by one. Many of the moral situations of life to which a student must respond are not easily linked to a particular virtue. And when there is more than one virtue embedded in a situation, they may conflict. A person, for example, may be forced to chose between being loyal to a friend and being honest about some aspect of that person's behavior, or between pursuing justice in a social situation and being kind and respectful to the people involved. Furthermore, when virtues are learned as ideals, with limited reference to the enactment of those virtues in the concrete situations that academic content introduces, students can be left with a desire to be good but no clear idea of how to achieve that goal.

In the case of service learning, oversimplification can occur when a service activity is rendered in the absence of both intellectual preparation for the activity and reflection on its significance. It is even possible that service learning without correlated academic study will misinform teenagers. "When the emphasis is on helping but not on the factors that create the need for help," observe Westheimer and Kahne (2000), "we risk teaching students that need is inevitable, that alleviating momentary suffering but not its origins is the only expression of responsible citizenship" (p. 32). The result can easily be a vague sense of moral commitment without a clear focus for action.

Oversimplification can give rise to another concern: the fear of indoctrination. Indoctrination was noted in Chapter 2 as one reason why any acknowledgment of the moral in schools draws more ire than the most contentious debates over academic content. It is not surprising that this issue surfaces here with reference to moral education approaches that tend to be direct and directive.

Indocrination is a threat linked to character education, some argue, because that approach exhibits "a conservative political and educational bias that is insufficiently sensitive to the diversity of the society" (McClellan, 1999, p. 93). It is not clear, however, that taking a multicultural viewpoint, putatively more amenable to respect for diversity, necessarily removes the potential for indoctrination. The Heartwood Institute represents a multicultural orientation, explicitly stating that the Institute's goal is to broaden the perspectives of children, and yet the issue of indoctrination remains pertinent to Heartwood, especially when the recommended lesson plan format is employed. There seems to be something about character education itself that opens the door to fears of indoctrination. The "something" is the shared opposition to ethical relativism that leads proponents of character education to insist that specific core virtues be demonstrated by all who claim good character.

One puzzling question is why more concern is not expressed about indoctrination in the case of service learning efforts grounded in a moral intention. It may simply be that "indoctrination" is a charge leveled more typically at conservative positions than at liberal ones. Perhaps service learning has a liberal tilt that prevents it from being a target of such criticisms. There is a more substantive explanation, however, that helps explain why service learning programs typically are not seen as engendering indoctrination.

The relevant difference between the two approaches may be that service learning programs tend not to make their underlying values explicit, nor do such programs require students to articulate specific virtues. What is required is participation. Some service efforts are designed to promote a sense of charity, others deal with social issues, and still others address environmental concerns, but the specific values motivating such varied service actions are rarely stated. No apparent attempt is made to shape the beliefs of students. Assisting others or fostering civic engagement tends to be identified as the purposes behind service learning. These purposes may be general enough and widely enough accepted that they are not seen as potentially indoctrinating. Thus, while exemplars of the SEPARATE category can engender the charge of indoctrination, the possibility of indoctrination seems to be reduced either when the core values are kept at a general level (a course of action recommended by William Bennett) or when the values themselves remain largely implicit (common in service learning efforts).

The politics of efforts that fall into the SEPARATE category warrant some comment here. All three of the clusters we have included—character education, service learning, and the ethics of teaching—are promoted with the claim that they are somehow not political, or at least not political in any controversial way. Character education and service learning both fly the flag of civic renewal; the ethics of teaching tends to ally itself with professional renewal.

The implication in all three cases is that all persons of goodwill can, of course, support these efforts. That may or may not be true.

What is true is that each specific effort and the three clusters in general are based on assumptions and beliefs that require articulation and analysis. They are not apolitical, whatever the rhetoric that accompanies them. David Purpel makes this point explicitly in a critique of character education in a 1997 Yearbook of the National Society of for the Study of Education, but his point applies equally well to service learning and to the ethics of teaching.

With regard to character education, Purpel (1997) says:

> Part of the strategy of [character education proponents] is to create a discourse in which the schools are blamed for not teaching values and families are blamed for teaching the wrong values. Implicit in such a discourse is the assumption that our social problems are not so much rooted in the failures of our social, economic, and political structures as in the attitudes and behaviors of individuals. (p. 140)

Purpel goes on to suggest that we ought to recognize that character education is an ideological and political movement rather than a debate about curricular and instructional matters.

Purpel's admonition is well worth our attention, but it applies to *any* effort to alter or preserve the moral and/or academic character of schooling. If character education is intended partly to hide the failures of our socioeconomic structures, perhaps service learning is intended to reveal those same failures. At least some who espouse service learning have a vision of societal well-being that requires recognition of the social determinants of being good and doing well. Instruction in the ethics of teaching, as conceived by Strike and Soltis, is not likely to encourage future teachers to critique the present system of schooling in any radical way—only to operate fairly and equitably within that system.

Thus efforts that treat the moral and the academic in schooling as separate realms also tend to be efforts that can mask political commitments in educational and psychological rhetoric. This is a danger perhaps more insidious than either oversimplification or indoctrination for two important reasons. First, such masking obscures the ways in which the moral is shaped and enacted in all educational efforts. Second, obscuring political commitments stymies the kind of careful conversation and dialogue about the moral in schooling that we believe is needed. The strengths of programs in character education, service learning, and the ethics of teaching are considerable, and they can stand up to the scrutiny of open and thorough debate that includes acknowledgment of their political and ideological underpinnings.

Whatever the attendant dangers, the SEPARATE approaches described here have lent significant weight to contemporary efforts to balance the academic and moral dimensions of teaching and learning. These initiatives and programs have generated awareness among educators and the public at large that the moral matters in American schooling and that it matters for students, for teachers, and for the community. They have done so in part by focusing narrowly on the moral, offering specific programs that are generally independent of and separate from the academic curriculum. Their contribution to making the moral visible is substantial.

4

The SEQUENTIAL Category

The assumption that the moral and the academic are separable domains is widely held, and examples of this kind of thinking are readily available in educational literature and practice, as illustrated in the previous chapter. However, not all who separate these two aspects of school life view their relationship in exactly the same way. While the previous chapter analyzed examples of programs and platforms that treat the moral and the academic as generally discrete and independently motivated elements in an educational effort, this chapter examines commentators and practitioners who view the two domains as distinguishable but related. They are related in a SEQUENTIAL manner. One is thought to precede the other in attention and effect. The moral typically comes first, although, as we shall see, it is possible for the academic to be the point of entry.

WHICH COMES FIRST?

Numerous educators see students' basic moral development as prior to—and instrumental to—the achievement of academic purposes. For some, the moral is the key that unlocks academic potential. For others, moral precepts set the stage for academic performance. The MORAL FIRST view comes in indirect versions and direct versions. The indirect versions require attention to encouraging responsive *teacher* attitudes and behavior or to building community in *schools* or to *funding* schools equitably; attention to the moral import of each of these is presumed to lead to higher academic achievement. The direct versions focus squarely on *students*. Good kids can become smart kids. Some even claim that good kids of modest ability *will* become smart kids.

66

This direct MORAL FIRST position is the view of choice of many teachers—whether they articulate this notion openly or not. A central tenet of teacher lore is that one ought not smile before Christmas. The point is not literal, of course. It simply means that to increase subsequent prospects for learning, a teacher should start the year by maintaining classroom order and expecting good behavior by the students. Most educators have moved beyond this rudimentary formulation, but the general point has validity. Teach students how to learn early in the school year (through cooperation, respect, tolerance, collaboration, and related practices), and you will see good academic results later on.

Here we examine several examples of programs and platforms that exemplify the MORAL FIRST perspective:

- *Character First* is Joseph Gauld's effort to ground, justify, and describe the work of the Hyde School, a private school in New England.
- Nebraska's Boys Town has exported a well-developed program for shaping the behavior of younger students and, in the process, published *The Well-Managed Classroom* and other support materials.
- James Comer's School Development Program begins from a developmental rather than a deficit perspective so that group goals, trust, and accountability for standards will lead to high-quality academic learning.
- Eva Midobuche represents those multicultural educators who, operating from a moral and political commitment to end racism, argue that teachers cannot be academically effective unless they recognize and value children's culture, heritage, and language through "culturally responsive pedagogy."
- Jonathan Kozol has spent the last decade illustrating the "savage inequalities" in school funding and children's financial circumstances that make equal opportunity for academic progress a false promise.

Each of these positions is described below.

It is possible to hold the opposite view—that light must shine first and primarily on the academic purposes of schooling if moral purposes are to be achieved. The roots of such a view lie deep, in ancient Greece and Rome, in what Bruce Kimball (1995) has called an oratorical view of learning and knowledge. For the orator, the source of virtue and morality can be found in the past, in the "great ideas." Rational thought grounded in great ideas clarifies moral principles. To learn those ideas and to reason about them is to make morality possible.

Our sole exemplar of the ACADEMIC FIRST position, *Paideia Proposal* (1982) author Mortimer Adler, advocates a common education for all, an education that is academically liberal and deeply moral. His plan focuses on children's personal (mental, moral, and spiritual) growth, their development as citizens, and their ultimate ability to make a living as well as live a good life. The path to both a good life and a good living is an academic one that interweaves knowledge, skills, and "enlarged understanding" (p. 23).

The Hyde School Way

When Joseph Gauld, founder of the Hyde School in Bath, Maine, titled his description of the school's work *Character First* (1993), he meant exactly what the title said—"that character excellence is the foundation of and the means to achieve academic excellence" (p. 19). Gauld defines character as "those qualities that help individuals develop their unique potential" (p. 19) but then goes on to be more specific.

Hyde expects all students to develop these traits: the *courage* to accept challenges, the *integrity* to be truly themselves, *concern* for others, the *curiosity* to explore life and learning, and *leadership* in making the school and community work. These "Five Words" are not only the vision for students but also the basis for evaluating programs and procedures.

In an anecdote describing his own teaching, Gauld makes clear how serious, and literal, he is in his view that if a teacher focuses on the moral concerns embodied in the Five Words, academic achievement of a fairly traditional sort is bound to follow. While teaching an Algebra III class, Gauld committed himself to evaluating students on "a productive attitude toward learning" rather than on actual academic performance. He observes:

> Each student faced a different challenge. One very creative but disorganized student was graded on discipline and follow-through. A student who was overly teacher-dependent was graded on self-reliance. Another student who "couldn't do math" was graded on self-confidence; and so on. I flunked the top achiever until he demonstrated genuine curiosity and learned how to share his gift with others. (Gauld, 1993, p. 48)

Gauld notes that at midyear his experiment seemed a failure, but fortunately he persisted. By the end of the academic year, his students' "math accomplishments—in terms of their abilities—were some of the best in my teaching experience" (pp. 48–49).

Gauld is not suggesting that developing character in and of itself increases academic knowledge; the two domains are separable. It is his continued efforts at academic instruction that resulted in the students' mastering academic knowledge. But he does maintain that a focus on issues of character is the key to students' willingness and ability to take on and master academic challenges.

Gauld's (1993) emphasis on character as the key to academic success is derived from his view that education should be about developing a person's "unique potential":

> A person's unique potential is akin to an inner calling and reflects his or her temperament, gifts, natural talents, dreams, aspirations, background, and traditions. It is the person waiting to be born in each of us out of our own unique amalgamation of background and experiences. (p. 16)

For Gauld (1996), character goals and academic goals both take shape within this broader context. Character goals are primary because they arise out of the imperative for unique potential; particular academic goals are expendable when they do not serve that imperative. Those academic goals that serve the development of unique potential for each student are pursued through the development of character.

In fact, the academic curriculum at Hyde School, though individualized for each student, is similar to that in most high schools. The school began with a traditional, discipline-based curriculum, and many Hyde students do achieve traditional academic excellence based in disciplinary learning. Still, Gauld (1993) insists that no academic "lesson would be more sacred than a student's unique potential" (p. 62).

The Boys Town Education Model

Father Edward J. Flanagan, the Founder of Nebraska's Boys Town, asserted in 1917: "There are no bad boys. There are only bad environments, bad examples, bad thinking" (Connolly, Dowd, Criste, Nelson, & Tobias, 1995, p. 2). Father Flanagan's attitude and commitment became the grounding for almost nine decades of work aimed at developing "good boys" (and, recently, "good girls") who were also smart and competent.

Over the past two decades, the educators at Boys Town have taken their methods on the road, promoting *The Well-Managed Classroom* (Connolly et al., 1995). As the subtitle for that publication suggests, their concern is to "promote student success through social skill instruction," particularly for troubled children. The premise of the Boys Town approach is clear:

> If students are motivated to learn, if they feel good about the classroom environment and the relationship they have with you, if they can manage themselves and accept responsibility for their behavior, and if they feel empowered to improve, then and only then can you effectively teach and your students truly learn. (p. 2)

This nexus of motivation, self-regard, caring relationship, personal responsibility, and self-improvement has much in common with the explicitly moral goals of those who espouse character education. But there is a difference.

The Boys Town claim is that the moral comes first, with academic achievement to follow. In fact, that claim is outlined in the very first paragraph of *The Well-Managed Classroom* (Connolly et al., 1995):

> In order for children to gain control of their lives and realize a sense of academic and personal fulfillment, they must first learn how to accept responsibility for their behavior, how to respect the rights of others, how to solve problems, and how to make choices and decisions that can benefit them or that are in the best interest of others. Teachers who maintain a well-managed classroom empower their students to attain these goals. (p. 1)

How is this to be accomplished? The Boys Town staff, in concert with researchers from the University of Kansas (Portner, 1996), identified 16 prosocial behaviors: following instructions, accepting criticism or a consequence, accepting no for an answer, greeting others, getting the teacher's attention, making a request, disagreeing appropriately, giving criticism, resisting peer pressure, making an apology, engaging in a conversation, giving compliments, accepting compliments, volunteering, reporting other youths' behavior, and introducing yourself. The teacher is to actively instruct individual students to use these behaviors consistently (particularly taking advantage of "teachable moments"); to offer students incentives for complying through a token economy; and to provide appropriate reinforcement and, when necessary, administrative intervention. The point of every element of this program—including administrative intervention—is to help students regain self-control. The focus is on keeping students *in* the classroom rather than removing them because they are "problems."

That is very much the reason Washington Elementary School in Lancaster, Pennsylvania, adopted the Boys Town Model. At Washington, a large school with a culturally diverse population in a neighborhood plagued by poverty and drug problems, student achievement scores were lagging. Committed to the belief that Washington's students could do better, principal Janette Hewitt adopted the Boys Town program as a way to create a common vocabulary and a common set of expectations among teachers and students about the classroom learning environment.

Hewitt and her school's discipline committee (personal communication, March 21, 2001) agreed that the "school climate was not conducive to students' learning at high levels." They were particularly worried about fighting and other forms of aggressive behavior because "the kids fighting were not learning, and the kids not fighting were distracted by the kids who were." They considered a variety of approaches that focus on kids' behavior but rejected them either because the model did not help kids learn to control themselves or because the program did not offer a concrete plan for teacher training. They settled on the Boys Town Model because it met both these criteria.

Six years later, Hewitt is happy with that choice. Disruptive incidents are down. Teacher satisfaction with this schoolwide program and its implementation is high. Fourth and fifth graders are able to explain why certain behaviors (e.g., violent responses) are inappropriate and certain social skills (e.g., accepting no for an answer) are valued. Hewitt suggests that shaping students' prosocial behaviors makes it possible to name those behaviors as caring actions; once named, students experience their own actions as well as teachers' and peers' concern as caring. A climate of caring creates a community of mutual respect, relationship, and dignity; that is, a moral climate that Hewitt insists precedes high-quality academic performance. That performance does not happen automatically.

The Boys Town Model, she concludes, "needs to be paired with high academic demand," including, in the case of Washington, a continuing attempt to change the perceptions and expectations of parents and guardians, students, and, sometimes, staff. Still, high academic achievement is not possible, believes the Washington Elementary staff, without the kind of individual self-control and the caring environment that is central to the Boys Town Model.

The Comer School Development Program

Child psychiatrist James Comer brings his African American experience and his background in public health and child psychology to bear on education in the School Development Program documented in *Child by Child: The Comer Process for Change in Education* (Comer, Ben-Avie, Haynes, & Joyner, 1999). Like Joseph Gauld, he maintains that contemporary schools are structured around a contrived definition of intelligence and academic achievement, thus missing the growth and development of individual children. Like the Boys Town Model, Comer's School Development Program (SDP) avoids moralistic language while nonetheless claiming prior importance for elements like trust, relationship, and mutual respect. Comer's schools differ from the Hyde School in that the wedge for change is not the individual child's character but the moral character of the school organization. The SDP is unlike the Boys Town Model in that it takes a more structural and systemic approach.

What SDP schools share with both the Hyde School and the Boys Town model is an assumption that if you take care of the moral dimensions of teaching, of school structure, and of personal development, then the academic will improve apace. The mission of the Comer SDP includes being "committed to the total development of all children by creating learning environments that support children's physical, cognitive, psychological, language, social, and ethical development" (School Development Program, 2002).

It is the focus on child development that dictates starting with learning environments. "Good" learning environments are those that support development of the whole child. In the prologue to *Child by Child*, Comer addresses the criticism that a child development focus without a standards-based curriculum and test data is of limited value. He maintains that research data support higher test scores in SDP schools "where the . . . mechanisms and processes are adequately applied" (Comer et al., 1999, p. xxv), even when there is no special attention paid to academic standards. This is because SDP schools attend to curriculum, instruction, and assessment using various approaches but *within* a set of predetermined conditions that can be described as moral. "Nothing helps the self-esteem of a child more than learning to read or to meet other academic challenges. But in schools serving underdeveloped children, the adults must know how to create the conditions to make high-level academic learning possible for all" (p. xxv). Learning matters, but it will not occur in the absence of prior conditions.

What are these conditions? How are they created? Comer espouses a nine-part process involving three mechanisms (school planning and management team, student and staff support team, parent team), three guiding principles for these teams (a no-fault approach to problem solving, consensus decision making, and collaboration), and three school operations (a comprehensive school plan, a staff development plan, and assessment and modification) (School Development Program, 2002). These elements embody a vision of schooling as moral work invested with democratic attitudes and practices, respect for others, communication and collaboration, a shared vision, teamwork, persistence, and other values.

Christine Emmons, a Yale researcher, and Belinda Carberry, the principal, tell the story of New Haven's Isadore Wexler School in "I Can Fly" (1999). Collaboration and consensus on the part of the adults in the school community lead to students who feel that they contribute significantly to school life and who are therefore motivated to be "disciplined and dedicated learners" (p. 81). Teacher Gloria Nobles says, "I've been at Wexler for twenty-eight years. All that time, I've felt that I had something to say, but no one was listening for many years. Now, because I'm part of the SPMT [School Planning and Management Team], people are listening" (p. 86). Staff developer Ralph Esposito echoes: "It goes back to the idea of the village again. . . . In the past, teachers were isolated in their classrooms. Now there is collaboration and sharing across the whole staff. We come to a consensus about the need first; then the committee follows. That's resulted in more productive work" (pp. 86–87).

Staff responsibility, collaboration, and productivity create conditions for constructive teaching. Programs such as the Pride Center, Wexler School's "version of in-school suspension, where the child has the opportunity to work on the eight steps of conflict resolution with an adult" (Emmons & Carberry, 1999, p. 89), extend similar conditions to students' learning. One student, Natrice Williams, reports that "teachers help you when you need help" (p. 92). Another, Terrence Biggs, says, "If I get in trouble at Wexler, they give me a counselor to talk to me. If I tell him something important, he can't tell nobody unless I want him to. And if I got kicked out or something, he could help get me back in a different program" (p. 93). Students learn to trust the adults around them; that trust makes academic learning possible.

When teacher–student relationships are strong, when teachers evidence the kind of moral regard for their students noted above, then the school is well on its way to constructing "a functional community" (Comer et al., 1999, p. 48). But a community needs structural supports, and that is what is provided by the mechanisms, principles, and operations outlined by Comer. Where the (moral) conditions for learning are attended to, academic achievement follows.

Culturally Responsive Teaching

Some writing and programming related to multicultural education contains seeds of the SEQUENTIAL view as well, particularly that work devoted to what is referred to as "culturally responsive teaching." Certain moral attributes and attitudes must be displayed *by the teacher* in order to make students' academic progress possible.

Eva Midobuche is a Mexican American teacher educator who describes her own experiences as a child to make the point that all children's cultural backgrounds should be understood, appreciated, and acknowledged by teachers. She recalls being punished for uttering Spanish words and having to lie about her breakfast food and hide her lunch to avoid being laughed at. She recalls the humiliation of non-native English-speaking classmates who were belittled when their native language inhibited learning to read in an English-only classroom. And she points out that Mexican American cultural references were utterly absent from the classrooms of her youth.

For Midobuche, this insensitivity is a failure of moral dimensions by teachers who lacked respect for her, her language, and her heritage. This failure will too often lead to another: student's failure to thrive academically. Conversely, only those teachers who treat students *con respeto* will foster academic achievement. She concludes:

Teachers who respect and appreciate the different cultures in the classroom accept, validate, and acknowledge the experiences, language, and traditions of linguistically or culturally diverse students. These students develop not only a sense of belonging but also a realistic and positive self-concept. They can then learn—and enjoy the experience. (Midobuche, 1999, p. 82)

For Midobuche, respecting children, especially their language and culture, "will go far in helping children and their families develop the skills necessary to succeed" (p. 82).

Rectifying Savage Inequalities

It may seem odd to include Jonathan Kozol in this category. He does not speak the language of morality in his detailed, graphic descriptions of disparities in school funding (*Savage Inequalities*, 1991) and of the life circumstances facing children who would be students in urban schools (*Amazing Grace*, 1995). Is he really suggesting that moral concerns are instrumental to academic concerns, educationally speaking? Isn't he addressing something that is political or economic but not moral?

Here we reiterate our earlier claim that attending to the moral in education does not require the use of the term *moral* or its cognates. Much that is moral—that is, any value-laden human action—goes unrecognized as such because it is not labeled as *moral*. The contemporary language of education actually discourages the use of moral-related terminology. Prescriptive moralism, often religious in source and character, renders moral language suspect in a pluralistic democratic community, and an individualistic understanding of morality places innumerable educational concerns on the outside of the moral circle. Educators and commentators who recognize that their values and perspectives are controversial often avoid the prescriptive and individualistic tenor of moral language in favor of political terminology and political action. Kozol is one of these. Still, his concerns are moral.

Savage Inequalities (Kozol, 1991) offers an extended descriptive comparison of several pairs of public school districts. Each pair consists of one urban, underfunded, and generally blighted school district and a neighboring (usually contiguous) suburban, well-funded, and generally attractive district. Kozol describes the physical environment, the physical facilities, the economic climate, the cultural and socioeconomic markers, and the attitudes of teachers and students in each district. Figures on per-pupil expenditures, local property tax rates, and state subsidies are comprehensively discussed.

For each pair of districts, the conclusion is the same: School is a very different experience for poor children of color than it is for White, middle-class children. For the latter, focusing on academic achievement makes sense; for the former, it is virtually impossible. Until the school environment for all students is conducive to learning, we cannot claim to be educating them at all, let alone educating them fairly for competition in a supposedly meritocratic economic and social system. This is a moral issue, an issue of what constitutes right action for a community, for a nation. And for Kozol this moral issue comes first.

That Kozol himself views his judgments as moral is evident in the title of his most recent book, *The Shame of the Nation* (2005). As the subtitle suggests, he argues that we have restored "apartheid schooling in America" by employing instructional methods that are "intellectually barren and indoctrinational in nature" in urban schools. The "shame" is that we use such methods in the schools attended by poor children of color but not in schools attended by middle-class White children.

Kozol's moral response to the inequalities he documents includes (1) fully funding (federally) preschool for all low-income children, (2) abolishing the property tax as the basic means of public school funding and replacing it with federal funding, (3) providing significant salary increments for teachers working in inner-city and poor rural schools, (4) enacting a $100 billion federal school reconstruction effort, (5) encouraging site-based management and generally decentralizing educational decision making, (6) avoiding tracking, and, most recently, (7) ensuring the use of intellectually stimulating approaches to teaching and learning in all schools (Kozol, 1991, 2005; Scherer, 1992/1993). This set of recommendations outlines the moral conditions that would enable *every* public school to be what a good suburban school is—a place where academic achievement is likely.

The Paideia Proposal

While we have found numerous and varied exemplars of thinking that can be characterized as MORAL FIRST, it is relatively rare to encounter an educator who argues that academic development gives rise to moral development. Mortimer Adler held and practiced such a position.

The Paideia Proposal: An Educational Manifesto begins with a message to the reader. As chair of the Paideia Group, Mortimer J. Adler says that his group's proposal will assuage virtually all the concerns about public schooling held by all the schools' constituencies. He implies that the Paideia Proposal will address low-quality basic education, classrooms that lack discipline, middle-class flight out of public schools, reform without increased costs, inequalities of educational opportunity, poor civic literacy and participation, weak job-skill preparation, and even the need for greater brainpower in the military! How can Adler claim so much for his reform proposal?

It is largely because Adler takes democracy seriously as a social and moral ideal. Despite his association with the classical works of the Great Books curriculum, his understanding of democracy is modern (aligned, for instance, with the thinking of John Stuart Mill rather than Plato or even Rousseau) and radical (applying to each and every person).

For democracy to become a social reality, each citizen must become educated:

> Democracy has come into its own for the first time in this [20th] century. Not until this century have we undertaken to give twelve years of schooling to all our children. Not until this century have we conferred the high office of enfranchised citizenship on all our people, regardless of sex, race, or ethnic origins. (Adler, 1982, p. 3)

Adler presses his radical egalitarianism further. Not only must each and every child be formally educated but their education must be substantially the same. Citing John Dewey and Robert Hutchins, Adler suggests that we know what constitutes the "best education for the best" (p. 6), but that we have not made that education available to all.

The best formal education is a general, liberal education (Adler, 1982, p. 18), one that ensures knowledge, intellectual skill, and enlarged understanding of ideas and values. These three—knowledge, skills, and ideas—constitute the "three columns" of the Paideia Program, each representing a different kind of teaching and learning. Students' acquisition of organized knowledge (in literature and fine arts, in math and science, and in history and social sciences) occurs by means of didactic instruction (lectures, textbooks). Students develop the intellectual skills (reading, writing, speaking, listening, calculating, problem solving, observing, measuring) that make critical judgment possible through coaching and supervised practice. Students' understanding of ideas and values is enlarged through maieutic (or Socratic) questioning, using rich texts (verbal, visual, musical, dramatic) as a basis for discussion. Adler (1984) insists that all three forms of teaching and learning must actively engage the learner to result in "genuine learning" (p. 47). Didactic instruction requires relatively less active engagement; Socratic questioning, in a seminar context, requires near-total engagement (1982, p. 23).

Adler envisions a significant reform of schooling, which is why he can claim so much for his program. While didactic instruction can be carried out with large groups of students, coaching and Socratic questioning cannot. While some kinds of instruction can occur in short time blocks, others require a substantial time. While classrooms with desks in rows might be useful for lectures, they are not appropriate for coaching. While textbooks can convey knowledge, they cannot serve as the basis for close questioning and the challenging of ideas and values. While lecturers need only know their audience in general terms, coaches must know the skills of their "players" quite precisely. Teaching and learning will change substantially in structure, material, and tone.

All of this is based in this self-styled "philosopher at large's" (Adler, 1977) vision of the good human life, for *that* is the end of education:

> Education is a lifelong process of which schooling is only a small but necessary part. The various stages of schooling reach terminal points. . . . But learning never reaches a terminal point. As long as one remains alive and healthy, . . . mental, moral, and spiritual growth can go on and should go on for a lifetime.
>
> . . . Schooling is the preparatory stage; it forms the habit of learning and provides the means for continuing to learn after all schooling is completed. (Adler, 1982, p. 10)

Adler (1988) articulates "three callings" that shape American lives for which *schooling* should prepare all: "(a) to earn a decent livelihood, (b) to be a good citizen of the republic, and (c) to make a good life for one's self" (p. 310).

The "good life," the examined life, is the crux of the matter for Adler (1988). It is a life committed to the search for truth. It is a life lived in freedom and responsibility in the context of democracy as the ideal form of government. It is a life lived in the world, not in the mind, but the mind is ever functioning in any truly human activity. Thus earning a decent living does not require specialized, vocational training as much as it demands the development of the inquiring, judging mind. Living as a citizen does not require mastering the mechanics of government as much as it calls forth the consideration and communication of ideas (equity, justice, law, etc.) about persons living together. Living well does not require carefully developed tastes unless those tastes have been subject to scrutiny in light of values and commitments.

Two elements of Adler's thinking open up to the moral: his understanding of and emphasis on ideas and his view that the end of human living is continued growth in the quest for truth. Knowledge and intellectual skills matter, but *ideas* are the point.

The consideration of ideas inevitably results in a heightened moral sensibility because this examination provides "basic moral lessons about the shape of a good human life" (Adler, n.d., para. 2). Coming to understand the nature of the "good life for man on earth" is the focus of human existence because it is the rational basis for all judgments of right or wrong and for all efforts at social reform and improvement (Adler, 2000, para. 8).

Thus the academic education that Adler recommends has as its ultimate purpose (beyond making a living, acting as citizen, and living well) the recognition of the "good life" in a universal sense. Adler states it baldly: "Liberal education is absolutely necessary for human happiness, for living a good human life" (Adler, 2000, para. 21).

One's knowledge, intellectual skills, and grasp of ideas are never complete, of course. The purpose of schooling is to ensure that each and every person will have the wherewithal—and the will—to continue the lifelong project of education. Adler's certainty resides in the quest for truth, in the mind used well, in the life lived well. He is committed to dialectic but not to dogma or doctrine (Adler, 1988), despite a personal manner and tone that many might view as dogmatic. Great Books contain error as well as truth, and the continuing challenge is to ferret out and distinguish the two. Adler (n.d.) would have no part of "the self-appointed guardians of the morals and patriotism of our society" (para. 9). Neither, however, would he tolerate relativism and subjectivism as stances toward moral truth. Moral philosophy seeks moral truth (Adler, 1988, p. xxix). Such truth, though perhaps not always accessible, exists and constitutes the human quest.

After a slow start, perhaps because of the kind of systematic change that Paideia points to, the circle of Paideia schools has widened. No accurate count is available, and rich descriptions of specific schools are not readily accessible. A book published by Terry Roberts and the staff of the National Paideia Center (1998) functions not to document the work of specific Paideia schools but to guide, both practically and theoretically, those who would attempt such a transformation. The materials that are available suggest that schools typically select aspects of the Paideia Program for implementation, rather than seeking wholesale transformation.

POSSIBILITIES AND DANGERS

It is relatively easy to find examples of MORAL FIRST thinking linked to varied aspects of the educational enterprise. We offer just a sampling here. Jonathan Kozol questions the moral quality of our system of public schooling as it is funded, populated, and instructed. Comer's School Development Program (primarily elementary) shifts that focus to the nature of the school and the relationship of the school to the community. Eva Midobuche and certain other multicultural educators focus moral light on the cultural knowledge and sensitivity of the teacher. The Hyde School (primarily secondary) and the Boys Town Model (elementary) attend to the moral development of the young.

The moral enters at different points in MORAL FIRST SEQUENTIAL approaches, but in each case the moral makes the academic possible. The nature of academic instruction and curriculum are not the focus of critical attention or the subject of significant questioning. The academic is taken as a given; it matters as much—perhaps even more so—than the moral. But the moral comes first.

It is much more difficult to locate ACADEMIC FIRST SEQUENTIAL positions, in large part because the logic of the ACADEMIC FIRST position is more idealistic and less pragmatic, and we are not living in idealistic times. Only an educator like Adler, who seeks to alter the logic of our present academic focus, is likely to speak out in such times.

What does a SEQUENTIAL view—either MORAL FIRST or ACADEMIC FIRST—offer educators and others who care about the moral purposes of public schooling? First, and perhaps self-evidently, the educator who views moral concerns as instrumental to academic concerns, or vice versa, *includes* rather than excludes the moral in educational deliberation. This cannot be taken for granted, as we suggest in Chapter 1.

Second, putting one domain before the other does not dictate the specific values (or hierarchy of values) that ground action, though identifying a proposal or program does require a specification of value. Order, respect, trust, caring, responsibility, family, community, equity, and cultural sensitivity are values that fuel, in greater or lesser degree, the MORAL FIRST approaches discussed above. ACADEMIC FIRST approaches might value fairness, democracy, cooperation, solidarity, good citizenship, and a host of other possibilities. The decision to approach the moral or the academic first leaves open the potential for social negotiation of the values to be encouraged and enacted.

Third, sequencing the two sets of concerns provides some concrete guidance for the educator who is feeling pulled in different directions. Whether one puts the moral or the academic first, at least one knows where to begin! In the face of multiple demands from students, colleagues, administrators, community members, and public officials, educators welcome clear advice on how to proceed.

Thus, finally, a SEQUENTIAL view goes beyond mere recognition of the moral alongside the academic and seeks to uncover potential links between the two. In other words, it seems to offer a more complex analysis than the views clustered in the SEPARATE category.

But there is also a downside. Educators who begin with the moral may never get to the academic; those who focus on the academic may lose sight of the moral target. When do you have enough order, respect, community, and so forth to let go and concentrate on learning to read? When do you know enough about the struggle for political rights over the course of American history to internalize and critique the demands of citizenship and equity? Ideological critics of education from both sides focus on exactly this point: Either teachers are so busy caring for kids that they do not get down to the basics, or teachers are so busy drilling (and testing) the basics that they crush young spirits. Juggling the two sets of concerns is not a simple matter, even when they come in ordered pairs.

It is at this point, in both theory and practice, that any analysis that separates the moral and the academic gets further complicated in at least two ways. First, are the moral and the academic equally important? If one comes first, does that make it more important or less important? If you do not have enough time to attend to all your concerns, which should be prioritized—the moral or the academic? Is one educationally central? Is one educationally peripheral or expendable? Second, isn't there overlap between the moral and the academic? Don't they get tangled up in each other? If not conceptually, then at least in practice?

These are not *our* questions. These are among the questions those interested in the moral contours of schooling have asked and answered over the past two decades. Answers to these questions have generated programs and platforms that can be categorized under the rubrics of DOMINANT (where one element in the academic/moral relation dominates) and TRANSFORMATIVE (where one element reshapes the meaning of the other). Each of these two categories comes in two variations: Either the moral is the moving force *or* the academic is the moving force in the relation of dominance or transformation. We take up DOMINANT in Chapter 5 and TRANSFORMATIVE in Chapter 6.

5

The DOMINANT Category

Several logical possibilities present themselves when one thinks about potential relations between the moral and the academic in schooling. We have explored two such possibilities in prior chapters. In Chapter 3, we examined instances in which the moral and the academic are SEPARATE but viewed as more or less equal; that is, both matter to a similar degree but each is achieved through a distinct set of efforts. In Chapter 4, we considered examples of SEQUENTIAL approaches, that is, approaches that put one or the other domain first in an instrumental relation to the other.

Here we consider another possibility: Either the academic or the moral commands so much attention that it overshadows or even dwarfs the other. From this perspective, which we call DOMINANT, the moral and the academic are generally separate but neither equal nor sequential. Rather, one domain "dominates" the other and in so doing controls attention and priorities. The dominated domain may be obscured and often is not well articulated but is never dispensable despite the imbalance of importance. Both ACADEMIC DOMINANT and MORAL DOMINANT positions are possible, and we have found instances of both in the discussion and practice of contemporary schooling.

ACADEMIC DOMINANT

In Chapter 3 we noted that the moral in schooling is not a point of emphasis for many parents, educators, and educational policymakers. Some go so far as to claim that schools are purely academic institutions with no moral dimensions:

> [Values] should be taught in the home and not as a separate curriculum in schools.

> To think that these values can be taught in a school environment in the same way math and science are taught is ridiculous. How will a student get a passing grade in Perseverance, for example? . . . To even think of teaching these subjects cheapens their meaning to students. (Kotecki, 1994, p. A17)

In this letter to the editor about the role of character education in the schools, John S. Kotecki (1994) offers what we believe to be a novel "take" on the situation:

> I see only one way in which these values can be taught in a formalized manner in a school setting. We will have to label kids as being either character- or values-deficient, such as we label other special education needs now, and pull them out of the classroom for special instruction. This way we will not impede the [academic] learning of the majority. (p. A17)

While the public generally agrees that the home should be the focal point for the teaching of values, most parents and educators would not go as far as Kotecki does in insisting that character and values ought not be part of the school program.

In reality, most educators acknowledge that schooling has some moral dimensions that cannot be avoided. Still, educators often do not directly address the moral dimensions of their work. The reasons the moral is diminished, even ignored, are various and complicated. Calls for "professionalizing" teaching and for identifying the "knowledge base of teaching" place considerations of knowledge and skill above those of character or manner. The press of such social problems as poverty and drug use has led some educators to avoid seemingly insurmountable social and moral challenges and focus on achievable academic tasks. Political forces demanding academic accountability leave little time or energy for anything besides test preparation. And, as we noted in Chapter 2, the push and pull of competing religion-based moral codes—and the church–state specter that accompanies such codes—drive many educators out of the moral arena altogether.

Such educational tendencies are *not* what we mean by ACADEMIC DOMINANT. It is probably most accurate to classify this vast array of practices, policies, and programs as *moral invisible*, implying not the dominance of academic concerns but a thoughtlessness about moral ones. We are concerned in this book not with business as usual in schooling and educational research, but with recent efforts to invigorate education and its research by acknowledging the moral dimensions of teaching and learning. Our fundamental purpose is to make visible the moral dimensions of schooling.

One prominent group of commentators and educators seems to have contributed to keeping the moral invisible by arguing for and trying to enact an enriched academic curriculum. They are decidedly *not* thoughtless about moral matters. Still, their focus on a renewed vision of the academic often means that specific efforts to enhance children's moral development are viewed as simply beside the point. Marva Collins and E. D. Hirsch are among those who share the view that the academic ultimately matters more than the moral; we characterize them as ACADEMIC DOMINANT. This approach is often taken in private school or charter school settings, but it can also be found in public school settings as well.

Marva Collins' Way

In *The Marva Collins Story*, a made-for-TV film released in the early 1980s, there is a memorable scene in which a second grader in Chicago's Delano Elementary School recites Marc Anthony's funeral oration from William Shakespeare's play *Julius Caesar*. When the child finishes, Collins praises her lavishly, and an engaging interchange follows between Collins and the class. She asks why Marc Anthony gave that speech, and the children reply "to sway the masses." She asks whether they will allow themselves to be swayed, and they say no. And when she asks what they will do instead, they recite in unison, "We will think for ourselves." Scenes like the one above are chronicled in her autobiography, *Marva Collins' Way* (Collins & Tamarkin, 1990), which is part memoir, part prescription, part pep talk. Such scenes illuminate the qualities that lead us to characterize Collins's teaching as ACADEMIC DOMINANT, while recognizing that her motivation, her methods, and her language leave open the door to the moral.

Movie, book, and press accounts of Collins's work, both in public school settings and in the private Westside Preparatory School she founded, make clear the rich and challenging curriculum that Collins favors for all children. She makes liberal use of Shakespeare, for instance, even with children in the primary grades. Collins tells the story to very young children, has early readers read a narrative adaptation aloud, or has fourth graders pulling meaning out of the text line by line. In each case, the lesson is never solely about Shakespeare and his play but also about human living. Lessons focus on the nature of evil, the importance of individual responsibility, the dangers of pride, and the vagaries of love. Shakespeare's plays, Collins believes, are "a gold mine of meaningful themes" (Collins & Tamarkin, 1990, pp. 156–157).

This is the stuff of a defensible academic education, but there are moral echoes throughout. For example, Ralph Waldo Emerson's essay *Self Reliance* introduces a lesson on the value of that character trait. Maya Angelou's *I Know Why the Caged Bird Sings* prompts one of her 8-year-old boys to reflect on the nature of freedom. She decries curricula that shelter children, excoriates calls for "relevance," and insists that children want and need meaning, meaning ("values, morality, and universal truths") that can best come from classical literature.

Reading lists at the end of *Marva Collins' Way* provide evidence of the rich literature that grounds Collins's teaching. Children as young as 4, 5, and 6 are read to from works by Leo Tolstoy, the Brothers Grimm, Roald Dahl, Mark Twain, Maurice Sendak, and Pearl Buck. Young readers tackle Aesop's Fables, Dante's *Divine Comedy*, Jane Austen's *Pride and Prejudice*, Anton Chekhov's plays, Victor Hugo's *Les Miserables*, Homer's *Odyssey*, Margaret Mead's *Anthropologists and What They Do*, Voltaire's *Candide*, *101 Famous Poems*, and assorted biographies.

Of course, such a reading list demands mastering not only the skills of decoding but also a sophisticated level of understanding. Collins has a theory and a method. Her method is based on "the roots of phonics." "Sounds make up words and words stand for thoughts" (Collins & Tamarkin, 1990, p. 117), and Collins instills this axiom as she drills children in letter sounds. She explains over and over that learning is no miracle, but rather a matter of hard work. From phonics and the sounds of words, she moves to homonyms and synonyms and antonyms and spelling. All 180 rules for consonant and vowel sounds are repeated and drilled relentlessly.

Collins knew from the beginning of her career that all children could learn if challenged and taught well and that the key was a rich and meaningful curriculum. What she came to realize more clearly later in her career was that the academic curriculum was what Dewey (1916/1980) called an end-in-view. After more than 20 years of teaching, she could say: "As a teacher I now try to teach children how to deal with life. More than reading, writing, and arithmetic, I want to give them a philosophy for living. But at twenty-one, I was too sheltered and too protected to know how to deal with life myself" (Collins & Tamarkin, 1990, p. 48). Ultimately her main goal became "to motivate the students to make something worthwhile of their lives" (p. 139). She emphasizes the uniqueness of the individual, the importance of character, and the value of high standards. She even admits that attitudes probably are more important than academic subjects.

But as an educator pushed to action, Collins returns every time to what generally would be called academic content. Academic content, however, is anything but sterile in Collins's hands. Every idea or author or text is a spark that lights the fire of inquiry about some other idea or author or text. She notes how she and her students segued from *Little Women* to the Civil War and *Pilgrim's Progress*, from Plato's *Republic* to Toqueville's *Democracy in America*, from triangles to Pythagoras to the transmigration of souls to Hinduism. She describes her approach: "I blitzed the children with facts, but I did not go into all subjects in detail. Mostly, I hit upon them in a generalized way. I wanted to get my students to see the flow of knowledge" (Collins & Tamarkin, 1990, p. 148).

Collins is well aware of the demand this kind of approach places on the elementary teacher who "needs to have a general knowledge about all fields of study" (Collins & Tamarkin, 1990, p. 150). She recommends "a solid liberal arts education" over Methods courses because "the object of teaching is to impart as much knowledge as possible. Students can only give back what a teacher gives out" (p. 150).

There is much in *Marva Collins' Way* (Collins & Tamarkin, 1990) that recognizes the moral contours of a teacher's work. Teaching is a vocation requiring devotion and commitment. Students should be disciplined with "a loving touch" (p. 224) and praised often. Schools must be "truly supportive of children" (p. 227). All students should be held to high standards of achievement and instilled with confidence and a positive attitude (pp. 139–141). As do others in the ACADEMIC DOMINANT category, Collins has called for a return to traditional values; she believes that children—both rich and poor—often lack any sense of values (Zahn, 1996). Her admitted ultimate goal—to feed students' need for meaning, to give each child a philosophy for living—is a moral one. But her action focus is clearly academic. For Marva Collins, the key to any reform of schooling is "overhauling the curriculum" (Reedstrom, 1997).

This academic dominance is readily seen in the schools that have tried a Marva Collins approach. For example, Milt Thompson (2001), the principal at Wilson Elementary School in Kenosha, Wisconsin, outlined a three-part basis for Wilson's "Marva Collins Project." The school relied on an accelerated approach to building academic knowledge and skills in all students, used Engelmann's method of Direct Instruction, and also adopted a Core Knowledge curriculum. The academic is clearly dominant, and it remained so even after Wilson dropped its affiliation with Marva Collins in an apparent dispute over licensing fees for using Marva Collins's name (Kranz, 2002).

But from Collins's perspective, the key issue is the proper implementation of her curriculum. She, for example, has objected when schools wanted to adopt "bits and pieces of too many programs" (Carr, 2004). Her traditional approach is also not amenable to the use of rap music as a teaching tool (Kane, 2004). In fact, Collins says that she has threatened to sue several schools that refuse to stop using her name (Amos, 2005). It may well be that no school except Westside Preparatory now has Collins's permission to use her name, yet the very schools that she has rejected have reputations for academic rigor drawn from her inspiration.

E. D. Hirsch and Core Knowledge

The Core Knowledge curriculum used at Wilson Elementary School is the curricular progeny of E. D. Hirsch's 1987 best-seller, *Cultural Literacy: What Every American Needs to Know*. In the late 1970s Hirsch began worrying about the declining emphasis on information in American schooling, or what he describes as a "documented decline in shared knowledge" (Hirsch, 1987, p. 10). He begins with the premise that "to be culturally literate is to possess the basic information needed to thrive in the modern world" (p. xiii). That information ought to cover all aspects of human activity and ought to be equally available to all students/citizens no matter their social class. Hirsch is careful to state that he is not prescribing an educational program or a high-brow reading list; he is, he asserts with a certain amount of political disingenuousness, simply describing what one must know to "get along" in modern America.

Hirsch believes that the influence of Jean Jacques Rousseau and John Dewey have shifted American schools away from the transmission of that information critically important to cultural literacy toward fuzzy views of child development. Without judging Hirsch's interpretation of Rousseau and Dewey or his assessment of the realities of school instruction, we can examine his central claim. Communicating (carried out through reading, writing, speaking, listening) is more than a matter of decoding language; it is also a matter of understanding references. Those who do not comprehend key references will not understand the ideas they hear or read and will not be able to frame substantive notions when speaking or writing.

Understanding references requires "background knowledge." This background knowledge need not be precise or detailed. In fact, Hirsch (1987) asserts:

> This haziness is a key characteristic of . . . cultural literacy . . . [because] much in verbal communication is necessarily vague, whether we are conversing or reading. What counts is our ability to grasp the general shape of what we are reading and to tie it to what we already know. If we need details, we rely on the writer or speaker to develop them. (pp. 14–15)

Hirsch's general argument for the importance and utility of background knowledge is widely accepted by educators. More problematic, however, is his unabashed use of "our culture" and his seemingly immodest effort to define "our culture" with the help of two colleagues similarly positioned culturally. The preliminary listing, in the Appendix of *Cultural Literacy*, of the "items" which constitute "cultural literacy" (p. ix) has long been a major source of controversy.

After *Cultural Literacy*, Hirsch compiled *The Dictionary of Cultural Literacy* (1988) and subsequently created the Core Knowledge Foundation (Mackley, 1999). The foundation's major activity has been the development of a Core Knowledge "Grader" Series for elementary students. Each book in the series—one per elementary grade—is titled *What Your Xth Grader Needs to Know: Fundamentals of a Good Xth-Grade Education* (e.g., Hirsch, 1991, 2005). The content of the seven books collectively is called the Core Knowledge Sequence.

Hirsch (1996), like Marva Collins, believes that making such background knowledge available to all children regardless of social status is a moral imperative. Only by understanding the dominant views and values can one challenge those views and values, Hirsch suggests, in an effort to respond to those who balk at the essential conservatism of his position. However, in *Cultural Literacy* (1987) Hirsch makes little specific reference to the moral dimensions of schooling except to contend that "universal literacy has never been a socially neutral mission in our country. . . . Universal literacy is inseparable from democracy" (pp. 12–13).

Hirsch's thinking changed little between 1987, when *Cultural Literacy* was published, and the early to mid-1990s, when initial volumes of the Core Knowledge "Grader" Series were published. But his moral and civic reasons in support of a Core Knowledge Sequence are more clearly articulated in the general introduction to that series. Not only does relying on commonly shared knowledge make schooling more effective, but this approach also "makes schooling more fair and democratic" because giving everyone the same subject-matter background means "all the students are empowered to learn" (Hirsch, 2005, p. xxiii). The "fair and democratic" assertion echoes Hirsch's earlier claims about equal access to important knowledge.

However, a new "cooperation and solidarity" justification addresses how diversity ought to be blended into our common culture:

> Diversity is a hallmark and strength of our nation. American classrooms are often, and increasingly, made up of students from a variety of cultural backgrounds, and those different cultures should be honored by all students. At the same time, education should create a *school-based* culture that is common and welcoming to all because it includes knowledge of many cultures and gives all students, no matter what their backgrounds, a common foundation for understanding our cultural diversity. (Hirsch, 2005, p. xxiii; emphasis in original)

This argument is Hirsch's response to those who have criticized his views as ethnocentric.

Thus Hirsch offers a moral argument for the teaching of important knowledge; that is, he argues on moral grounds that the academic (read "content") should dominate apparently moral concerns (read "process") in teaching. Hirsch and dozens of Core Knowledge Schools, located in almost every state, are responding to a perception that "mere facts" do not count in today's educational system. Hirsch wants to argue that facts do count in a way that is more significant than any other single aspect of schooling.

There is none of Marva Collins's care for children in Hirsch's work (1993, 1996). His more recent writing (e.g., 2000) is more clearly located in contemporary politics, even as he denies that the issue of acquisition of background knowledge has political undertones. But Hirsch and Collins, despite some differences in rhetoric and role, share a core commitment to the importance of the academic as the dominant force in all educational efforts. The dominance of the academic is needed to achieve cultural literacy (Hirsch) or autonomy and responsibility (Collins), thus making possible civic, moral, and economic community.

More urban schools (39%) use Core Knowledge than either suburban (37%) or rural (24%) schools (Core Knowledge Foundation, 2005a). Urban educators may be responding to the contention by those characterized as ACADEMIC DOMINANT that children in less privileged circumstances are often shortchanged when knowledge is distributed. In today's educational climate of high-stakes testing, magnified by the impact of No Child Left Behind, urban schools are under extreme pressure to raise student test scores. What is not clear at this juncture is how well most states' standards are aligned with Core Knowledge content and whether the use of this curriculum furthers or hinders schools' efforts to comply with state requirements. The Core Knowledge Foundation (2005b) is currently engaged in a major effort to align the Core Knowledge Sequence with the state standards for all 50 states.

In the last decade, the Core Knowledge Foundation has recruited numerous schools—public and private—to a strong focus on the academic. In May 2004, the schools using the Core Knowledge Sequence were 79% public, 14% private, and 6% parochial (Core Knowledge Foundation, 2005a). Starting in August 2003, schools had to make formal application to be an official Core Knowledge School, culminating 2 or 3 years later in a formal school visit by foundation officials to confirm that all requirements had been met. By July of 2005, more than 125 schools had been identified on the Foundation website as official Core Knowledge Schools, establishing that they had achieved 80% implementation of the Core Knowledge curriculum. (In recent years, the Core Knowledge Foundation has given increased attention to staff development.) This accreditation process should help ensure a certain consistency of approach across schools, including the kind of focus we have identified as ACADEMIC DOMINANT.

MORAL DOMINANT

Just as some educators focus on academic concerns to the relative neglect of moral ones, so, too, do others stress moral concerns over academic ones. We call them MORAL DOMINANT because they are willing to subordinate their academic concerns and efforts to moral mandates. The academic is not absent from a MORAL DOMINANT view of schooling; neither is the academic significantly altered in the light of moral concerns. Rather, the academic program is simply overshadowed, diminished in importance; if anything, academic efforts are taken for granted. Careful attention is reserved for matters that we have characterized as moral. Talk to MORAL DOMINANT educators, and they will tell you that their academic programs are good but are not the point.

The point, they would say, is having a faith-based view of human living. That view of human living is typically based in a particular religious tradition and renders the academic of value only insofar as it serves the call of the faith-based life. Two examples—a Catholic school and Christian homeschoolers—illustrate this position in its contemporary form. MORAL DOMINANT views need not be religiously based, but secular perspectives that reflect moral dominance are far less common in American schooling than religiously oriented views.

"Exceptional" Education in a Catholic School

Today, parents send their children to parochial schools for myriad reasons, but religious admonition played a key role in the past. Early in the 20th century, immigrant families were directed to do so by the priest from the pulpit. Only in the Catholic school would children learn the faith, as well as the discipline and behavior that accompanied that faith. After one generation of a family was educated in a local parochial school, family tradition, as well as concern for the value of faith-based education, led subsequent generations to continue the line.

Lancaster Catholic High School is similar to many other parochial high schools. It is relatively small (about 700 students) and draws students from nine surrounding parishes. In general, parents select Lancaster Catholic not so much for its academic program as for its moral mission to make their children into "good" adults. Lancaster Catholic High School (2004), according to its school philosophy, "offers a quality education which helps students integrate their faith with the knowledge they acquire and the skills they develop, so they may serve the community as responsible adults."

The Catholic focus is evident both in the school's physical plant and in its program. Both main entrances have a significant religious symbol—a crucifix outside the gym and a statue of the Virgin Mary outside the office. There is a chapel, and crucifixes adorn the walls of every classroom. Mass is celebrated on a regular basis for the entire school community. Every child, Catholic or not, is required to study religion—Old Testament, New Testament, The Church, and Christian Ethics.

The academic program is traditional in conception and is similar to what is offered in neighboring public schools. This generalization refers not only to Algebra II, English III, and American History, but also to Biology (there is minimal concern about evolution in Catholic schools). Teachers are mostly state-licensed. Differences in academic activity include the prayer that begins each class session, the more traditional pedagogy typical of Catholic schools, sporadic references to matters religious, and a faith-based emphasis on service learning.

Nonetheless, the moral vision—the mandate to be and become truly Catholic—dominates the educational landscape. The moral, expressed in religious language and practice, takes precedence over academic concerns. The previously stated philosophy declares that moral vision in principle; the principal expressed it in practice in a 2001 newsletter. The principal was proudly reporting an academic accomplishment—a Quiz Bowl team that had won the Pennsylvania State Championship and finished seventh in a national tournament. But he goes on to put this achievement in a MORAL DOMINANT perspective:

> Our Academic Quiz Bowl team's journey to such lofty heights is one that will be recounted with admiration for years to come. . . . And yet, it is only the second most important trip Catholic High students made this year. Even more significant was the all-school pilgrimage to the Basilica of the National Shrine of the Immaculate Conception in Washington, DC. . . . It was a remarkable experience that exceeded all expectations for the 700+ pilgrims who set out that morning seeking a closer relationship with our ever-loving God.

He continues:

> These two diverse and worthwhile journeys define the essence of this exceptional place. Catholic High is an institution where students are encouraged and pushed to achieve at the outer limits of their abilities, but where they learn that the ultimate bottom line is that Christ loves and values them no matter what.

This last paragraph suggests a feature of the thinking of those who take MORAL DOMINANT positions or construct MORAL DOMINANT programs. It is the sense, sometimes seemingly self-congratulatory, that their position or their program is "exceptional."

The sense of being a very special school was also captured in a newspaper advertisement for a new teacher. The ad heading reads, "Social Studies Teacher for the World's Most Civilized Kids." The text notes that the successful candidate will "join a superb faculty, teaching the world's most teachable students in a cheerful, purposive environment. We will give you a 100% guarantee of respectful, polite students in return for your 100% commitment to their growth and well-being." This is a bold claim—at once refreshing and a bit off-putting—and one that would be difficult to support. It is not clear on what basis the principal viewed the students as "the world's most civilized kids," but it does seem clear that he views the religious focus as the basis for an exceptional educational experience.

This perspective is typical of many diocesan Catholic schools. An article subtitled "Catholic Education Tries to Head Off an Identity Crisis" (Archer, 1997) describes a dilemma faced by Catholic schools that succeed in academic terms. Sister Louise Levesque, who runs training sessions for Catholic school leaders in the Providence diocese, notes, "We've been getting a great deal of positive press . . . and the fact is that many studies show that Catholic schools are excelling [academically]. But we must not ever lose sight of why we're here just because we're excelling" (p. 33).

In diocesan Catholic schools, the academic does matter; such goals are pursued with vigor. But the academic is neither foremost nor controlling. Its place is secondary to, and generally independent of, the schools' moral focus. The curriculum is not significantly altered by the dominance of moral concerns, but it tends to be overshadowed by them. The academic warrants attention because of its link to one's ability to be a Catholic in this life and beyond. Talents, academic and otherwise, come from God and are to be developed in the service of God; the primary educational goal is eternal salvation. Lancaster Catholic High School is typical of the thousands of diocesan Catholic elementary and secondary schools throughout the country. The moral is dominant.

Christian Homeschoolers

Homeschooling, the education of school-aged children at home rather than in school, is on the rise and numbers about 1 million youngsters (Walsh, 2002). According to one homeschooling proponent (Lyman, 1998), the increased interest in homeschooling reflects two kinds of "broadening dissatisfaction with formal education" (para. 5). On the one hand "public schools are turning out a poor product—illiterate and unprepared graduates" (para. 7), and these "public schools have become crime scenes where drugs are sold, teachers are robbed, and homemade bombs are found in lockers" (para. 8). While issues of learning and school safety often do contribute to parents' decision to homeschool, ideological reasons may also prompt such a choice (Paulson, 2000; Stern, 2003).

Parents on the "libertarian left" view any form of schooling as infringing on their parental prerogative to educate their children and as designed to make the young compliant to the state. Libertarians believe that today's schools fail utterly to educate for autonomy, self-respect, and free will—the moral mandate of the libertarian. John Taylor Gatto is a folk hero to many libertarian homeschoolers. Gatto spent 29 years working in public schools and was once named New York State Teacher of the Year. As a public school "turncoat," Gatto (n.d.) has real credibility when he criticizes the "public school ideology" that allows the State to prescribe a "value code for all."

Gatto and other libertarians do offer a view of schooling that privileges the moral over the academic, but the moral plays a transformative rather than dominant role. To begin with autonomy, self-respect, and free will as the greatest "good" transforms both the nature of school (libertarians advocate "unschooling") and the academic goals and content of that experience. Homeschoolers of the libertarian left are better understood as MORAL TRANSFORMATIVE (see Chapter 6).

Homeschoolers from the Christian Right do tend to fit the MORAL DOMINANT mold. Homeschooler and university professor Jim Muncy (1994) explains the motivation of Christian homeschoolers by delineating the recent history of American public schooling:

> Throughout most of public education in America, Christians felt that the environment of the school reinforced their efforts to raise up Christian children. However, starting in the 1960's, public life in America began to dramatically change and many of those changes carried over into the schools. In the 1950's, public schools were leading their children in prayers and the recitation of Bible verses. By the mid 1960's such practices were declared unconstitutional. And other changes occurred. Curriculum evolved taking on more of a "secular humanist" philosophy. Discipline in the schools changed. Sex education entered the schools. The very intellectual, spiritual, and moral teachings that were so important to Christian parents were no longer being reinforced in the schools; to the contrary, many parents felt that the public schools were actually undermining what they were teaching with such great passion at home. (para. 6)

Muncy notes that this dissatisfaction with the public schools gave rise to a widespread network of Christian schools. The programs and priorities of these Christian schools are similar to those of Lancaster Catholic High School.

This dissatisfaction has also helped fuel a thriving Christian home-schooling movement. Educational efforts within individual Christian families who view the home and family as the best environment where "Christian values can be taught, modeled, and reinforced" (Muncy, 1994, para. 8) have been transformed into a cohesive movement. Key to this movement is the involvement of such institutions as Bob Jones University, the creation of advocacy organizations, and Internet access to a variety of support groups and teaching resources. Internet searches turn up any number of individual family websites, parent groups, and homeschooling forums both private and commercial, including, for example, Classical Christian Homeschooling (http://www.classicalhomeschooling.org), the Christian Homeschool Community (http://christianhomeschoolcommunity.com/), and the CHF Web (http://www.chfweb.net/). At all these sites, the emphasis is on the importance of the Christian message and the Christian way of life. Academic matters are addressed in the shadow of Christian moral commitments. The Home School Legal Defense Association is a major legal and political advocate for Christian homeschoolers, although its efforts on behalf of Christian Right political issues (such as limiting the authority of child welfare services) do not necessarily represent the interests of all homeschoolers, or even all Christian homeschoolers.

Substantial diversity exists within the Christian homeschooling movement. Some take the militant political perspective of the Exodus Mandate Project and argue that all Christian parents must withdraw their children from a public school system that "is currently unconstitutional, is not reformable, has no Biblical mandate, and has become a tool of statist social engineers" (Exodus 2000, n.d., para. 4). Others, like longtime homeschooling proponents Raymond Moore and Dorothy Moore (recently deceased) have defended a nonpartisan view of homeschooling that is hospitable to Christian homeschoolers but welcomes and supports parents of all faiths (for example, a significant contingent of Jewish homeschoolers) or various moral persuasions (the libertarian segment mentioned above). Moore and Moore (1981, 1982) "advocate a firm but gentle approach to home education that balances study, chores, and work outside the home in an atmosphere geared toward a child's particular developmental needs" (Lyman, 1998, para. 19).

Whatever the political attitude of Christian homeschoolers, their ultimate motivation may be best captured by Jim Muncy when he suggests that Christian parents desperately want their own children to live as Christians with them in this life and to be with them in heaven after death. Muncy (1994) declares:

> Christians who are totally committed to their faith receive an indescribable joy and meaning for life from this faith. It is, in a very real sense, the very reason for their existence. Many of them have tried to live a life apart from God; but, when they found God, they couldn't possibly imagine a fulfilled life without a walk with Christ. Indeed, to the Christian parents, their all encompassing

passion and their greatest reward is knowing that their children find a fulfilling life walking with Christ and then having them there on the other side to
enjoy eternity with them. If this happens, then life is a success. (para. 4)

It is this passion and this interpretation of success that result in a view of
homeschooling that we characterize as MORAL DOMINANT. The moral elements, captured in committed Christian faith, dominate the academic dimensions of education.

POSSIBILITIES AND DANGERS

At the beginning of the section on ACADEMIC DOMINANT, we noted that much
of today's educational research, commentary, and even practice might be
classified as moral invisible. This descriptor can be applied, for example, to
the contemporary political thrust toward state standards and high-stakes
testing. This movement has none of the moral justification, egalitarian orientation, or supportive tone of those whose position is ACADEMIC DOMINANT.
To view the academic as dominant is not to denigrate or even to ignore moral
concerns; rather it is to see the academic as the key to social success of any
kind and the moral as subsumed into this understanding of success. The
opposite can be said of the MORAL DOMINANT view. To view the moral as
dominant is not to denigrate or even to ignore academic concerns; rather, it
is to see the moral as the key to social success of any kind and the academic
as subsumed into this understanding of success.

The MORAL DOMINANT and ACADEMIC DOMINANT positions appear to
have little in common. Exponents of a MORAL DOMINANT view usually start
and end in religious language and practice (remember that secular versions
of MORAL DOMINANT are possible in principle but uncommon); exemplars
of an ACADEMIC DOMINANT view rarely mention religion or its practice.
Those espousing a MORAL DOMINANT view tend to operate outside the
public school system and within explicitly religious settings; ACADEMIC
DOMINANT educators are active in both public and private school settings.
Most important, the MORAL DOMINANT view is centered on the moral as
the key to worthwhile education, while the ACADEMIC DOMINANT view
considers academic matters primary.

But to focus on their distinctions would only obscure some significant
similarities:

- Both MORAL DOMINANT and ACADEMIC DOMINANT exemplars tend to
  view curriculum, both content and structure, in more or less traditional
  ways. The focus is on what John Dewey called "funded knowledge."

- Both MORAL DOMINANT and ACADEMIC DOMINANT exemplars hold a clear and inspiring vision of human living and the education it requires. There is no waffling or tentativeness in their views.
- Both MORAL DOMINANT and ACADEMIC DOMINANT exemplars trade off complexity for focus. Complexity may well be acknowledged, but the educational path to be pursued is easily resolved by reference to clear curricular mandates (ACADEMIC DOMINANT) or clear religious ones (MORAL DOMINANT).
- Both MORAL DOMINANT and ACADEMIC DOMINANT exemplars border on being "true believers" who project a sense of self-confidence that some might view as arrogance.
- Both MORAL DOMINANT and ACADEMIC DOMINANT exemplars deal explicitly with American cultural diversity, though in opposite ways. ACADEMIC DOMINANT exemplars argue that their vision of human living and the kind of schooling that makes this vision possible ought to be available to all Americans whatever their race, class, or gender. MORAL DOMINANT exemplars view religious and political diversity as inimical to American (their own) well-being and create structures for schooling that keep their values in and other values out.

These similarities reveal both the possibilities and dangers of DOMINANT positions.

ACADEMIC DOMINANT and MORAL DOMINANT exemplars offer clear and compelling answers to parents and educators who are bewildered by the seemingly disparate tasks assigned to schooling. By choosing to rely on a carefully delineated vision of *either* the moral *or* the academic, they offer a standard by which educational responsibilities can be assumed (or discarded).

Moreover, the programs they prescribe appear to work according to typical measures of school success. Catholic schools, particularly those in urban areas, have earned a reputation for higher levels of academic achievement than their public counterparts. Christian homeschoolers represent the lost ideal of the two-parent family educating children who seek and attain academic excellence, according to a study by Lawrence Rudner (1999). And these results come from educational settings that often claim not to care overmuch about academic concerns! Marva Collins has achieved personal notoriety for turning around the lives of individual at-risk children and for altering classroom culture by demanding academic excellence in the context of rich academic curricula. E. D. Hirsch has attracted numerous schools to his Core Knowledge Sequence by specifying precisely what each child, at various ages, should know.

Does this mean that a DOMINANT position is the most productive one for educators to take? Not necessarily. Both MORAL DOMINANT and ACADEMIC

DOMINANT involve a traditional academic curriculum that "fits" contemporary assumptions about testable academic achievement. Perhaps a more limited claim is possible. DOMINANT positions can be successful in specific ways, in specific circumstances, and with specific student populations. But in what sense are such positions successful? Are Catholic schools and Christian homeschoolers successful in encouraging a joyful Christian life and a blessed life after death for their students, since this is the ostensible goal of such schooling? Are such educational settings more successful in achieving this goal than public schools? Data are not available to answer this question. Are children educated under the programs advocated by Marva Collins and E. D. Hirsch more knowledgeable and more able to live as active democratic citizens than those educated in other schools. Again, data are difficult to pin down.

Even if we accept these programs and positions as successful on their own terms, there seem to be limits and dangers that are the flip side of their strengths. All DOMINANT positions either presume or prescribe a kind and level of cultural homogeneity that cannot be taken for granted—even as an ideal—in the fractured American social landscape. When, for instance, E. D. Hirsch claims access to "what every child should know," it is fair to ask about his authority in this matter. This preference for homogeneity is precisely what makes such positions problematic to the postmodern sensibility.

It is also true that conviction can impede conversation with others; that is, the confidence and clarity expressed by those we have characterized as both MORAL DOMINANT and ACADEMIC DOMINANT easily "put off" educators who do not share their convictions. Careful and deliberate consideration of the strengths of such positions may be lost through closed-mindedness on both sides.

Both MORAL DOMINANT and ACADEMIC DOMINANT are vulnerable to concerns about indoctrination (see Chapter 2). Those who possess the truth—the truth of the best that has been thought and done in the world or the truth of eternal life—aim to share that truth. From one perspective, this seems only right, even generous. From another, it has the look and feel of indoctrination. We do not here suggest that either MORAL DOMINANT or ACADEMIC DOMINANT educators intend indoctrination. Nothing in their words or practice suggests so. We only note the fear of such indoctrination from both the secular and religious sides.

It is clear that MORAL DOMINANT and ACADEMIC DOMINANT positions make sense, take root, and are successful in some communities. It is an open question whether positions of this sort are broadly applicable to schooling in a pluralistic democracy.

6

The TRANSFORMATIVE Category

TRANSFORMATIVE positions, programs, and practices are different from any we have considered thus far because they are characterized by a melding of the moral and the academic. In any particular TRANSFORMATIVE position, the moral and the academic are interconnected, but one element sets the agenda, altering the meaning and impact of the other. Thus we might say that the moral "transforms" the academic so that a particular position is MORAL TRANSFORMATIVE. Nel Noddings, for instance, embraces a view of the moral, an ethic of caring, which is so fundamental to her thinking that it leads her to rethink and recast the academic curriculum in terms of centers of care. The opposite is true of an ACADEMIC TRANSFORMATIVE position. For example, Ted Sizer's central commitment to developing particular habits of mind not only clarifies and orders his view of the academic curriculum, but these habits of mind have moral stances embedded in them and set a moral agenda as well. Since the melding can go in either direction—from moral to academic or from academic to moral—the approaches introduced in this chapter are called either ACADEMIC TRANSFORMATIVE or MORAL TRANSFORMATIVE.

This melding of the moral and the academic distinguishes TRANSFORMATIVE positions from DOMINANT ones. DOMINANT positions do not presume the existence of a significant connection or relationship between the moral and the academic realms. Instead, in an ACADEMIC DOMINANT position such as that of E. D. Hirsch, the academic is so central that it pushes aside any concern Hirsch might have for the moral. Hirsch recognizes the moral realm, even acknowledges its importance, but this realm is not the focus of attention and is not viewed as interrelated with the academic. Similarly, the MORAL DOMINANT thinking that underlies Lancaster Catholic High School does not ignore the need for an academic curriculum, but that curriculum, with the exception of religious education, is not generated from the moral vision to be (and become) Catholic. Those who hold DOMINANT positions simply do not give much attention to the nature of that element—either moral or academic—that is of lesser interest.

DOMINANT and TRANSFORMATIVE positions, however, do share several characteristics. First, positions representing both categories can use either moral or academic considerations as a point of departure. Second, for both DOMINANT and TRANSFORMATIVE positions, the point of departure—either moral or academic—is selected because that realm is key to establishing a particular educational program or view of practice. For TRANSFORMATIVE positions, the realm—either moral or academic—that serves as the entry point activates and orders the other realm.

In the following discussion, we look first at three examples of MORAL TRANSFORMATIVE thinking (the Community School, Nel Noddings, David Purpel) and then conclude with an example of ACADEMIC TRANSFORMATIVE (Ted Sizer).

C-SCHOOL'S RELATIONAL EDUCATION

Founded in 1973 by Emanuel Pariser and Dora Lievow, the Community School, known as C-School, is located in a Victorian-style home at 79 Washington Street in Camden, Maine. C-School is a 6-month residential program designed for "kids who have not 'fit' anywhere" (Pariser, 1998). Many have battled drug and alcohol abuse, some have learning disabilities, and still others are bright youngsters who are bored in school and/or feel boxed in by the rigidities of the public school system (Booraem, 2004).

These students are part of "a whole group of teenagers out there who are really disconnected and they need to belong, to feel connected" (Pariser, 1998). Pariser (1999) believes that this disconnectedness is rooted in enormous social changes that have occurred over the past half-century. Disintegration of the nuclear family, the decline in meaningful contact between teenagers and adults, and other societal changes have left adolescents increasingly adrift. The conventional model of schooling, perfected in the early 1900s, has been extraordinarily slow to respond to these massive changes in the American social landscape.

The C-School response is to place "a primary focus on the development of trusting, supportive, and resilient relationships between all members of the learning community" (Pariser, 1999). This approach is labeled by its cofounders, Dora Lievow and Emanuel Pariser, as "relational education." In relational education, the teacher no longer plays the traditional role of information provider but rather becomes a listener. In fact, faculty members at C-School are called teacher/counselors, an acknowledgment of the importance attached to receptivity and responsiveness in relational education. To structure the listening process, each student is assigned a "one-to-one," an adviser who meets regularly with the student (the eight young people at C-School each term are matched with five or six staff members). The adviser's manifest task is to discuss the student's progress in the program, but "on a fundamental level" the adviser tries to develop "a trusting and supportive relationship in which the student can begin to experience her life as having meaning" (Pariser, 1999, para. 15).

The focus on relationship building does not mean that subject matter is unimportant, but such study is organized by C-School personnel to meet the needs of their disaffected and disheartened students. Buck O'Herin, formerly a teacher at C-School, notes that in historical study the stress is not so much on facts, which are easily forgotten, as on "understanding implied meanings and analytical skills. We want to teach people to think" (in Verde, 1990, p. 95). However, even more important than this cognitive outcome is the role subject-matter study plays in increasing each student's self-confidence and willingness to explore new ideas. Academics at C-School are designed "to revitalize the learning process for students: to help make them less afraid of making mistakes, to encourage them to take risks in thinking about things, to build their self-confidence and trust in others so that they can engage in the genuine dialogue which is at the heart of all learning" (Pariser, 1990, pp. 12–13).

An Individual Graduation Plan is used to personalize the program of study for each student. While this plan includes such required academic courses as literature, science, social studies, mathematics, and grammar, the diverse personal interests of C-School students lead to including differing content within any particular required course. Content can also vary because courses address specific subject-matter deficiencies of students, ranging from fractions in math to difficulty with writing. One-to-one tutoring is the most common form of teaching, and competency tests are frequently used to verify successful completion of courses. An Individual Graduation Plan also addresses the social, personal, and interpersonal issues that have contributed to a student's previous lack of success in school. Topics can range over such areas as conflict resolution, communication and decision making, assertiveness training, anger management skills, and substance abuse counseling. Performance assessment is commonly used to check competence in these skill areas.

The Individual Graduation Plan is not the only requirement for graduation. To receive high school diplomas, students at the Community School must meet "independent living and work requirements, as well as paying a portion of their own room and board expenses" (Community School, 2000). C-School induces responsibility by having students hold jobs in Camden, jobs that students must find and keep. Similarly, students are held accountable for their behavior in the C-School community and for doing such daily chores as cooking meals and washing dishes (Pariser, 1990). The intent of these policies is to break down the barriers between school and the "real world." As one student reflected, "What's the point of taking us out of the Real World, if the idea of school is to prepare us for it" (in Pariser, 1999, para. 19).

It is not surprising, therefore, to hear Dora Lievow say "our goal is to launch people into independent living" (in Hatch, 1999, para. 7). In a fundamental way, the "curriculum" of C-School is only partly a matter of traditional subject-matter study, which is relegated to the evenings in any case. One student told a visiting reporter, "Classes aren't really that intense. They're probably the least focused-on part of the program" (in Verde, 1990, p. 93). At the core of the Community School "curriculum" are life skills. These skills include the ability to get and hold a job, which entails consistency and perseverance, but also the ability to live within a group and to regularly assume responsibility for the daily tasks of living at C-School.

With such ambitious goals, C-School does not always succeed; some semesters all students finish the program, but other times less than half do so. Perhaps surprisingly, about 80% of the 500 C-School students have earned their high school diplomas (Booraem, 2004). This level of success is possible only because the Community School is a 16-hour-a-day effort grounded in a comprehensive view of learning. As Emanuel Pariser (1990) put it, learning at C-School

> does not fit into neat packages. It comes as life is lived from day to day, and as we make the choices which give our lives shape. . . . The teaching staff is on hand as much to facilitate these choices as it is to create a useful and relevant lesson plan. The emphasis on the personal, the intimate human encounter, results in an affective intensity and warmth which are singular. (pp. 17–18)

C-School's educational design is an interconnected moral and academic effort. When considering any piece of the C-School structure and program, it is easy to see how that piece fits within the larger picture. C-School, for example, is deliberately constructed as a mini-society, a society that provides its adolescent students with a variety of cognitive, affective, and life challenges. Teacher/counselors are there to help students address these challenges, even as the ultimate responsibility for coping with these challenges resides with each student. Traditional subject-matter content is personalized to individuals, and this content not only serves cognitive ends but also addresses the psychological need for students to become self-confident and their social need to become a critically aware citizenry. The overall curriculum is viewed as preparing adolescents for life; in fact, the curriculum basically *is* life, to the extent that life can be replicated in a residential home for adolescents. In this way, the idea of the academic—C-School's attempt to create common understanding—includes some subject-matter content but goes beyond that to entail the preparation adolescents need for living a healthy and productive life.

Even though C-School is an interconnected educational effort, this effort can be fully comprehended only if we begin with the underlying moral vision of Emanuel Pariser and Dora Lievow. This vision centers on countering the disconnectedness and disaffection experienced by many youth, and every aspect of the school is transformed by the moral goal of engendering a meaningful and independent life for these youth. The structure of C-School (socially as well as educationally), its approach to subject-matter study, its emphasis on relationships and life skills—all these components are activated in an attempt to meet the needs of those youth who have thus far failed at life. C-School is an exemplar of what we term a MORAL TRANSFORMATIVE position.

We cannot help but wonder if the need for a meaningful and independent life is not an appropriate moral vision for *all* of today's youth. Disaffection and boredom are widespread among youth, including many, if not most, of those who appear to succeed in high school. A school like C-School—personalized to the needs of varied audiences of American youth—might finally bring about the kind of school reform that has eluded those who aspire to regenerate the American high school. Yet to move in that direction would require a substantial broadening of the conventional view of the academic. Pariser and Lievow achieve that broadening by allowing a moral vision to guide their thinking.

NEL NODDINGS'S CARING CURRICULUM

Just prior to retiring from Stanford's School of Education, Nel Noddings was asked how schools could be made more meaningful. She offered few suggestions "except making school more home-like," with increased opportunities for exploring topics that are "at the center of life" such as personal commitment, family, children, friendships, and neighborhoods (O'Toole, 1998). It is not surprising, therefore, that Noddings (1992) believes the main aim of education should be to produce "competent, caring, loving, and lovable people" (p. 174). Although this goal echoes the commitment of Pariser and Lievow to relational education, Noddings focuses far less on the affective elements of caring than do the founders of C-School.

In contrast to any "soft, fuzzy notion" of caring, Noddings (2001) views caring as a relation pointing "to something far deeper and more important —a way of being in the world" (pp. 101, 99). In addition to rejecting a "sentimental" view of caring, Noddings (2000) also contrasts her work with a view of caring rooted in virtue ethics. With character education obviously in mind, she distinguishes between two forms of caring: "caring as virtue" and "caring as relation." Caring as virtue means that "we act from our own framework and try to do what we think the other needs." In contrast, in "caring as relation," we "work with the needs expressed by the cared-for." Thus, caring as relation leads us to "judge what we do not from the perspective of our own virtue but by the response of the cared-for" (n.p.; see also Noddings, 2002).

In her philosophical writing, Noddings (1984) is careful to point out how an ethic of "caring as relation" entails a reciprocal relationship between the person who cares (the "one-caring") and the recipient of care (the "cared-for"). The one-caring tries as best that person can to act in the interests of the cared-for, although that does not mean being permissive and not attempting to influence the cared-for. Rather, the one-caring attempts to "feel with" the cared-for and respond appropriately, an experience Noddings calls "engrossment." Moreover, the caring relation only becomes complete when the person being cared-for recognizes the care that is being offered by the one-caring. Noddings sees the reciprocal relation between the one-caring and the cared-for as appropriate to a variety of human relationships.

It is not sufficient, therefore, for the teacher to have good intentions; the teacher must develop trust with students. "That doesn't mean," Noddings (2000) notes, "that we [teachers] don't guide them, but we use their interests to motivate them. We have to get away from the idea that we can just impose a pre-set curriculum on kids and say that we 'care.'" But if the curriculum is not predetermined, does that mean each classroom will have its own curriculum? And what preparation do teachers need to work toward the fundamental goals of education, namely, the creation of "competent, caring, loving, and lovable people"? We turn now to addressing what Noddings's ethic of caring means for curricular practice and teacher preparation.

Belzer Middle School's homepage has a quote from Noddings that captures her sense of the centrality of the moral: "Moral education must precede and guide all others" (Belzer Middle School, 2000). The ethic of caring —that is, caring as relation—is the moral stance that undergirds Noddings's conception of teaching (Boostrom, 1994; Noddings, 1984). Caring as relation is both the proper basis of the teacher–student relationship and the potential core of the school curriculum. Our young people, for example, need to address the "moral task" of learning "the skills needed to care effectively for others" (Noddings, 1988, p. 32).

In *The Challenge to Care in Schools: An Alternative Approach to Education*, Noddings offers a vigorous critique of the long-established structure of liberal education. Liberal education, she argues, "puts too much emphasis on a narrow form of rationality and abstract reasoning" (Noddings, 1992, pp. 42–43). In addition, this overemphasis on the life of the mind "leads successful students to believe that they are truly superior to those living more physical lives" (p. 43). Third, the traditional liberal arts curriculum "is largely a celebration of male life" while "activities, attitudes, and values historically associated with women are neglected or omitted entirely" (p. 43). However, instead of trying to correct the flaws of liberal education, Noddings proposes a new curricular structure.

Education should be "organized around themes of care rather than the traditional disciplines" (Noddings, 1992, p. 173). The key is to engage students in a general education that "guides them in caring for self, intimate others, global others, plants, animals, and the environment, the human-made world, and ideas." These "centers of care" entail a range of study, with some centers focusing on care outside human relationships (e.g., animals and plants) and others emphasizing care from a distance and at a high level of abstraction (global others and ideas). Making caring central leads to a reconstructed curriculum and recasts the purposes of schooling as moral. Noddings believes that half of each school day should be focused on issues of caring.

She supplies no content outline for the centers of care because such a preset curriculum would be inconsistent with the caring relationship between teacher and student. For Noddings, a teacher in concert with students would "forge a curriculum without any need for control, or rules, or disciplines" (Boostrom, 1994, p. 112). The openness of teacher–student curriculum development will make some teachers uncomfortable, but others will be stimulated by the challenge to create and implement a curriculum responsive to their students. In *The Challenge to Care in Schools* (1992), Noddings provides minimal guidance on the process of cooperative curriculum planning, but subsequently she (Noddings, 1995) did recommend the use of interdisciplinary units.

Besides grounding her school reform agenda, the idea of centers of care also suggests why caring ought not be solely a parental responsibility. Should the liberal arts curriculum remain intact, then it might cancel out the effects of a caring-based home life. Noddings (1988) also believes that "the traditional structures of caring have deteriorated" and that "schools must become places where teachers and students live together, talk with each other, take delight in each other's company" (p. 32).

Noddings's ideas on teacher preparation flow logically from what a teacher needs to know and be able to do in order to develop a curriculum organized around centers of care. Teachers-in-preparation need an integrated education, one that provides them with "a superbly well-trained capacity for inquiry and a Socratic willingness to pursue wisdom" (Noddings, 1992, p. 178). When she observes that teachers need a curriculum adapted to "the existential heart of life and to their special interests" (p. 177), she is recommending two kinds of study for prospective teachers. On the one hand, their college curriculum could be grounded in centers of care. What better way for teachers to be prepared to offer their students a care-based curriculum than for these teachers-in-preparation to be educated through that very curricular design? On the other hand, the special interests of teachers require rigorous and in-depth subject-matter preparation attuned to the specific academic needs of K–12 teaching (Noddings, 1998).

Noddings represents a clear-cut instance of a MORAL TRANSFORMATIVE position. Her educational recommendations are generated out of a moral ethic of caring, and whenever she confronts an educational issue, Noddings returns to this ethic for guidance. Hers is fundamentally a moral stance, as revealed by her quotation on the Belzer Middle School (2000) homepage that "moral education must precede and guide all others." At the same time, she takes questions of academic study very seriously, although her approach rejects the organization of this study around the traditional liberal arts disciplines. She wants academic study to flow from and be consistent with her conception of the centers of care. In contrast to the MORAL DOMINANT position of Lancaster Catholic, where academic study is also important but remains essentially the same as academic study in public high schools, Noddings hopes to replace study of the liberal arts disciplines with study oriented around centers of care.

Noddings also differs from the typical MORAL DOMINANT position in that she lacks the sense of certainty that is so common among MORAL DOMINANT exemplars. For Noddings, little in life is settled. She observes: "I am fairly sure about some things, but not very many. . . . If you were to visit me on the New Jersey shore, we would take a long walk and we would be talking about this uncertainty that is part of life as a moral quest" (in O'Toole, 1998, para. 12).

DAVID PURPEL AND THE TEACHER AS PROPHET

In contrast to Nel Noddings, who stresses themes of care, David Purpel (1997) looks first and foremost to the global goal of "creating a just and loving society and a culture of joy and fulfillment for all" (p. 152). Focusing on the broader society and culture may seem a long way from classroom life, but Purpel cautions against basing our educational thinking exclusively—or even primarily—on what traditionally has been referred to as "moral education." That is, he argues against starting our moral discourse and analysis by examining "the specific ethical implications of living in schools—as in what happens when students cheat or steal" (Purpel, 1991a, p. 311). To ground our moral thinking about schools in moral education can easily lead to separating moral education "from the moral aspects of the larger school and social settings" (Purpel, 1997, p. 152).

In fact, Purpel (1997) believes that the idea of "moral education" is "largely redundant" (p. 151). For him, "moral" and "education" have a common origin: "Education is at root a moral endeavor" (Purpel, 1989, p. 65). Schooling of necessity involves moral decisions, including questions of grading, tracking, curriculum, and proper student behavior (Purpel, 1991a). At the same time, Purpel (1997) contends that "deliberate intervention in the behavior and character of students is a central if not dominating theme in the history of public schooling in the United States" (p. 141). Thus education is a moral endeavor because both the daily activities of schooling and the institution of schooling are integrally moral. (Purpel often does not distinguish education from schooling, suggesting that he gives primary attention to the formal aspects of education, that is, to schooling [Griffith, 1991].)

In *The Moral & Spiritual Crisis in Education* (1989), Purpel begins by outlining the multifaceted crisis that grips American society. Underlying this crisis is a set of value paradoxes, involving tensions between such competing values as individuality/community, worth/achievement, equality/competition, ethnocentrism/universalism, among others. These deeply rooted value tensions make it difficult to develop a common moral vision for our society, particularly in light of the enormity of such social issues as privilege, pollution, the horrors of war, moral callousness, injustice, hierarchy, and poverty (Purpel, 1989, 1991a, 1991b).

To his social analysis—influenced by the ideas of Paulo Friere, Henry Giroux, Maxine Greene, and others—Purpel adds a religious and spiritual dimension. For Purpel (1991a), the fundamental search in life is a quest for meaning: "Simply put, the most important and troubling of all human tasks (and hence a challenge for educators) is to be able to know what it means to live the virtuous life" (p. 309). In *The Moral & Spiritual Crisis in Education*, Purpel does not pursue a sectarian view of religion but rather seeks to engage central religious issues and hopes that society can reach consensus on basic religious principles. Purpel's (1989) desire is to "sacralize the educational process" (p. 78; see also Purpel, 1991b).

Yet our society is unable to embrace any common moral vision, except at the most general level. Our commitment to the Enlightenment ideals of reason and science has ultimately led to the deconstructing, contextualizing, and relativizing of knowledge and virtue and to our being "alone, fragmented, and lost" (Purpel, 1991a, p. 309). This predicament is a "catastrophe in the face of our current massive social and cultural crises" (p. 309).

Purpel is not, by any means, the first person to develop a social and spiritual critique of American society. In particular, as he notes, a number of "radicals have boldly and forcefully developed a powerfully illuminating discourse of political and economic domination, social oppression, and intellectual hegemony" (Purpel, 1991a, p. 311). However, he contends these radicals have often failed to go beyond social critique to identify a spiritual and religious vision for American society. It is this vision that Purpel thinks is critical if we are not only to address the social shortcomings of our society but also to provide a sense of meaning that can bind us together.

Purpel does propose a vision—a moral and religious framework—that might provide meaning and social purpose for Americans. Drawing on several ancient traditions and current theological movements, Purpel (1989) describes his effort as seeking an "overarching mythos of meaning, purpose, ultimacy that can guide us in the creation of a vision of the good, true, and beautiful life" (p. 68). In many ways, what Purpel does is to outline the parameters of such an "overarching mythos" rather than put forward a specific mythos, all the while noting that we are a nation of diverse ideas and heritages. From the "overarching mythos" Purpel moves to educational implications. He casts these implications as six general goals for education, ranging from the contemplation of the wonder and mystery of the universe to the development of attitudes of outrage and responsibility in the face of injustice and oppression (Purpel, 1989). Teachers, as suggested in the section heading, are to engage in "education in a prophetic voice."

Since his six general goals involve assumptions, beliefs, and values, Purpel considers indoctrination to be an ever-present danger. Rather than avoiding indoctrination and thereby surrendering their prophetic calling, teachers are better advised to give away, as much as possible, their coercive power over students, especially the "primitive practice of 'grading' students" (Purpel, 1989, p. 120). Students could then study key educational issues with less fear of being dominated by teachers, and teachers could express their passionate convictions with less concern about overpowering their students.

In the last two chapters of *The Moral & Spiritual Crisis in Education* (1989), Purpel outlines the content for a curriculum focused on social justice and compassion. Whatever occurs in schools "should be in harmony with a society's most emancipatory and visionary goals" (p. 122), evidence again of how small a distinction Purpel draws between education and schooling. Purpel identifies specific educational goals and objectives that range over a variety of areas, including intellectual processes and forms; a sense of historicity; the development of social skills; the assimilation of critical knowledge; critical consciousness and competence; and imagination, creativity, and play. In all of these areas, Purpel (1989) believes that the educative process must affirm and celebrate the basic moral vision yet also entail "free, open, and continuous inquiry" (p. 137).

Purpel (1989) supports the study of a common core of knowledge, starting with all people learning how to "read, write, and figure" (p. 129). He also believes everyone should know "seminal statements about our moral commitments" (p. 129) such as the Ten Commandments and the Declaration of Independence. Further, everyone should learn about "the major geopolitical features of our world" (p. 129) and have "a broad historical perspective" (pp. 129–130). He adds that he is "comfortable with teaching students knowledge which the culture believes gives one cachet" (p. 130). Purpel believes that developing a sense of community and universality is a reasonable rationale for a core curriculum, but he calls the determination of appropriate content an "issue of practice" (p. 129) that professionals need to address.

Purpel (1989) is ambivalent about whether his curriculum for social justice and compassion can be offered within the context of the traditional subjects, and he offers an alternative that organizes the educational program around "important and key heuristic and critical questions" (p. 153). As examples, he provides such timeless questions as "By what process do we discern reality?" or "What is the nature of the good?" (p. 154). Even his more specific questions are daunting, such as "What is the nature of language?" or "What are the causes of wars, depression, and creative genius?" (p. 154). He provides few details about the curriculum, once again returning to his theme that teachers can "meet the challenges of design and implementation inherent in our framework" (p. 156).

As in the case of Noddings and C-School, Purpel represents a clear-cut instance of a MORAL TRANSFORMATIVE position. His ideas for educational reform, including academic study, are always rooted in a moral vision. Again and again he returns to social justice and compassion to reassert their importance to all issues of schooling. In a personal essay, Purpel (1999) is forthright about the centrality of moral purpose: "My professional work is totally concerned with grounding educational policies and practices not in critical thinking and not in creative expression but in moral commitment" (p. 248). Purpel takes questions of academic study seriously, but such academic considerations always serve fundamental moral purposes. Interestingly, Purpel's conception of a core of knowledge stresses the kind of perspective and intellectual habits that Ted Sizer takes as his starting point. We now turn to Sizer, our only example of ACADEMIC TRANSFORMATIVE thinking.

TED SIZER AND HORACE'S SCHOOL

Ted Sizer's credentials as an educator are well known. Public school teacher, college professor, education school dean, private school headmaster, founder of an institute for school reform, chair of a school reform coalition, and co-founder of a charter school, Sizer has put his ideas into print and into action in a very public way throughout his career. His interest is secondary education; his goal is reform.

For Sizer, the central life "skill" needed by American youth is development of their intellectual abilities. He argued in *Horace's Compromise* (1984) that high schools exist not merely "to subject the pupils to brute training . . . but to develop their powers of thought, of taste, and of judgment" (p. 4). In *Horace's School* (1992), he contended that high schools ought not be "cradles of all virtuous habits" but rather focus on the intellect. "It is the habit of thoughtfulness, of bringing an informed, balanced, responsibly skeptical approach to life, that schooling addresses" (p. 69). Similarly, the Coalition of Essential Schools, initially chaired by Sizer, based its school reform work on 10 principles, beginning with "Schools should focus on helping adolescents learn to use their minds well. Schools should not attempt to be 'comprehensive' if such a claim is made at the expense of the school's central intellectual purpose" (Sizer, 1992, p. 207). To the extent that high schools fail to foster thoughtfulness in students—and Sizer believed many do fail—these schools are ineffective and in need of reform.

Sizer (1992) would heal high schools by focusing on the academic, conceived not as "core knowledge" but as habits of mind. While readily conceding that thinking is never empty (pp. 25–26) and that content therefore matters, Sizer's emphasis remains steadfastly on "intellectual work" (p. 87). He explains, "A wise school's goal is to get its students into good intellectual habits" (p. 73). He cites eight habits: perspective, analysis, imagination, empathy, communication, commitment, humility, and joy. That Sizer views these as intellectual habits suggests something quite interesting about his understanding of the academic and its link to the moral, and it helps to explain why we view Sizer as ACADEMIC TRANSFORMATIVE.

Terms like *empathy, commitment, humility,* and *joy* are not evocative of what most people would call "academic" (Sizer calls these terms "intellectual" concerns). Even terms such as *perspective, imagination,* and *communication* seem to meld the moral and the academic. Only analysis connotes an approach that can be easily distinguished from moral matters. Yet Sizer is insistent that these habits are the work of the mind. When Sizer and the Coalition of Essential Schools articulate the principle of "student as worker," the point is not that students must take on practical activity (though they often do) but that learning is mental work. "'Working' means working the mind" (Sizer, 1992, p. 87). The mind, to Sizer, is not abstract intelligence. Rather, *mind* refers to skills of observation, of persistent attention, of thoughtful conduct, of willing and skillful collaboration. These are "habits of learning to use ideas," and "schools must give students practice in the craft" (p. 95).

Sizer's understanding of the mind as a functional tool for responding to lived challenges emphasizes concerns that typically might be considered academic, using the language of intellect. At the same time, his understanding of the mind transforms what counts as academic and what counts as moral, marking them as ultimately inseparable. His curricular and school structure recommendations illustrate this point.

Most high schools continue to divide their instructional time among an array of school subjects with names (English, mathematics, biology) derived from the academic disciplines. Teachers are presumed to be experts in a single discipline, and teacher-constructed and -conducted student assessment is linked to each course of study. A student who passes a discipline-based course accumulates credits; the student with the right—and the right number of—credits then graduates.

Sizer recommends two significant changes in this arrangement. First, in order to make meaningful student–teacher relationships possible and to ensure the meaningful consideration of content, instruction is to be blocked into three lengthy sessions per day: history/philosophy, math/science, and the arts. Teachers are to be well prepared in a related academic discipline but will not necessarily, or even probably, be expert in all facets of the history/philosophy, math/science, or arts curriculum.

Second, Sizer disconnects assessment from these blocks of integrated instruction. To graduate, a student must demonstrate intelligence-in-use through a series of exhibitions determined by the school's faculty at large and assessed by a team that includes persons outside the school faculty. In *Horace's School* (1992), Sizer describes sample exhibitions that are either memory-based or life-based. The memory-based exhibition (just one exhibition but involving multiple tasks) requires performance prompted by such standard academic tasks as reciting a particular poem or drawing and labeling a map of the world. Life-based exhibitions (with a focus on human issues and problems) range from the completion and audit of a federal tax return to the analysis of a community need and the creation of a corresponding community service. All exhibitions—memory-based or life-based—require that students be thoughtful.

Sizer believes that schools can be thoughtful places only if there is time for thought and there are opportunities for communication. Using longer instructional blocks creates the needed time. Teaming teachers and students fosters long-term communication. Having a teacher/adviser meet daily with a small (15-student) advisory group makes one adult responsible for the overall progress of each student. And linking graduation to exhibitions encourages a student to work with particular teachers over time on major projects of personal interest. To talk about teams, about meaningful relationships, and about caring and responsibility is to venture into territory that is often considered moral. However, for Sizer (1992), all of these ideas have an academic purpose, that is, a "central focus . . . on the intellect, on helping each young citizen learn to use his or her mind resourcefully and well" (p. 142).

The use of the term *citizen* is not accidental. Sizer recognizes and readily admits that particular values undergird his proposed reforms. These values grow out of an understanding of what it is that democracy requires, and this requirement has a moral character (Sizer, 1992, p. 124). In *Horace's Compromise* (1984), Sizer considers the history of public schooling and its purposes in American social life. He notes the broad range of purposes proposed in the 1918 Cardinal Principles but maintains that a narrower focus is needed in contemporary schools. "One purpose—education of the intellect—is obvious. The other—an education in character—is inescapable" (Sizer, 1984, p. 84). While Sizer understands that moral purposes are served in any educational program, it is concern for the education of the intellect, not character, that drives all of Sizer's recommendations.

And so Sizer defends his curricular and structural plans on academic grounds (developing habits of mind) rather than on moral grounds (e.g., acting in a way that is caring). He argues the importance of academic grounds based on usefulness. In *Horace's Compromise* (1984), Sizer asserts that "intellectual training is eminently 'useful'; it opens means to educate oneself in any sphere of interest or importance. Without it, one is crippled" (p. 85). For Sizer, as we suggested at the outset, intelligence-in-use is the goal of schooling because it is the sine qua non of a life lived well, whatever one's circumstances.

What is it that sets Sizer apart from educators like E. D. Hirsch and Marva Collins, whom we have characterized as ACADEMIC DOMINANT? Their views do have much in common. All three educators, for example, believe academic concerns are central to the purpose of schooling and also share an equity concern that all students receive a similarly challenging and empowering education. Yet there is one key distinction. Where Collins and Hirsch tend to focus on the content of the curriculum, Sizer takes on the structure of the school. Rather than asking what children should learn, Sizer asks what circumstances encourage the habit of thoughtfulness in students and teachers. This significantly different question results in an academic thrust that is TRANSFORMATIVE rather than DOMINANT. Sizer's consistent focus on the habit of thoughtfulness calls into question and eventually transforms every other aspect of the school experience, moral as well as academic.

In fact, it is the emphasis on the (behavioral) context for thoughtfulness that enables Sizer to bring academic and moral concerns into focus at the same time. Thus respect among teachers and students is both a moral goal and a feature of a thoughtful academic environment (Sizer, 1992, p. 125). Ferreting out the truth rather than passively accepting apparent certainties is both an academic goal and a moral, civic commitment in a democratic society.

Sizer may have begun his educational career with the kind of views we have classified as ACADEMIC DOMINANT (e.g., Sizer, 1973). His experience as a teacher and, especially, as headmaster at Phillips Academy seem to have effected a shift as he explains in the Acknowledgments in *Horace's Compromise* (1984): "My many Phillips Academy associates . . . [taught me] that high standards and personal caring for students need not nor cannot be separated" (p. 226). He also learned from his own attempts to redesign the high school, but especially from "an extraordinary group of school people, able risk takers of a remarkable sort" (Sizer, 1992, p. 229), including Dennis Littky (Thayer High School) and Deborah Meier (Central Park East). Sizer's academic focus, born of his own experience as a student, was clearly tempered by persons who shared his concern for thoughtfulness but understood thoughtfulness in a way that opened the door to moral considerations as well as traditionally academic ones.

In 1999, Sizer and his wife, Nancy Faust Sizer, published a book that directly addresses the moral import and impact of schooling. *The Students Are Watching: Schools and the Moral Contract* makes clear what is sometimes latent in the Horace volumes, that "the moral and the intellectual are inextricable" (Sizer & Sizer, 1999, p. 15). But even here, Sizer's vision of the transformative power of the academic goal of thoughtfulness remains clear and consistent.

POSSIBILITIES AND DANGERS

There are several points of significant contrast between the views we have characterized as TRANSFORMATIVE and DOMINANT. In the previous chapter, we noted that those who adhere to a DOMINANT perspective—either MORAL DOMINANT or ACADEMIC DOMINANT—tend to look at curriculum in more or less traditional ways. That certainly is not the case for the ACADEMIC TRANS-FORMATIVE and MORAL TRANSFORMATIVE educators we have discussed, all of whom see much to criticize about conventional curricular approaches. Earlier we also observed that those classified as DOMINANT hold clear and inspiring visions of human living and the education these visions entail, with little tentativeness in their viewpoints. While those classified as TRANSFOR-MATIVE also have strongly held social and educational positions, they often reveal a sense of caution about their educational work, expressed variously as a declaration of personal uncertainty (Noddings), a deep concern for preventing indoctrination (Purpel), a recognition that their educational efforts sometimes fail (Lievow and Pariser), or an acknowledgment of how important others have been to developing one's perspective (Sizer). As compared to the pursuit by DOMINANT educators of widely accepted curricular approaches, TRANSFORMATIVE educators tend to propose dramatic reforms in the school curriculum, yet concurrently seem to lack the single-minded focus and sense of certainty so common among those classified as DOMINANT.

Why do TRANSFORMATIVE educators express wariness and restraint even as they make proposals for dramatic change? This cautious stance may be a consequence of TRANSFORMATIVE educators viewing school reform in the United States as a complex and far-reaching task. A TRANSFORMATIVE solution is never a simple and straightforward solution. For example, either a MORAL TRANSFORMATIVE or a ACADEMIC TRANSFORMATIVE position requires attention to both moral and academic considerations. TRANSFORMATIVE positions, of necessity, are comprehensive in scope. Moreover, the consideration that is subsidiary in a TRANSFORMATIVE stance is nevertheless transformed by the attention given to the primary consideration. Remember that Lievow and Pariser not only argue that schools must become relational communities but also use this vision to expand our conventional conception of the academic to include a variety of life skills. Remember also that Sizer not only challenges our common understanding of the academic by emphasizing intellectual habits of minds but also includes several habits that seem to be as moral as they are academic. This last attribute of Sizer's thinking reveals a third form of complexity in TRANSFORMATIVE thinking: The academic and the moral tend to be melded together. The interplay between the moral and the academic in transformational thinking leads to a level of educational complexity not characteristic of the perspectives considered in the previous three chapters.

The practical value of TRANSFORMATIVE solutions depends heavily on whether current schooling conditions require coherent yet comprehensive educational reforms. Do we need an entirely new vision for the high school as both Sizer and Pariser and Lievow would have us believe? Have we failed to link our ideas for public schooling to the moral and spiritual crisis of our time as suggested by Purpel? Ought the ethic of caring, as outlined by Noddings, not only guide relations among teachers and students but also lead to abandoning the discipline-based curriculum and replacing it with a curriculum grounded in centers of care?

The widespread use of student test scores as our major form of accountability indicates that public policy is headed in a different direction. Relying on state standards and high-stakes testing presumes that what we need is not so much fundamental reform in schooling as increased rigor and equity of outcomes in the academic curriculum as traditionally conceived. Earlier we characterized the contemporary focus on test-driven accountability as *moral invisible*. It is quite possible, perhaps even likely, for a school faculty to be committed to a MORAL TRANSFORMATIVE (or ACADEMIC TRANSFORMA-TIVE) stance and still be able to obtain good student test results. However, contemporary accountability policy reinforces conventional views of academic achievement, and as the provisions of No Child Left Behind require higher and higher levels of student test results, we are likely to see increased emphasis on teaching to the test.

None of the TRANSFORMATIVE theorists discussed in this chapter favor accountability based on student test results. Purpel, Noddings, and Sizer have spoken and written directly and critically about the recent path of accountability policy in the United States. Similarly, Pariser and Lievow's broadening of curriculum to include life skills as well as subject-matter content suggests they oppose educational accountability as currently conceived. At the same time, all of the TRANSFORMATIVE orientations that we have discussed, including C-School, want to preserve the prerogative of teachers and students to work through the implications of transforming a curriculum. This reliance on the creativity of teachers is an attribute that differentiates TRANSFORMATIVE thinking from the more prescriptive manner of DOMINANT approaches. Recommendations by TRANSFORMATIVE reformers tend to be limited in specificity, primarily because TRANSFORMATIVE approaches are too complex and interconnected to be amenable to blueprints for educational change.

Indeed, one danger is that TRANSFORMATIVE positions might be adopted by would-be reformers in incomplete and superficial ways. Caring, for example, has become a part of the mainline reform agenda, as indicated by the call for the preparation of "competent, *caring* and qualified teacher[s]" (National Commission on Teaching & America's Future, 1996, p. 21; emphasis added). However, this widely promulgated view of caring tends to be grounded in "virtue ethics" (the teacher interprets the needs of students) rather than a caring-as-relation view (the teacher attends to the perspective of the cared-for student as well as to his or her own intentions). To use Noddings's work to bolster this mainline view of a "caring" teacher, as often is the case, is to accept a truncated conception of caring as relation. Similarly, the great difficulty the Coalition of Essential Schools has had in helping schools follow the 10 coalition principles is another example of incomplete adoption of a TRANSFORMATIVE position, this result occurring despite the coalition's substantial support for these schools (Muncey & McQuillan, 1993, 1996).

Instead of stressing the incomplete and superficial adoption of TRANS-FORMATIVE ideas, perhaps we should be surprised that TRANSFORMATIVE positions have had any practical effect. To have even a modest impact on the conduct of schooling can be viewed as a major achievement in light of the overwhelming emphasis on accountability for conventional academic outcomes. TRANSFORMATIVE positions also fly in the face of the commonsense belief that the moral and the academic are independent realms. TRANSFOR-MATIVE thinking and action, moreover, entail a willingness to accept that either the moral or the academic realm can lead to reconceiving the other realm. Neither this latter dynamic, which we earlier identified as the "moving force" issue, nor the melding of the academic and the moral are widely accepted perspectives. TRANSFORMATIVE solutions are not only complex solutions; they are also solutions that challenge our "folk theory" of how the moral and academic are related to one another.

At the same time, we need to note that TRANSFORMATIVE positions can be criticized as being incompletely developed and articulated. For example, after identifying a broad moral vision for the future of American schooling, Purpel provides minimal information about a curriculum design for realizing this vision. He turns over the entire task of curriculum planning to the teaching profession, leaving himself open, as one reviewer notes (Egan, 1990) to the "accusation of 'idle theorizing'" (p. 126). Kieran Egan worries that if Purpel does not provide a strong sense of how to realize his ideas in practice, no one will. "If no one will," Egan continues, "what's the point?" (p. 126). Egan might also be disappointed by Noddings's failure to supply no more than general advice for designing a curriculum based on themes of care. Only in the case of Pariser and Lievow, who seem to have theorized and developed C-School concurrently, do we get a strong sense of the educational practices consistent with a particular MORAL TRANSFORMATIVE or ACADEMIC TRANSFORMATIVE position. More detail would be welcome by many educators if the authors of these positions are to help us both address the complexity of their reform solutions and overcome barriers to change created by current accountability practices.

Although we found many similarities between MORAL DOMINANT and ACADEMIC DOMINANT views, we did outline several differences between these two types of DOMINANT positions. In the case of TRANSFORMATIVE positions, we propose no significant points of contrast between ACADEMIC TRANSFOR-MATIVE and MORAL TRANSFORMATIVE variants. These two variants tend to be similar since both meld together academic and moral considerations, differing only in the point of entry. We turn now to positions we characterize as INTEGRATED. INTEGRATED positions, like TRANSFORMATIVE ones, meld together the moral and the academic. However, INTEGRATED positions have no identifiable entry point, and moral and academic considerations influence one another in an interactive and dialectical way.

7

The INTEGRATED Category

When Alan Tom published *Teaching as a Moral Craft* in 1984, few educators were focused on the moral dimensions of their work. Today, one can discern a chorus of voices that apparently cannot talk about school experience in ways that are discretely academic or discretely moral. This is, in fact, the thesis of a qualitative research report published in 1993 by Jackson and colleagues entitled *The Moral Life of Schools*. The authors looked at classroom events through a moral lens, revealing the moral influence exerted on students by apparently "neutral" actions. They concluded that all schools "explicitly seek to have a moral influence on their students" and that "the moral influence schools and teachers actually have is far from limited to those explicit efforts" (p. 237). They followed this conclusion with some recommendations about how educators might "cultivate expressive awareness," that is, how they might realize this moral influence in *conscious* action. Jackson and colleagues do not replace an academic focus with a moral one. Instead, they complement the academic picture with its moral reflection. Look from this side and the scene makes sense academically; look from over there and the same scene makes sense morally.

The category we characterize as INTEGRATED is rooted in teaching practice and encompasses views in which (1) the moral and the academic seemed blended (though each may be distinguishable for analytic purposes) and (2) changing one changes the other in action, in effect, or in meaning. This melding of the academic and the moral reflects bidirectional—and dialectical—influence. One shapes the other; neither takes precedence.

The characteristics noted above—blending and transformative influence—are found in the previous category, TRANSFORMATIVE, but TRANSFORMATIVE positions operate predominantly from one direction to another. The positions described in this chapter defy categorization as ACADEMIC TRANSFORMATIVE or MORAL TRANSFORMATIVE because *both* the moral and the academic are always present, are always important, are always transformative. Exemplars we introduce include the following:

- Bob Peterson is a fifth-grade teacher at *La Escuela Fratney* in Milwaukee who has been heavily influenced by his reading of Paulo Freire. His work, like that of teacher educator Landon Beyer, relies on the concept of social justice to integrate the moral and the academic.
- Deborah Meier is a former kindergarten teacher turned school principal and school reformer at Central Park East Secondary School in Harlem and, later, at Mission Hill School in Boston. Meier enacts an educational program that she identifies as education for democracy.
- Lisa Delpit argues for the moral responsibility to teach *all* children academic "codes," basic linguistic forms and communications skills, that ensure entrance to the "culture of power."
- Jared Stallones, former academic director at Austin's Grace Covenant Christian School, is convinced that liberal, democratic education and Christian education can be mutually supportive.
- Rachel Kessler relies on Parker Palmer's view of the soul as the reality that focuses teachers' academic and moral intentions and students' academic and moral development.
- David Hansen analyzes teaching as a practice and maintains that removing the moral is not possible.

Although each case is an example of INTEGRATED, elements of other categories are evident. Deborah Meier sounds ACADEMIC TRANSFORMATIVE, but she also attends to moral community and the importance of relationship. Jared Stallones invites characterization as MORAL TRANSFORMATIVE or even MORAL DOMINANT by starting with a Christian ethic, but his appeal to logic, Latin, and democracy confound that judgment. Only by reading each case through can integration be seen as the critical descriptor, largely because we have no language of integration in educational practice. We have instrumental language and we have expressive language, we have academic terminology and we have moral terminology, but few terms convey both perspectives. The integration that is an intrinsic part of educational action for these exemplars is not easily explained, but it can be described.

TEACHING FOR SOCIAL JUSTICE

Bob Peterson is both a classroom teacher and one of the editors of *Rethinking Schools*, "a non-profit, independent newspaper advocating the reform of elementary and secondary public schools." This journal identifies itself as emphasizing "urban schools and issues of equity and social justice."

Peterson became committed to critical education as a high school student in the late 1960s and early 1970s, heavily influenced by his reading of Paulo Freire. That reading led him to realize that progressive education "could be more than just 'relevant' and 'student-centered'" (Peterson, 1991, p. 156). A decade later, the impact of his 1980 trip to Nicaragua moved Peterson to apply Freire's critical ideas to his fourth- and fifth-grade bilingual classrooms in inner-city Milwaukee.

Peterson experimented with Freire's dialogic "problem-posing" method of education in which both teacher and student(s) become "actors in figuring out the world through a process of mutual communication" (Peterson, 1991, p. 157). This dialogic approach contrasts with a "banking" method of education in which the teacher has the right answers and regularly "deposits" this knowledge in the minds of students. In a Freirean approach, the lived experience of students is central and the teacher respects students' culture and language. Students, moreover, should have "the maximum amount of power that is legally permitted and that they can socially handle" (p. 158). Instead of stressing answers, Peterson tried to make open-ended questions the core of his curriculum in order to "prod students to critically analyze their social situation and encourage them to ultimately work towards changing it" (p. 157).

In planning, Peterson looked for issues or topics—an incident from a student's life, a community problem, an idea that a student picked up from the media—that were immediately engaging to students. He often started off the school year with a unit on his students' backgrounds and families. One year, on the first day of school, his students wrote a book about a topic that he and the class jointly selected. He always had students putting their own ideas and experiences on paper, often publishing the results in the student newspaper, the city newspaper, or children's magazines. Even when he felt compelled to teach a specified curriculum or used a required instructional approach, Peterson found ways to appeal to the life experiences of his students. For example, while using basal readers, he had his students compare their lives to those of characters in the readers.

Peterson acknowledged the challenges inherent in his organic approach to teaching. The first was his students' limited life experiences. "Given the class oppression in our society, poor children usually have a narrower range of experiences than those from more affluent homes" (Peterson, 1991, p. 161). He rejected the notion that these poor children were culturally deficient, but he did try to stretch the limits of their experience by taking them out into the world through field trips or the study of current events or by bringing the world into his classroom through speakers and movies.

A second cluster of difficulties flowed from Freire's assumption that what most inspires the learner is examination of personal experience, particularly the learner's own oppression. For many urban children, Peterson believes, this oppression is centered in the key institutions of school, family, and community. Thus the teacher who seeks to use students' experience of oppression as a springboard to understanding the world is simultaneously representing an oppressive institution. Peterson did develop two approaches to reveal and defuse this contradiction. The first way was openly to explore power relationships and "oppression" in his own classroom; the second way was to introduce questions of societal conflict and inequity into the classroom through the discussion of specific issues in Milwaukee.

But bringing the broader world into the classroom forced Peterson to confront a third challenge in the problem-posing method. The enormous impact of the visual media means that generative themes that appeal to children may be more linked to video games and topics on television than to life in their own community. The visual media not only impact the topics of interest to children but also lead children to rely on instantaneous, simple, and even violent solutions to social issues. In addition, the imaginative abilities of children are deadened. These potent and destructive influences of the visual media led Peterson to engage students in considering how the media impact their thinking (Peterson, 1994).

Peterson's fourth difficulty arose from the temptation to cover too much content too quickly while simultaneously realizing that his organic approach to teaching required in-depth study. Peterson's most successful experiences, he found, occurred when he centered class activity on one concept or aspect of a problem situation. He used a variety of focal points, ranging from a word for the day to a cartoon or a news article. Through word webbing, Peterson could link the topic of study with the life experiences of the students. The students might use the focus term as a "password" as they move through the day. Focusing on one word, especially in a bilingual setting, helps students become aware of language as a tool for cognition and metacognition (Peterson, 1991).

In the face of each of these four challenges, Peterson sought to integrate moral concerns and academic goals. His students *would* learn to read critically, to speak well, to think carefully, to appreciate cultural references, to understand current events. And *in that process*, they would name oppression, recognize conflict, criticize inequity, and imagine (and enact) liberation. In Peterson's hands, both the academic and the moral had an overtly political form and quality.

Peterson persevered with his personal problem-posing approach and, in the late 1980s, joined with others to create a site-managed, democratic, multicultural, two-way bilingual school (Peterson, 1995). The difficulties facing *La Escuela Fratney* have been significant: the tendency for English to become dominant, tensions between White parents and parents of color, the construction of a truly multicultural curriculum, reaching some balance in the influence of mainstream and dominant cultures, even the choice of a particular approach to the teaching of reading. While differences arose about how to implement a school governance scheme that emphasized the role of teachers and parents, parental involvement has been substantial, though segmented (Peterson, 1995). Despite the challenges and sometimes failures, *La Escuela Fratney* is a reminder that democratic education grounded in a vision of social justice is worth working toward.

Bob Peterson persisted in his effort to educate for social justice in a way that brings moral considerations (justice, power, respect, and reform) together with academic considerations (literacy, language competence, and communicative skill), always locating the integration in the experience of his students. Peterson, though unusual, is not alone in his commitment to educate for social justice. What Peterson is doing for school children, Landon Beyer does for future teachers. First at Knox College and then at Indiana University, Beyer was intent on educating persons who will be teachers in the Peterson model.

Over two decades, Beyer (1997) spoke and wrote about the "moral contours" of teaching, arguing that any educational effort is inescapably moral and inescapably political. He is open about his own political views, which could be characterized as critical liberal. Beyer's students are now in the schools attempting to enact teaching as reflective moral action. He invited some of them to share their reflections in a book he edited: *Creating Democratic Classrooms: The Struggle to Integrate Theory and Practice* (Beyer, 1996).

A pattern of struggles, challenges, and conceptual expressions emerges through the reading of their multiple personal reflections: *empowerment* of teachers, students, and parents; *voice* that can be cultivated and heard; *community* that is only possible when democracy marks every aspect of classroom practice. A catalog of useful tools for creating communities of learners emerges as well: journaling, class meetings, dialogue, cooperative learning, peer tutoring, peer editing, cooperative researching, discourse space, thematic teaching, writing workshops, and rule-generation strategies. These are the kinds of tools that Bob Peterson has discovered by necessity. Like Peterson, these new teachers generally recognize that their efforts to teach for social justice are incomplete, always in progress. Beyer recognized this as well, and, in his conclusion to *Creating Democratic Classrooms*, he suggests that teachers pay particular attention to four elements of their own experience if they are to teach for social justice: the quality of community both within the classroom and with other educators, the unpredictability of democratic action, the value of continued knowledge growth, and the promise of collaboration.

Peterson and Beyer root the integration of the moral and the academic in the Freirean concept of *praxis*—that place where theory and practice are brought together by critical values. Their moral commitment to social justice shapes understanding of academic goals and how to achieve them. Their academic goals for growth in critical understanding contribute to possibilities for social change.

HABITS OF MIND FOR DEMOCRATIC EDUCATION

High School II, Fred Wiseman's 1994 documentary about Central Park East Secondary School, includes a remarkable scene in which four school personnel sit talking with a female student, her mother, and her brother. The student is returning to school after giving birth to a daughter. The conversation is focused but not hurried; it covers a wide range of concerns that might arise when a student returns to school, especially a student who is now a mother. School personnel express pleasure at her return and probe her perspective on this change in her life. Gently but insistently, they raise questions about whether she can successfully make the transition back to school and examine her reasons for saying "yes." They encourage her to connect her decision to return with the impact on her child, her mother, and herself. They ask whether things would be better if she changed schools to one that provides on-site child care. They wonder what her reentry will mean to her, to her brother, and to the baby's father, who is also a student in the school. All of the probing and encouragement suggest care and concern for this young woman. And all of this discussion is about her academic prospects and performance. There is no divide between academic concerns and moral ones. Significant time (more than 20 minutes visible on tape) is invested by seven people who think together about how this student can be both good and smart in response to a particularly challenging set of circumstances.

Deborah Meier was one of the participants in this scene. She was, in 1992 at the time the film was shot, the co-director (and co-founder) of Central Park East Secondary School (CPESS). This scene is one scrap of evidence for what seems to be Meier's broader position. Taking care of students entails challenging them intellectually (even when the subject is not an academic one); teaching them to think takes care of them and enables them to care for and with others. Democracy demands that every child in every school be challenged and cared for in these ways. Both Meier's written views and recorded practice support our characterization of her as taking an integrated approach to the moral/academic relation.

Central Park East Secondary School was affiliated with Ted Sizer's Coalition of Essential Schools, and Meier herself is often associated with

Sizer's thinking. Thus, we might categorize Meier with Sizer as ACADEMIC TRANSFORMATIVE. But Meier often sounds like the MORAL TRANSFORMATIVE Nel Noddings, suggesting that caring relationships inevitably reshape academic vision and practice. She is able to articulate both these voices and still seem consistent because her overall approach is INTEGRATED. The principle that holds the moral and the academic together for Meier, that presents them as mutually transformative domains, is her radical democracy in conjunction with her personal predilection for dialectic and ambiguity.

At the start of *The Power of Their Ideas* (1995, p. ix), Meier proclaims herself a "democrat" and "socialist." There, and in an essay entitled "Educating a Democracy," Meier outlines what she considers to be "indispensable traits of a democratic society: a high degree of tolerance for others, indeed genuine empathy for them, as well as a high degree of tolerance for uncertainty, ambiguity, and puzzlement, indeed enjoyment of them" (Meier, 2000, p. 16). These empathetic and intellectual qualities ought to be at the core of education for children. Such an education involves "responsibility for one's own ideas, tolerance for the ideas of others and a capacity to negotiate the difference" (Meier, 2000, p. 5). For Meier (1995), "Ideas—the ways we organize knowledge—are the medium of exchange in democratic life, just as money is in the marketplace" (p. 8).

Like Ted Sizer, Meier is explicitly concerned with the intellectual life of students. And like Sizer, she believes that the most direct route to invigorating the lives of both students and teachers is to change the structure of schools. She notes:

> Human learning, to be efficient, effective, and long-lasting, requires the engagement of learners on their own behalf, and rests on the relationships that develop between schools and their communities, between teachers and their students, and between the individual learner and what is to be learned. (Meier, 2000, p. 9)

Therefore, schools must be small, parents and students should have a sense of both autonomy and responsibility, coaching is the preferred model of instruction, curriculum must be linked to life, and assessment should be authentic.

In one newsletter piece addressed to "students, parents and staff," Meier (1995, p. 155) writes: "That's how we at CPESS define being well-educated: getting in the habit of developing theories that can be articulated clearly and then checked out in a thoughtful way" (p. 155). Developing, checking, and acting on theories requires habits of mind. Central Park East relies on five: perspective, evidence, connection, supposition, and significance. These habits are not only developed with regard to algebraic equations or fruit fly reproduction or Shakespearean characterizations, however. A look back at the scene described earlier reveals the use of the same five habits in making sense of the young woman's return to school. Meier will do whatever it takes to ensure that students use their minds well in the pursuit of all facets of their lives.

Like Nel Noddings, Meier (1995) articulates the moral imperatives of caring and compassion as worthy and challenging educational ends:

> Caring and compassion are not soft, mushy goals. They are part of the hard core of subjects we are responsible for teaching. Informed and skillful care is learned. Caring is as much cognitive as affective. The capacity to see the world as others might is central to unsentimental compassion and at the root of both intellectual skepticism and empathy. (p. 63)

In Meier's (1995) complex educational world, the meaning of "moral" and the meaning of "academic" shift as one's perspective changes:

> The goal is educating, and that means knowing what we're educating *for*. . . . It's not enough to keep saying our goal is "academic excellence" as though that means something sufficiently neutral and obvious that none can disagree. It doesn't. . . . We need to replace the word "academic" with a new word, maybe more than one, for what we're after—with language that carries a different set of connotations. (p. 161; emphasis in original)

Meier is not an opponent of what currently counts as "academic," that is, the traditional school subjects. But she also insists:

> Once we recognize and acknowledge that academia is but one form of intellectual life, we can begin to imagine the other possibilities. Other possibilities don't mean that all traditional disciplines are now unimportant to us; quite the opposite, they force us to ask how such disciplines are relevant to our inquiries. They make the discipline, however, second to the intellectual inquiry. What determines what we study, the driving criteria, should be the demands of a democratic citizenry, not the requirements of academia. (Meier, 1995, p. 168)

This brings Meier back around to the habits of mind, habits that are for her intellectual in a way that incorporates concerns of value (the moral) with concerns of fact (the academic). Such habits should be developed because living well, living democratically, requires them.

ACCESSING THE "CULTURE OF POWER"

In Baton Rouge, Louisiana, Dalrymple Boulevard once separated Baton Rouge's White community from its poorer, Black neighborhoods. Lisa Delpit was born on the "wrong side" of that dividing line. The Baton Rouge in which she grew up was thoroughly segregated, as were the Catholic schools Delpit attended. She recalls how "some of the black nuns we had would tell us, 'Act your age, not your color,'" indicating how deep was the "internalization of society's views of black people" (in Viadero, 1996, p. 40). Delpit believes that this kind of racism persists throughout the United States and continues to pose severe problems for today's African American children (Delpit, 1999), though often in more subtle forms than was true for the Baton Rouge of her youth.

As an adolescent, Delpit crossed Dalrymple Boulevard when she integrated first one and then another Catholic high school in Baton Rouge. And when it came time to go to college, she continued her border crossing by selecting Antioch, known for its radicalism. At Antioch, she was exposed to radical politics and progressive teaching strategies. She began her teaching career in a racially mixed school in Philadelphia with the belief that "the open classroom was the most 'humanizing' of learning environments, that children should be in control of their own learning, and that all children would read when they were ready" (Delpit, 1995, p. 12). She was committed to "teaching black children and teaching them well" (p. 14).

Delpit was one of the few Black teachers in the school, and the other Black teachers tended to be older and to use "traditional" teaching techniques. Instead of loosely structuring learning environments to induce children to flourish intellectually, these Black teachers "focused on 'skills,' they made students sit down at desks, they made students practice handwriting, they corrected oral and written grammar" (Delpit, 1995, p. 13). The young White teachers tended to see the established Black teachers as a bit "oppressive" and believed these teachers did not realize how smart the kids really were.

Following the "progressive" lead of her Antioch training and her White colleagues, Delpit found that her White students prospered while her Black students floundered. She stayed in Philadelphia for 6 years, and each year her teaching became less like that of her young White colleagues and more like that of the older Black women teachers. As her classroom became increasingly "traditional," the reading and writing of her Black students steadily improved but never matched the achievement of her White students. Delpit blamed herself, and eventually left classroom teaching—first to take an administrative job in Louisiana and then to attend graduate school.

In 1984, with a doctorate in hand, Delpit obtained a position as a university-level literacy instructor, taking an approach that emphasized "process" over "skills," as her graduate study and research suggested. Once again, she was forced to confront the question of progressive and traditional approaches in teaching Black children. And once again, she arrived at the conclusion that strictly following progressive approaches did Black students a disservice.

Prompted especially by encounters with experienced Black educators, Delpit reconsidered her earlier failure in teaching Black youngsters. Delpit's 1986 essay "Skills and Other Dilemmas of a Progressive Black Educator" told the story of her journey in trying to teach Black children as effectively as White students. Using personal experience, the experience of other teachers, and reasoned argument, Delpit made the case that progressive educational ideas often do not serve Black youth well, even that the attempt to impose these ideas on the teachers of minority youth marks a callous disregard for these children's access to education.

But Delpit's contention that all children do not prosper with the same teaching techniques is only one part of her message. In an equally controversial essay, "The Silenced Dialogue: Power and Pedagogy in Educating Other People's Children" (1988), Delpit concluded that issues of power, not pedagogy, are central to the belief among teachers of color that skills and skill-related content need to be highlighted for many non-White and non-middle-class children. By emphasizing skills, Delpit does not champion meaningless drill. She expects teachers of minority youth to develop their students' abilities "to critique the way the dominant culture affects their lives and the larger society, while at the same time making sure their students have mastered the gate-keeping skills the dominant society has established for entrance" (Freedman, 1999, p. 25).

Children who are already part of the cultural mainstream arrive at school with—or learn from their families—what Delpit calls a "culture of power." This culture involves access codes—accepted linguistic forms, communication strategies, and ways to present the self. Success in school or in other societal institutions is predicated "upon acquisition of the culture of those who are in power." Children from middle-class homes tend to outperform those from non-middle-class homes because "the culture of the school is based on the culture of the upper and middle classes—of those in power" (Delpit, 1988, p. 283). Focusing on process, fluency, or student empowerment was fine for children who learned those codes at home; those who did not needed, initially at least, to master the linguistic, communication, and reasoning skills that filter entrance to the dominant culture.

Access to the dominant culture comes through acquisition of basic academic skills. Delpit does not propose a change in the school or the broader society. She seeks to ensure that Black children are not excluded from it. Once Black youth acquire the codes of the dominant culture, they can enjoy the social and economic benefits of that culture. Still, she seems to welcome the critical spirit that educated Black adults will bring to the way that social life is organized and structured.

In any case, Delpit believes that being either "good" or "smart" will not be an adequate guide for the teacher who wants to succeed at teaching all children. Both the moral and the academic are joined in an understanding of power and its dynamics in social and economic interaction. For this reason, Delpit's approach can rightly be characterized as INTEGRATED.

DEMOCRACY AND CHRISTIAN TRADITION

The exemplars above can be loosely classified as radical (Peterson and Beyer), liberal (Meier), and neoliberal (Delpit) in the context of modern American politics, but someone who demonstrates an integrated view need not share that left-leaning political orientation. Jared Stallones, the former academic director of a Christian school in Austin, Texas, is such an exception. Grace Covenant Christian School has as its logo a lion and as its slogan: "Come further up and further in, beyond the Shadow-Lands." Both of these are references to C. S. Lewis's *Chronicles of Narnia*, inviting students to follow the lion, a symbol of Christ, into the land of faith (Stallones, 2000c). Its mission statement is clear: "to minister to families by creating a nurturing, Biblically-based learning environment, to achieve excellence in academics and reinforce Christ-centered values" (Grace Covenant Christian School, n.d.). Based on this bit of information, Grace Covenant Christian presents itself as a school with a MORAL DOMINANT orientation, not unlike that of Lancaster Catholic High School.

But there is more. The school's website makes it clear that Biblically based and Christ-centered values transform the curriculum. Each traditional subject is cast in terms that place God at the center of understanding. God is in control of human history. God made the universe in an orderly manner, one that is mathematically verifiable. The arts reveal a people's relationship to God. Based on this curricular transformation, we might surmise that Grace Covenant Christian School evidences a MORAL TRANSFORMATIVE stance toward the moral and the academic. The moral—specifically, a Biblical orientation—does not merely dominate but also reshapes the academic.

But there is still more. Latin and logic are both taught as part of the elementary- and middle-level curriculum, celebrating both tradition and reason. Inference, analysis, and problem solving are an integral part of each child's development, apparently without concern that reason might contradict faith. The school's newsletter asserts that "all truth is God's truth" (Stallones, 2000d) and suggests that seeking the truth through an expansive academic program shapes both Christian thought and Christian action. Perhaps Grace Covenant Christian's claim to "promote academic excellence and spiritual growth in each of its students" is a claim of mutual integration rather than separation.

The views of Jared Stallones support an integrated interpretation. Stallones (2000d) authored a column in Grace Covenant Christian's newsletter in which he clearly articulated a vision of what it means to be a Christian school. He insists that both the Christian worldview and the scholarly perspective be taken seriously simultaneously, and he is not afraid to be critical of his own or other Christian schools that slight one or the other element (Stallones, 2000a).

Stallones has also raised his voice in contemporary scholarly discussion over the role of schooling in a democracy and the relationship between religion and schooling, both public and private. In talks given at the National Council for the Social Studies Conference and the Conference on Curriculum and Pedagogy, Stallones (2000a, 2000b) argued that democracy, community, and faith are "a three-legged stool" and that to neglect religious interests and values is both to sell democracy short and to fail to achieve academic excellence.

Stallones (2000a) makes the first case by articulating the "democratic dilemma." Respecting individual rights and prerogatives threatens community cohesion; community constraints threaten individual creativity. Stallones suggests that religious traditions have dealt with the questions of authority implicit in this dilemma by an appeal to divine authority. He argues, "Religious conviction provides a place to stand and objectively assess human society" (p. 4). The presence of this "objective" authority results in principles that ground "action to correct injustices" (p. 4). Self-regulation is achieved when individuals' religious traditions govern behavior prior to and independent of the constraints of law or force. In this way, individual rights and prerogatives do not threaten community cohesion.

Stallones is not arguing that government designate a divine authority or dictate religious conviction. Rather, his point is that any failure to encourage the development of mature religious faith on the part of democratic citizens impoverishes democracy and threatens its effective functioning. Faith and democracy go hand in hand, generating social justice. Thus Grace Covenant Christian School, Biblically based, can focus on "the development of such democratic attitudes toward the worth of all individuals, service to others, self-control, and principled objectivity by children" (pp. 4–5). These goals and values are both Biblically based and democratically demanded.

This moral view, in which the Bible and democracy support each other, transforms the academic curriculum, and Stallones describes faculty efforts to reconceive what and how they teach. For instance, in seventh-grade Life Science, students investigate both naturalistic and religious accounts of the origins of life. They then investigate the philosophical, spiritual, and social ramifications of adopting each account; that is, they learn the uses of and the limitations of scientific and religious ways of viewing the world. This approach takes students far deeper than is typical in a state school or common in Christian schools, helping students to think critically about the implications of belief systems.

To read to the end of this remarkable description (and there is much more than is noted above) is to understand that the academic curriculum is surely altered by Grace Covenant Christian's Christian-democratic worldview, while at the same time, that moral world view is open to critical review. Both teachers and students are encouraged to engage, without fear, in social critique based in a Christian "ethic of love."

Stallones makes his second case—that academic excellence is undermined when religious influences and interests are not explicitly taught and taken seriously—by examining the social studies curriculum. He charges that we "teach about religions from behind a screen of pseudo-academic detachment that robs religious ideas of their force and appeal" (2000b, p. 1). This is, of course, when we are willing to acknowledge the existence of religious belief and practice at all.

Two things are lost when we adopt such a stance of "pseudo-academic detachment." The first is historical accuracy and the historical self-understanding that goes with it. The second is a rich democratic sensibility, simultaneously based in the integrity of the individual and the primacy of community. Because, as argued above, religious traditions engender an understanding of the many and the one, religious faith typically grounds democratic appreciation.

While Stallones acknowledges religious indoctrination as a danger, he seems more concerned about the alternative. "To do less [than teach about religion] is to present an incomplete explanation of the world to children and to rob them of the richness that a knowledge of religion can provide to their lives" (2000b, p. 9). Yes, the academic curriculum that includes a careful consideration of religious concerns and motivations may "spark students' interest in religion" and may "spark the teacher's religious sentiments" as well (p. 10). But for Stallones, the academic exists to stimulate an interest in what matters in human living. "Our goal as teachers is to help children develop as accurate and functional a world view as possible. Ignoring religion, or dealing with it on other than its own terms, defeats our purpose" (p. 11).

For Stallones and his former colleagues at Grace Covenant Christian, to remove religious influences from the moral and academic life of the school is "unfortunate" because it violates democratic freedom of thought, because it undermines democratic values of tolerance and self-regulation, and because it weakens an academic curriculum that should be built around what matters. The academic and the moral are equally implicated when religious interests are fully unacknowledged.

EDUCATION AS SPIRITUAL JOURNEY

For the educators at Grace Covenant Christian, schooling is a spiritual experience rooted in a Christian ethic of love that is congruent with an American
democratic ethic. Jared Stallones contends that all students and teachers, not
just those in parochial schools, need a meaningful education, an education
that addresses them as spiritual as well as cognitive beings. Some educators make this case without recourse to organized religion or to democratic
principles.

In 2000, the Association for Supervision and Curriculum Development,
the professional organization of thousands of educators in teaching, leadership, and curricular positions, published *The Soul of Education: Helping
Students Find Connection, Compassion, and Character at School* by Rachel
Kessler. Kessler's book, with a foreword by Parker Palmer, decries the fact
that modern classrooms are spiritually empty by design and lays out strategies for teachers who wish to promote students' spiritual development.

Kessler's discussion is largely dependent on Palmer's work as summed
up in this passage from *The Courage to Teach* (1998):

> Our knowledge of the world comes from gathering around great things in a
> complex and interactive community of truth. But good teachers do more than
> deliver the news from that community to their students. Good teachers repli-
> cate the process of knowing by engaging students in the dynamics of the com-
> munity of truth. (p. 115)

Knowing, teaching, and learning are all essentially communal. "Gathered
around great things" and oriented toward "truth," persons "think the world
together" (Palmer, 1998, p. 62). This gathering and thinking implies—and
generates—individual participants with well-formed identities and integrity. Palmer begins with identity and integrity and moves through the nature of knowing, the power of the sacred, and the possibilities for teaching
and learning.

Kessler agrees with Palmer that education is connection. She accepts his
analysis that today's educational institutions are marked by disconnection—
grading and evaluation, fragmented fields of knowledge, competition, and
bureaucratic procedures. To counteract this state of affairs, she suggests that
teachers attend to seven gateways to the soul in education: the yearning for
deep connection, the longing for silence and solitude, the search for meaning and purpose, the hunger for joy and delight, the creative drive, the urge
for transcendence, and the need for initiation (Kessler, 2000). In individual
chapters, she explores each gateway, making use of concrete examples of
student questions and conversations from her own work as a teacher and
educational consultant.

Kessler is convincing in making the case that young people of all ages, particularly adolescents, resonate to the "great things" she has identified as gateways to the soul. She is less successful in demonstrating how these "teachable moments" constitute an integral part of what we typically take to be academic subject matter. One danger is that an overburdened teacher, reading Kessler, would respond, "I'd love to have these conversations with the kids, but I have no time. This is just one more thing." Another is that a skeptical teacher will say, "I'm not about to talk about souls with kids in a public school classroom. *That's* not my job." In both responses, the moral and the academic are separated out again.

But this is not the soul-based vision that animates Kessler's recommendations (see Oldenski & Carlson, 2002; Palmer, 1993, 1998). A spiritual point of view—a focus on students' inner landscapes, on their souls—alters one's understanding of academic goals (understanding the world) and moral purposes (achieving selfhood and integrity). Both the academic and the moral reside *in* one's relationship to the world. Both are always implicated in the spiritual journey that is education.

THE MORAL INHERES IN THE PRACTICE

David Hansen—a teacher educator and philosopher of education and one of Philip Jackson's co-authors of *The Moral Life of Schools* (Jackson et al., 1993)—has been one of the strongest, most consistent academic voices explicitly articulating the integration of the moral and the academic in teaching. He has maintained repeatedly that "the moral is *in* the practice" of teaching, a phrase that became the title of his 1998 article in *Teaching and Teacher Education.*

Sometimes arguing philosophically, sometimes relying on his observations of and interviews with teachers, Hansen suggests that we need look only as far as the role of teacher to understand education's moral dimensions. If we consider carefully what we know about what teaching is, the moral side is as evident as the academic side. Whether a teacher leads students to new knowledge, helps them articulate new ideas, coaches them to perform new skills, or promotes new attitudes or the reconsideration of old beliefs, the teacher is acting on a moral vision that seeks to enrich students' lives and their relationships with other human beings.

Hansen (1998) maintains that "teaching has its own characteristic set of responsibilities and obligations which practitioners learn through preparing for and enacting the terms of the practice" (p. 648). If teachers actually do the things Hansen suggests, then they will come to realize that the terms of the practice call on them to act in certain ways and to fulfill certain responsibilities. Patience, attentiveness, humility, and fairness are "built into" teaching, Hansen suggests, because those who cannot evidence such virtues will not be up to the task. Serving students by supporting their intellectual and moral development is an indispensable feature of teaching; fail to do it and you are no longer teaching. Recognizing each student's dignity and gifts is a requirement, not as an extrinsic moral stricture but as an intrinsic professional demand. Making pedagogical decisions reasonably in light of some vision of human flourishing is critical; blind or arbitrary decision making does not embody the point of teaching.

Note that Hansen is not relying on moral philosophy to recommend an ethic for teachers. Rather, he suggests, to choose to teach at all (as differentiated from indoctrination, conversion, or command) is to take on a moral orientation—that of a teacher, that of *all* teachers. This point is expanded in his recent book *Exploring the Moral Heart of Teaching*, where he begins with the claim that teaching is a moral and intellectual practice and carries that through an exploration of the kind of deliberation and action that shape teachers who understand the dual demands teaching places on them. Hansen (2001a) makes explicit his integrated view of the moral and the academic as he attempts to "fuse what are often treated separately in both the scholarly literature and in the classroom: theory and practice, philosophy and action, ideas and conduct" (p. 19).

POSSIBILITIES AND DANGERS

What is gained when we understand the moral and the academic as intertwined, as fused, as dialectically linked? What educational possibilities do Bob Peterson and Deborah Meier, Lisa Delpit and David Hansen, and the others included here present to us that have not been apparent in other positions? The great strength of the various INTEGRATED approaches sketched above is what they include in the circle of teaching and learning. Each portrait incorporates moral, spiritual, and political commitments with an academic, intellectual vision. The incorporation is so thorough that it is very difficult to pry apart the moral and the academic elements, let alone to stipulate independent meanings for the two terms. These elements are fused in action. In other words, an INTEGRATED stance seeks to represent fully and richly the complex reality educators face as they interact with children in classrooms and communities.

Thus the exemplars of an INTEGRATED approach think broadly rather than narrowly about the goals of education and their work as educators. This is especially helpful in a time when the press for accountability threatens to limit our educational vision.

We see this breadth when we consider how those we classify as INTE-GRATED consider things moral. There are no codes of conduct to be followed or sets of virtues to be emulated. The moral comes in many faces; it has many facets. The faces are political, spiritual, and ethical. The facets are social justice, personal access to the culture of power, democratic participation, Christian love and service, identity and integrity in a community of truth, and unavoidable questions of responsibility. What is true in each case is that the moral domain spills into the academic as both ideal and check; the academic takes shape against some understanding of the moral. A quality of human living is implied in each vision of the moral.

Similarly, the exemplars described here take no narrow view of the academic task, of the academic domain. There is no discussion of specific facts to be mastered or tests to be administered, though content always matters and paying attention to students' thinking and students' experience is featured prominently. The academic starts with students' experience of the world, takes account of what they must know and be able to do to function across cultures of power, requires that students learn to use their intelligence fully and habitually, incorporates any meaningful dimensions of human living such as religious faith and practice, implicates the soul, and inevitably gives rise to questions of moral responsiveness and responsibility. Academic functioning arises out of and gives rise to a vision of the moral. A quality of human living is implied in each understanding of the academic.

Clearly, our exemplars of INTEGRATED do not think alike. Their moral visions (to the extent that these can be characterized independently) are more or less traditional, more or less political, more or less religious, more or less spiritual, more or less radical. Their academic actions are more or less conventional, more or less substantive, more or less reformist. What all share is a refusal to leave out important elements of their educational and pedagogical experience even when these elements cannot be easily explained or theorized. While the exemplars reflect different kinds of thinking, they *do* all practice and respect the kind of thinking that John Dewey (1916/1980) called the "method of intelligence." Inquiry marked by "directness," "open-mindedness," "single-mindedness," and "responsibility" is evident in the positions taken by those described in this chapter.

Such habits may explain the emphasis on teaching practice, on the everyday actions of teachers, that seems to be another common—and particularly valuable—feature marking our exemplars of the INTEGRATED approach. They are not theorizing abstractly about how teaching and learning ought to be; they are reflecting on how it is in their experience. Their reflection is both pragmatic and phenomenological. They are attuned to the institutional and cultural contexts in which they work, but also attuned to the personal possibilities that give meaning to action. This, too, is a strength of this category.

Schools are not always truly educational institutions, and a public requirement that all children be schooled does not ensure educative experience. The
exemplars of the INTEGRATED category seem fixed on education, not just
schooling.

In fact, distinguishing the moral and the academic in any stable way is
quite difficult in an INTEGRATED mind-set, in part because the focus on what
is truly educative insists on keeping them together. We constructed our category scheme on a distinction between the moral and the academic, and, as
we reach the last category, we are forced to admit that the distinction does
not hold up for the educators featured in this chapter. Deborah Meier's discussion with the new mother returning to school was the right thing to do. It
was right for many reasons, but we would be hard-pressed to separate out
which reasons were moral and which academic. The Grace Covenant Christian faculty's curriculum reconstruction effort is the right thing to do—for
moral reasons *and* for academic reasons. They will reshape and enrich their
entire curriculum, and their students will flourish as a result.

This blending that presents itself as a strength in the INTEGRATED approach also suggests some pragmatic dangers. Three are evident. The first is
the issue alluded to several times above and clearly articulated by educational
researchers Deborah Ball and Suzanne Wilson (1996) in a joint reflection on
their own elementary teaching:

> How can we reshape the very language about practice to blend the moral with
> the intellectual? How can we represent the complicated and dynamic nature
> of pedagogical reasoning to reflect not only what teachers know and believe
> but also what they are committed to and think is right? Doing this means
> developing a more adequate language, a rhetoric of inquiry that honors both
> knowing and caring and seeks ways to embrace and illuminate the connec-
> tions among ideas and understandings, concerns, and values, wishes and
> dreams. (pp. 187–188)

Ball and Wilson are right that we have no language that says "moral" and
"academic" at one and the same time. The INTEGRATED category becomes a
purely descriptive one with no useful theory when there are no terms to construct such a theory. Our exemplar educators can "do" the moral and the
academic together, but they cannot talk about it except descriptively. The
language we do have, the language of schooling, has become technical and
instrumental, as we noted earlier. That language is not always hospitable to
the concerns of the moral. Neither is it always hospitable to concerns of intelligence understood in a Deweyan sense as habits of reasoning in the face
of real issues. Couched in instrumental terms, morality is absent and the
academic is shrunk to sets of discrete skills and informational lists.

The second and third dangers are related. Our exemplars of an INTE-GRATED approach provide us with a sense of what might be but little guidance about how to get there. We read David Hansen's claim that the moral is in the practice, in what teaching calls us to be and do, and it rings true. Now what do we do? We are inspired by Bob Peterson's or Deborah Meier's efforts but know that emulating them does not mean doing what they do. Even directions for emulation are descriptive or narrative, as in the case of Rachel Kessler's guidance for teachers who wish to foster their students' spirituality.

Further, the educators who populate this category are persons who can tolerate ambiguity, who can live in the messiness resulting from multiple educational goals. They can think in both/and rather than either/or terms. They understand and appreciate the creative power of maintaining the tension of what seem to be competing claims on commitment and action while being unbothered by the confusion that can accompany such competing claims. The fact that the moral and the academic shift meaning is viewed as fruitful rather than frightening.

Not all educators can or want to think this way, however. Ambiguity gives rise to discomfort for many and raises the question of relativism for others. Can individuals be trusted to respond to specific circumstances and challenges in fitting ways, in ways that bring an inspiring educational vision to reality? If there are no clear guidelines, when will we know that we have gone too far? Not far enough? This could limit the practical usefulness of the INTEGRATED category as a conceptual place to bring competing concerns together, despite its character as the broadest, most inclusive of our categories.

That broad reach is the element of this category worth holding on to. We are challenged, in our considerations of the moral and the academic in teaching and learning, to keep both elements in the picture all the time. This is difficult since we have no shared discourse that encourages us to do so. But it matters, as these educators teach us, because the moral and the academic are fused in the practice of teaching.

8

Mapping the Moral Terrain

In the five preceding chapters, we have surveyed a wide range of efforts to address the moral dimensions of American schooling. As we consider the results, two basic conclusions seem inescapable. First, many educators are as concerned about the moral dimensions of schooling as they are about the academic, despite the current policy focus on a narrow conception of academic goals and accountability. Second, these educators think about and act out their concerns in varied ways. The richness of their programs and proposals is clear to the observant reader and might well prompt the desire to implement similar programs.

We are interested in more than providing an inventory and emulation of model programs, of course. By paying careful, conscious attention to the relation of the moral and the academic, we hope to further communication among those who share a concern for the moral in schooling and to prompt conversation with those whose focus is primarily academic.

We began our work by broadly defining the moral and the academic. Our intention was to include a wide variety of efforts to develop kids who are both "good" and "smart" and to do so in ways that are good and smart. Our formulation of categories to sort out these efforts developed as we surveyed them. Certain relations between the moral and the academic presented themselves logically; others appeared in concrete cases. Over time, our categories took the shape we have presented, a shape we believe is supported both conceptually and empirically.

Still, any category system generates questions, and ours is no exception:

- Are SEPARATE, SEQUENTIAL, DOMINANT, TRANSFORMATIVE, and IN-TEGRATED the only possible ways of configuring the relationship between the moral and the academic in schooling? Do our categories adequately map the territory?

- Does the academic/moral analytic frame clearly mark the significant elements and worthy goals of schooling? Are such realms as the political, the religious, and the economic adequately addressed in this frame or does the emphasis on the moral and the academic exclude these goals for schooling?
- What does this configuration of categories tell us about the present state of thinking and practice regarding the moral dimension of schooling? About how we may address current realities in interesting and productive ways?
- Do the survey of programs and the analytic framework of categories facilitate making sense of moral matters in school and acting as though the moral matters? Do they, for example, help us to make sense of the vignettes with which we opened this book? Do they push us to deeper, more nuanced interpretations of what is at stake?
- In what ways and to what extent is the value of this map limited by our own definitions, assumptions, and ideology?
- What gaps exist in our efforts to make sense of schooling as moral in the 21st-century United States. What is the role of theorists and practitioners in filling these gaps?

In this chapter, we take up these questions with reference both to the adequacy and the usefulness of the framework we have introduced.

IS THAT ALL THERE IS?

We have offered a portrait of five possible ways of viewing the moral/academic relation in schooling. Three of the five—SEQUENTIAL, DOMINANT, and TRANS-FORMATIVE—have both academically oriented and morally oriented variations. The other two categories—SEPARATE and INTEGRATED—either split the moral and academic or fuse them. Our implied claim is that these five categories exhaust the possibilities when consciously considering the moral contours of schooling.

In addition, we have acknowledged that educational expectations and efforts in the early-21st-century United States often fall outside the territory we have mapped here, in a space we have referred to as *moral invisible*. It is true that many educators, theorists, and researchers have no conscious focus on moral concerns as they pursue instruction, inquiry, and investigation. It is even true that some educators, particularly in public schools, consciously choose to segregate moral concerns in response to perceived professional, legal, and societal limits. The *moral invisible* suggests that although moral concerns may be neither apparent nor acknowledged, they are still present.

A not-so-hidden feature of our agenda is to highlight the links between academic matters and moral matters in schooling, making that which sometimes is "invisible" more difficult to set aside or ignore.

Is this all there is? Have we missed other ways of thinking about the relationship between the moral and the academic in schooling? Obviously, we think not, with two caveats. First, the categories we offer are ideal types. They represent the range of possibilities for thought and action but do not necessarily occur in pure form and on a consistent basis *even in the work of the exemplars we have chosen to illustrate each category*. Are they nonetheless useful? Yes, the categories are useful as a heuristic; that is, they serve "as an aid to learning, discovery, or problem-solving" (*Merriam-Webster Online Dictionary*, 2005). The real value of these categories lies in their ability to further careful reflection and constructive conversation about the moral dimensions of schooling.

Second, we readily acknowledge that the practices of educators are likely to be eclectic in approaching schooling from a moral point of view. That is, specific recommendations and concrete programs of action may well draw on approaches relevant to more than one of our categories. In Chapter 1, we referred to the Character Education Partnership; this group is an eclectic effort to guide educational practitioners' work in moral education. Here we consider two other well-known examples of eclectic practice that rely on multiple conceptions of the moral dimensions of schooling.

In 1991, Thomas Lickona published a widely used textbook, *Educating for Character: How Our Schools Can Teach Respect and Responsibility*, and solidified his identification with the character education movement. When character education was attacked several years ago by Alfie Kohn (1997), Lickona published a vigorous response. In this rejoinder Lickona (1998) spoke in an approving manner about the "Word of the Week" program at Allen Academy and defended character education against Kohn's charge that it tended to be narrowly focused on drilling students in specific behaviors and values.

Lickona's self-identification with the character education movement and his affirmation (1993) of such personal core values as respect, responsibility, trustworthiness, and fairness seem to place him squarely among the approaches we identified in Chapter 3 as SEPARATE. However, his recommendations to educators extend beyond the conventional boundaries of character education. In *Educating for Character* (Lickona, 1991), he links the moral and the academic in a variety of ways. He endorses school and community service grounded in altruism; he places substantial emphasis on moral reflection; he recommends conflict resolution and the creation of a democratic classroom environment; he offers an image of teacher as caregiver; and he identifies the academic curriculum as rich with moral possibility.

His most recent work, *Smart and Good High Schools: Integrating Excellence and Ethics for Success in School, Work, and Beyond* (Lickona & Davidson, 2005), continues in an eclectic vein. The language of the title, "integrating excellence and ethics," suggests that the academic and the moral will be related somehow and they are, especially through his use of "character" as an attribute of both moral and academic functioning. However, the "practices for building 8 strengths of character that help youth lead productive, ethical, and fulfilling lives and ethical behavior" include many of the approaches and strategies recounted throughout this book (see Lickona, n.d.). Lickona sometimes focuses on the moral as separate from the academic, but just as often he links them substantively or procedurally.

In 1996, the state superintendent of instruction in Wisconsin began a program designated as the Wisconsin Citizenship Initiative (2004). A task force of representatives from religious, educational, political, business, labor, and public interest groups was convened to make recommendations for promoting citizenship for youth. The statewide task force recommended that each community establish a public group, reflecting a range of interests, to identify a set of core citizenship values to be promoted by home, school, and community. To guide these local committees, the statewide committee suggested illustrative values: honesty, courage, respect, and responsibility.

This citizenship effort, therefore, had elements of character education, which we label SEPARATE. However, the statewide task force also identified other characteristics of schools that develop good citizens. Schools should (1) adopt a core set of values, (2) be safe and orderly places, (3) involve parents/caregivers and other segments of the community, (4) address societal issues, (5) develop positive relationships, (6) engage students' minds, keeping them connected to the schooling experience, and (7) develop high expectations for students and staff. This diverse set of academic and moral expectations yielded a wide variety of local citizenship efforts, including schools that developed mentor–mentee relationships, instituted drug-free programs, devised a simulation of an entire town, created a good citizen award, worked to restore a local river, and piloted a social studies ethics unit (Gee & Quick, 1997). The drug-free programs are probably an example of SEQUENTIAL and an ethics unit could be an instance of SEPARATE, but the other practices seem to be distributed over all five of our categories. Thus the Wisconsin citizenship practices, generated out of a single set of characteristics, represent a wide range of categories from our system.

The routine presence of eclectic approaches in schooling practice does not negate the importance of identifying distinguishable conceptual elements and possibilities. Nor does it erase the value of allowing those concepts and the categories that arise from them to stimulate novel (and sometimes recycled) ways of imagining moral matters in schooling. At this juncture, we present the five categories as a faithful mapping of the actual state of distinguishable efforts to address the moral, that is, the *moral visible*. Together with the complementary domain of *moral invisible*, our categories cover the territory of schooling.

It might also be asked whether these categories form a continuum. Can they be construed as or transformed into stages of action or development as category systems so often are? Our answers are a qualified no to the former and a clear no to the latter.

Viewed simplistically with regard to the relation between the moral and the academic, our categories can be seen as located on a continuum from SEPARATE to INTEGRATED. SEQUENTIAL, DOMINANT, and TRANSFORMATIVE do seem to represent lesser to greater degrees of the intertwining of moral matters and academic matters. But our categories also capture two other qualities that confound simple classification on a continuum. We have characterized not just the degree of interaction between the moral and the academic but also the quality of that interaction. TRANSFORMATIVE does not simply represent greater interaction between the moral and the academic than does SEQUENTIAL; it represents interaction of a different kind. Moreover, we recognized that even within the same kind of interaction, one or the other element may be preeminent. Three of our categories are bimodal. Thus it is best to be cautious in thinking about these categories as forming a continuum based on the extent to which moral and academic concerns are intertwined.

It is especially important that these categories not be viewed as stages of development or as phases that educators pass through as they become increasingly more sophisticated about moral concerns in schooling. From our vantage point, there are complicated political, philosophical, professional, practical, and perhaps even psychological reasons why one might take or espouse one of the approaches we have characterized here. We are, as an educational community, far from the place where we might claim what constitutes some higher or later stage of development. For now, the best we can do, what we have attempted here, is to take a comprehensive and comparative look at the ideas and conceptions available to us, identifying where we see dangers as well as possibilities.

CRITICAL MARKERS

Even if we are correct that the map we lay out here is adequately extensive, one might question whether our categories mark the important features of the geography of schooling—or at least those features that are relevant to moral matters broadly construed. By simplifying our analytic framework to rely only on the academic and the moral, have we omitted other significant concerns?

When Horace Mann (1848/1957) reported for the 12th time to the Massachusetts Board of Education, he argued that schooling had *five* significant purposes: physical, intellectual/economic, political, moral, and religious. Note that Mann does include a moral purpose, but he does not include an academic one. Are we justified in using *the academic* and *the moral* as realms for all that is expressed in these five purposes?

In truth, Mann's priorities previewed those contemporary policymakers who are primarily interested in the power of schooling to alter economic realities. His reference to "intellectual" purposes was meant not as an expression of the power of thought for its own sake but "as a means of removing poverty, and securing abundance" (p. 84). In a well-known phrase, Mann described schools as "the great equalizer of the conditions of men—the balance-wheel of the social machinery" (p. 89). He believed that schools would not merely diffuse old wealth but would create new wealth: "For creation of wealth, then—for the existence of a wealthy people and a wealthy nation—intelligence is the grand condition" (p. 89).

Joel Spring (2000) identifies, with less approval than Mann, roughly the same set of purposes for contemporary schooling. In fact, Spring's discussion of purposes, compiled a century and half later, is decidedly more critical than Mann's. That the economic purposes of schooling are prominent is not viewed positively by Spring (1972), who has long been skeptical about educational goals based on corporate interests. From his perspective as a *small-d* democrat, Spring believes that the specific social, political, and moral goals around which schools are structured are economic (corporate capitalism) in origin and act to inhibit the development of democracy.

Both Mann and Spring acknowledge moral goals for schooling but rely, Mann positively and Spring critically, on a narrower understanding of "moral" than we have drawn here. For both, moral goals are served when students take on the values and norms that mark conventional (dominant) social groups and interaction. We use the moral to call forth all aspects of schooling that lend meaning to life, that enable all involved to make sense of their lives in interaction with others. The moral resides not merely in the values and behavior of individuals but also in the quality of human interaction and the institutional structures that shape that interaction. This broadened view of the moral brings at least some elements of what might otherwise be identified as the religious, the social, the political, and even the economic under the moral umbrella, as can be seen throughout the preceding five chapters.

What about the academic? Neither Mann nor Spring directly addresses the academic as an educational goal, but this omission is at odds with our commonsense view of schooling. What are parents and teachers talking about when they discuss students' academic progress? How can one make academic progress when one has no academic purpose? Perhaps we should speak instead of students' social, political, and economic progress? Why don't we? Does this mean that *academic* has only an instrumental meaning —instrumental to social, political, economic, and even moral action? Or is *academic*—as it appears in everyday use—simply a code word for the total school program?

As we argued in Chapter 2, the meaning of *academic* is closely linked to the action and self-understanding of educators in a way that terms like *social*, *political*, and *economic* are not. The latter terms come from the realm of policy and research, from the outside. *Academic* comes from the interaction of teachers and students, from the inside. It is about school subjects, and basic skills, and great ideas, and habits of mind, and critical thinking, and academic standards even when these formulations appear to contradict one another. It is about patriotism and about political resistance. It is about the structure and theory of human life and about the historical struggles, physical and intellectual, that competing views have spawned. The academic is fundamental to the school's agenda, a vision of shared understanding set out in advance and subject to progress checks. As is the case with the moral, our definition of the academic is an inclusive one. There is room under this umbrella for most, but perhaps not all, of what Mann and Spring view as the purposes of schooling.

Dividing the territory of schooling into the academic and the moral is a conceptual move made for very specific purposes. We do not disagree with Mann and Spring that the social, political, religious, economic, and moral purposes of schooling can be identified. They can be identified and distinguished, and there are reasons to do so. We do claim that for the analytic, deconstructive, and communicative purposes we have *here*, it is more fruitful to begin with a distinction between the academic and the moral. We recognize that the academic may encompass goals Horace Mann would identify as economic; we recognize that the moral may encompass goals Joel Spring would identify as political. Our use of the academic and the moral is rooted in the lived reality of the teachers and students who do the work of schooling.

WHAT THE CATEGORIES TEACH US

Where, then, do we find ourselves after mapping contemporary efforts to take the moral contours of schooling seriously? What does the survey framed by our categories reveal? At the end of each category chapter, we discussed possibilities and dangers inherent in the approach captured by the category. Here we comment on those lessons in an overall way.

The term "moral" has multiple meanings for those who care about the moral contours of schooling. The moral can be about individual student character and behavior or individual teacher ethics, in school or outside. It is about values and virtues. It is also about economic and social justice, cultural sensitivity, community support, educational efficacy, and even human wholeness. It is *in* student–teacher relationships and *in* curricular materials and *in* classroom rituals. The moral in schooling demands not only students' moral education but also educators' moral responsibility. The moral encompasses doing right and doing good. It demands knowing the good, which may be based in religious teaching, existential decision, or human relation. It requires caring for, being with, and thinking well by all those who are players in the task of schooling, whatever the nature of the school. Those who explore moral matters in school may mean any or all of these mutations of meaning.

"Academic," similarly, can be viewed in varying ways. The academic is about content and coverage; it is "what your 1st grader needs to know" (Hirsch, 1991). It is also about basic skills, great ideas, habits of mind, and centers of care. The academic is expressed in standards and measured by tests. It is also expressed in Great Books and dissected in dialogue. It is expressed in student action and captured in portfolios. The academic is shaped, even governed, by values and achieved through character. As is true of the moral, the academic is a moving target. If we forget the shifting nature of these terms, we will not understand each other. Our hopes of finding firm ground on which to construct a shared understanding of the moral in schooling will be diminished. Without that hope, our individual visions of schooling are less, our common view of schooling weakened, even fragmented.

The relation of teacher and student alters as the relation of the moral and the academic shifts. Simply stated, those who hold the moral distinguishable from the academic (SEPARATE, SEQUENTIAL, DOMINANT) tend to view the teacher and student as independent agents. The educator (teacher, principal, parent, etc.) has power *over* the student, a power rooted in presumed moral and academic maturity and wisdom. In this view, legitimate authority yields an appropriate and benevolent power, exercised in the best interest of the student. The context in which such power is exercised is viewed as politically and ideologically neutral. Those who emphasize the intertwining of the moral and the academic (TRANSFORMATIVE, INTEGRATED) are more likely to see the relation between the student and teacher as dialectic, as contributing to the mutual constitution of the social selves who act morally or academically. Teacher and student can respond and resist. Each has power *with* the other in a common, ideologically charged context and in pursuit of common educational goals. To the extent that either is powerful, both are powerful. These issues of individual agency, the social constitution of the self, and power relations lie beneath the discussion of the moral and the academic but are worthy of our direct attention.

Conceptions of knowledge and knowing interact with understandings of moral and academic. The agency and power described above are also implicated in views of what counts as knowledge and how one knows. Knowledge can be understood as the static product of others' inquiry, transmitted by the expert to the novice. This is the view embedded in the thinking and action of those who distinguish the moral and the academic. Knowledge can also be understood as a dynamic residue of one's own inquiry, constructed and negotiated in interaction with others. This is the view that marks the thinking and action of those who blend the moral and the academic. Recognizing these significant differences can assist the kind of engagement we have been recommending.

The quality and structure of schooling is implicated in the expression of moral concerns. Whether public, private, parochial, or home-based, a school is a setting constructed of values expressed through a mission statement, curriculum, physical structure, staff selection, student population, recommended relations, and appropriate behaviors. The comprehensive positions provided by James Comer (SEQUENTIAL) and Ted Sizer (ACADEMIC TRANS-FORMATIVE) illustrate how distinctive values can be consciously embedded in the design of a school. At the same time, when a school is fashioned within a particular homogeneous culture, the school appears to be a neutral institution, but it is neutral only with respect to that subculture's taken-for-granted values and mores. Nonetheless, a school always exemplifies a particular intellectual and/or cultural perspective (defined by race, class, gender, religion, political commitment, sexual orientation, physical or emotional disability, historical understanding, cognitive theory, anthropological view, or some combination of these). Schooling cannot be value-neutral. In contemporary America, schooling is compulsory, publicly mandated, oriented toward the dominant culture, and increasingly regulated (for both teachers and students as well as administrators and even school board members). Because this is so, some moral possibilities remain in play while others are excluded.

Social, political, and economic contexts impact moral possibilities. As suggested above, schools *are* sociocultural settings. They also operate *within* social, political, and economic contexts—nationally, regionally, and locally. In communities where cultural practices are shared, social conditions are comparable, and values are held in common, the moral dimensions of schooling exist in implicit agreement, without identification or controversy. Only when cultures collide does the presence of the moral come to consciousness; it comes to consciousness *because* there is difference and conflict.

That conflict is as likely to be about the meaning of sociocultural "reality" as it is about the proper response to it. William Bennett espouses character education because he perceives a loss of traditional values and a pattern of inappropriate behavior. Lisa Delpit and Eva Midobuche call for cultural sensitivity as a moral imperative in a time and place where they see cultural minorities experiencing discrimination. Jonathan Kozol, Bob Peterson, and Paulo Freire remind us that economic justice matters because educational resources and educational goods seem to be unevenly distributed in conditions of apparent scarcity. Those who do not perceive the same reality will not accept the proffered response. The moral matters that command our attention will be different depending on the context in which they arise *and* on our understanding of that context.

These observations are gleaned not from one category or another but from the entire array of possible ways of making the moral visible in schooling. They are foundational; that is, they point to a set of essential questions that we can ask together in considering the moral dimensions of schooling: What do we mean by the moral? What do mean by the academic? How are teacher–student relations shaped by our conception of the moral vis-à-vis the academic? What is the link between knowing (the academic) and doing (the moral)? How is the quality of schooling (structure and curriculum) shaped by our assumptions about the moral? What is the context (social, political, economic, professional, personal) for our efforts to make the moral visible while addressing the academic with integrity? And how does that context shape moral possibilities?

While the framework as a whole reveals certain foundational generalizations, each of the individual categories we sketch in this book captures its own "truth" about the moral dimensions of schooling (Table 8.1), and certain specific observations are worth restating. SEPARATE reminds us that the moral deserves its own spotlight. SEQUENTIAL productively links the moral and the academic and highlights the importance of concrete guidance for educators who are not sure where to begin in addressing both the moral and the academic. DOMINANT expresses the power of focus, of clear vision, of confidence in that vision. TRANSFORMATIVE calls us to combine complexity of understanding and comprehensive view with concrete action by providing a starting point for reimagining schooling. INTEGRATED insists that the moral and the academic are neither contradictory nor separable in action but intrinsic to the intention to educate.

And each of the five categories also bears a warning to those who limit their thinking and action to a single category. SEPARATE tends to equate the moral with direct instruction of children, an understandable but restricted perspective. SEQUENTIAL runs the bimodal risk of rendering the moral instrumental to the academic or leaving the moral unattended in the shadow of the academic. DOMINANT trades complexity for focus and raises the specter of indoctrination. TRANSFORMATIVE is trapped in an idealism that is at

Table 8.1. Possibilities and Dangers

Category	Possibilities	Dangers
SEPARATE	Spotlights moral	Moral limited to direct instruction
SEQUENTIAL	Links moral and academic; provides practitioners with a starting point	Risk of treating one dimension as instrumental to the other
DOMINANT	Highlights the importance of having confidence in a vision	Trades complexity for focus; raises specter of indoctrination
TRANSFORMATIVE	Combines complexity, comprehensive view, and concrete action	Idealistic; may not seem doable
INTEGRATED	Both academic and moral intrinsic to the educational intention	Complicated and ambiguous; lacks specific guidance

odds with the realities of contemporary schooling. INTEGRATED may be too complicated and ambiguous for many practitioners who want and need help in figuring out where to start and what to do next.

We do not pretend that there is some easy way to combine or synthesize the insights of the individual categories. Our public debate regarding the moral in schooling remains too simplistic and too oppositional to make that possible. What we can offer is a set of questions to be asked and answered as educators collaborate with communities to revitalize schooling as moral.

ACTING AS IF THE MORAL MATTERS

If you are an educator (or policymaker or parent) who wants to participate in the moral renewal of American schooling, how have we helped you? This, after all, has been our motivation in writing this book. We wanted to make sense out of the recent stream of ideas and initiatives that have highlighted the moral dimensions of schooling and to do so in a way that fosters productive communication and minimizes weaknesses of interpretation. We wanted to start with answers—in the form of programs and proposals—and see whether those answers might lead us back to the questions that educators are wrestling with as they attempt to make the moral visible in American schooling. We hope we have engaged you in a fresh look at a wide range of efforts to reinstate the status of things moral in schools.

Reconsider the stories of Wake County and the Board's efforts to implement character education, of Rodney Morris and Mary Brown and their common struggle to claim a professional morality, of the Potomac School and the pressures on students and staff to cheat their way to academic "success." After thinking through the relationship of the moral and the academic using a wide range of examples, your reading of these narratives is bound to be different.

Perceptions will be broadened and sharpened. The meaning of both the moral and the academic could be stretched, allowing new possibilities to emerge. You might, for example, notice that the moral can generate references to students' character development, teachers' professional action, curricular content, classroom environment, school structure, and public support for schools. You might recognize that academic standards and habits of mind can be alternative academic possibilities. You might observe examples of the thinking we have categorized as SEPARATE, SEQUENTIAL, DOMINANT, TRANSFORMATIVE, and INTEGRATED. You might also notice that some believe that the moral should be invisible in schools.

Were we to employ these diverse perspectives in conversation, we might ask interesting, substantive, and engaging questions of each other, the kinds of questions our categories seem to generate. This discourse can be punctuated not just by the distinctions our categories suggest but also by the foundational issues that mark the moral/academic fault line. We might abandon the effort to immediately "fix" the situation and instead try first to understand the situation—and each other. This kind of conversation has the potential to be richer and less defensive than the ideological debates so common when we address the moral and the academic in the context of U.S. schooling.

We suggest two ways, then, in which the work recorded here is helpful. First, it strengthens the interpretive power of individual educators and policy-makers; that is, it informs what I see and understand. Second, it enhances the communicative power of groups of educators; that is, it informs at once what we see and understand and what we believe about what the other sees and understands.

As Hans Georg Gadamer teaches us in *Truth and Method* (1975), interpretation and conversation are bound up in the language, in the sets of concepts and categories, which we use to interpret and converse. By shifting the central concept that guides consideration of the moral with regard to schooling (from ideological stance to moral/academic nexus) and by suggesting a set of categories to express observations, we are breaking open the hermeneutic circle, making alternative forms of interpretation, conversation, and action possible. We are, in Gadamer's terms, addressing the conditions for understanding; we are making understanding possible. Where there is understanding (even when there is disagreement), there is no need to demonize or dismiss.

We have used the relation between the academic and the moral heuristically here because, however understood and even deconstructed, these two concepts capture important intuitions about what is desired, what is needed in raising the next generation. These concepts set us to thinking. Our hope is that they also set us to communicating more carefully and more honestly about schools as they might be. We hope, too, that our categories and related ideas will facilitate dialogue among those interested in the moral in contemporary schooling.

Note that the possibility of dialogue cannot be established for all times and places by the introduction of any set of categories. The analytic "tool" we provide is embedded in the context of 21st-century U.S. schooling. Note, too, that our observations and questions are not moral in any narrow sense. We do not simply ask what is the "good" or "right" thing to do; we do not look for principles or rules to be obeyed. Rather, our questions are radical (root) questions, teasing out what we often take for granted about human nature and human flourishing.

As we argued earlier, there is much that binds us if we are willing to seek it. There is no need to obliterate difference in the process, and we are not recommending a false effort to smooth over legitimate difference in belief or action. In fact, we view difference as a condition for growth; it is only when there is disagreement that new possibilities can arise. What we do recommend is a concerted effort at interpretation, at stepping back from action to first understand the situation. When interpretation is neglected, communication fails and action is likely to be unresponsive. When interpretation is neglected, we are less likely to discover common assumptions and understandings.

IDEOLOGICAL STANDPOINT(S)

We are commenting on ideology in two senses: how it has affected discussions of the moral in schooling and how our own ideological stance shapes the present work.

Earlier we observed that issues related to the moral dimension of schooling and, in particular, to students' moral development are frequently debated in political or ideological terms. For example, several years ago an exchange in the *Phi Delta Kappan* pitted conservative advocates of character education (Edward Wynne, Thomas Lickona, and others) against those with liberal views (Alan Lockwood and Alfie Kohn). This interchange, often argumentative, proceeded over several issues of the magazine and featured charges by one group, countercharges in response, and occasional questions about the goodwill and even the honesty of those on the other "side."

Robert Nash's *Answering the "Virtuecrats"* (1997) characterizes approaches to moral education as neoclassical, communitarian, and liberationist and offers a postmodern alternative. He locates each contemporary approach on a political spectrum from conservative to liberal but argues that all established approaches ultimately fail because "the worldviews they represent are far too large, monolithic, and prescriptive" (p. 148) for the purpose of moral conversation. In point of fact, he seems to be criticizing all three perspectives for their common ideological underpinnings. In his postmodern alternative, he advocates "moral bricolage" (a language and conversational style that is nonfoundational, multifunctional, and nonexclusionary) as the only sensible approach to cultivating the moral in a secular pluralist democracy.

By grounding our analysis of moral/schooling efforts in the concepts of the moral and the academic as intrinsically educational concepts, we earlier contended that some "hot button" political and ideological divides can be defused. More thoughtful consideration of what is at stake may also become possible. Nonetheless, we readily admit that ideology and politics are not to be avoided in human deliberation. Thus three questions emerge:

- Are we defusing these issues or simply sidestepping them?
- What are the ideological parameters of the way we have chosen to frame the issue?
- What is gained or lost by this shift in perspective?

We address, in turn, each question about our own ideological stance.

Our hope has been to defuse taken-for-granted political and ideological categories (e.g., conservative/liberal, dominant culture/dominated culture) just long enough to make possible fresh views of the underlying issues. Political stances tend to harden into stock responses, and ideologies privilege some views over others. We *are* sidestepping standard political reactions and deconstructing conceptual assumptions, not because we think we can avoid politics and ideology but because we believe it fruitful to disrupt that which is taken for granted. Alternative proposals for action are more likely to emerge when old categories do not constrain the consideration of possibilities.

If we admit that any conceptual apparatus is ideologically bound, what are the ties that bind the analytic framework we have constructed here? We began to answer this question in Chapter 2 when we acknowledged our own presuppositions. Primary among them is that schooling matters and that schooling would be better if the moral matters relevant to and intrinsic in schooling were taken seriously. In other words, we privilege the moral in a way that is not evident in contemporary school policy. However, by locating the moral in all aspects of schooling that lend meaning to human interaction, we are privileging not a particular set of values but the very possibility of value-laden activity. We do not oppose the moral to other aspects of schooling (specifically, the academic) but open the moral to all aspects of schooling.

To raise the question of the relation between the moral and the academic is to open up the possibility that they are related—and even that they are intertwined. The more one sees the moral and the academic as potentially intertwined, the more one can problematize the categories of the academic and the moral themselves. When the academic and the moral lose their preconceived shape and meaning, then the nature and purpose of education generally and schooling in particular becomes an open question. Opening up that door—raising that kind of radical question—allows similarly radical alternatives for schooling to slip in.

That is the ideology that undergirds this project. We want to get at the root of schooling by attending to moral matters as we attend to academic ones. By relying on what we view as two inescapably educational concepts—the moral and the academic—we encourage radically rethinking the social context for and the fundamental purposes of schooling.

MINDING THE GAPS

What we offer to educators interested in moral schooling is straightforward: an analytic tool (the moral/academic relation), a return to the root questions that move us to action, and a plea to prescind from action long enough to engage in shared interpretation. We readily admit that the moral/academic relation and a commitment to interpretation in specific settings by specific groups of educators are not enough. Our analysis has revealed three significant gaps in efforts to make sense of schooling as moral in 21st-century United States.

The first is regular, thoughtful dialogue on what democratic schooling demands vis-à-vis cultural diversity and religious belief and practice. Both moral discussions and discussions about the moral, as we suggested in Chapter 2, are grounded in those ways in which persons construct meaning in life. Religious faith and cultural identity are two critical facets of meaning making. The combativeness and rancor that accompany discussion of religion and culture predictably spill over into considerations of public morality and public education. We hope that our categories can facilitate dialogue among those educators and members of the public who want to bridge areas of social and cultural difference.

The second gap is a language of schooling that tends toward the technical and instrumental, typically bifurcating the moral and the academic. Deborah Ball and Suzanne Wilson (1996) insist that one cannot complete any careful study of educational practice without attending to the moral as well as the academic, and they call for a language that blends the moral with the intellectual. We do not have space here to address the nature of such an educational language, but serious attention is starting to be applied to the moral dimension of this issue (see, e.g., Sockett & LePage, 2002). The exemplars cited in this book are participating in this process by drawing on such terms as *caring*, *character*, *community*, *service*, *stewardship*, *social justice*, *vocation*, and *responsibility*. This extraordinary language can act as a wedge, decentering taken-for-granted terminology and the specific practices that this terminology supports. We invite readers to participate in this process.

Developing such a language is a complex and ambitious goal, a goal that cannot be fulfilled by designating once and for all the "right" terminology. A language cannot be designed by theorists and imposed on the community of educators; the language will need to emerge from the practice and discourse of educators. But theorists—and innovators—can subject the community's concepts, terms, and practices to a hermeneutic of suspicion (Ricoeur, 1987) by juxtaposing taken-for-granted terminology with novel, challenging words and phrases.

The third gap can be seen in the conflict between the exploration of moral matters in schooling and the current policy thrust toward standards and testing. This observation is obvious, but it warrants blunt statement. Standardized testing seems superfluous at Deborah Meier's Central Park East Secondary School, where students are publicly demonstrating their competence in exhibitions and excelling in postsecondary study. Content standards do not match Nel Noddings's vision of caring, competent young people as the goal of schooling. "Adequate yearly progress" seems bloodless and sterile when viewed against the background of David Hansen's vision of teachers pursuing their vocation, intrinsically moral, of educating the young. Certainly, some of the work we have discussed here leaves room for standards and testing, but much of it, pursued vigorously, seems to render the standards movement, as currently constituted, as at best peripheral. Many of the efforts we have documented here seem to suggest that what is needed today is not the cold compression of the academic into specified standards and tests to match but heated attention to and expansion of both the moral and the academic.

CONCLUSION

We suggested in the Introduction that this book might be useful on several levels. We believe we have fulfilled that promise.

Put simply, the contents of this book are useful as a survey of the territory that is the moral in U.S. schooling. One can see and appreciate the richness of ideas and initiatives put forth by a wide range of educators around the country. Educators can identify ideas of interest and consider implementing them, drawing on our discussions of the possibilities and dangers associated with particular approaches.

Probe more deeply and the analysis reported here serves as a model for thinking about educational practice through the lens of the moral/academic relation. Deconstructing taken-for-granted views of the moral and the academic extends the interpretive power of individual educators, decenters the assumed consensus that hastens overquick solutions to complex problems, and breaks the oppositional frame of those who cast disagreement in partisan political terms. It sets an agenda for dialogue, defuses dichotomies, and makes strange bedfellows out of some who seem to have little in common. Both individual agency and effective collaboration are strengthened.

Our analysis also generated a series of foundational considerations about the moral/academic relation that can be stated in essential question form for those who are just beginning to think about the moral dimensions of their work. To ask oneself and one's colleagues and constituents about the meaning of the moral, the meaning of the academic, and the ways these notions are implicated in school relations, structure, knowledge, and context is to ground future action in a shared understanding that has been negotiated rather than assumed.

Dialogue and collaboration require a shared understanding and a language to express it. At present, those seeking common ground with regard to the moral do not have a common language. The point is not that we cannot act until we create a language. Rather, language is both a tool and a product of the community of discourse that is making the moral visible. Our work, then, is an invitation to those who are trying to make the moral visible to be self-conscious about the way they verbalize what they are doing.

Finally, this work will itself generate a range of positive and negative responses, prompting (we hope) continued efforts to wrestle with the moral dimensions of schooling. We look forward to this conversation.

We claim a modest contribution to the effort to revitalize schooling as moral, to make the moral visible in American schooling. But there is nothing modest about the broader conclusion that our work supports. While it is sometimes difficult to remember in the specification of academic standards, in the rhetoric of high-stakes testing, in the jargon of instructional methods, in the calls for the professionalization of teaching, and even in the demands for "zero tolerance" in school discipline, the moral matters.

References

Abington v. Schempp, 374 U.S. 203 (1963).

Adler, M. J. (1977). *Philosopher at large: An intellectual autobiography*. New York: Macmillan.

Adler, M. J. (1982). *The Paideia proposal: An educational manifesto*. New York: Macmillan.

Adler, M. J. (Ed.). (1984). *The Paideia program: An educational syllabus*. New York: Collier.

Adler, M. J. (1988). *Reforming education: The opening of the American mind*. New York: Macmillan.

Adler, M. J. (2000). *Mission*. Retrieved March 10, 2006, from http://www.thegreatideas .org/mission.html

Adler, M. J. (n.d.). *A moral and an educational revolution*. Retrieved March 10, 2006, from http://www.radicalacademy.com/adlereducation.htm

Allison, D. (1992). *Bastard out of Carolina*. New York: Dutton.

Amos, D. S. (2005, March 23). Marva Collins wants name back. *Cincinnati Enquirer*, p. 1C. Retrieved July 26, 2005, from http://www.enquirer.com/

Anderson, K. (2000, September). *Prayer at football games*. Retrieved September 20, 2001, from http://www.probe.org/docs/c-football.html

Apple, M. W., & Beane, J. A. (Eds.). (1995). *Democratic schools*. Alexandria, VA: Association for Supervision and Curriculum Development.

Archer, J. (1997, February 26). Keeping the faith. *Education Week*, pp. 31–35.

Ball, D., & Wilson, S. (1996). Integrity in teaching: Recognizing the fusion of the moral and intellectual. *American Educational Research Journal, 33*, 155–192.

Belzer Middle School. (2000). *Caring about character education*. Retrieved January 8, 2001, from http://www.msdlt.k12.in.us/belzer/character.html

Bennett, W. J. (Ed.). (1993). *The book of virtues: A treasury of great moral stories*. New York: Simon & Schuster.

Bennett, W. J. (Ed.). (1995). *The moral compass*. New York: Simon & Schuster.

Bernardo, R., & Neal, J. (1997). In pursuit of the moral school. *Journal of Education, 179*, 33–43.

Beyer, L. (Ed.). (1996). *Creating democratic classrooms: The struggle to integrate theory and practice.* New York: Teachers College Press.

Beyer, L. (1997). The moral contours of teacher education. *Journal of Teacher Education, 48,* 245–254.

Booraem, E. (2004). Life lessons. *Hope Magazine,* No. 44. Retrieved August 4, 2005, from http://www.thecommunityschool.org/articles/Hope_Article.pdf

Boostrom, R. (1994). A curriculum of caring. *Journal of Curriculum Studies, 26*(1), 97–114.

Boyer, E. L. (1995). *The basic school: A community for learning.* Princeton, NJ: Carnegie Foundation for the Advancement of Learning.

Bush, G. W. (2001, April 18). *President's Remarks at Central Connecticut State University.* Retrieved July 27, 2005, from http://www.whitehouse.gov/news/releases/2001/04/20010418-3.html

Cahir, B. (2001, March 25). Bush's plan for student testing draws fire. *Denver Post.* Retrieved March 27, 2001, from http://www.denverpost.com/news/news0325f.htm

Canedy, D. (2003, May 13). Critics of graduation exam threaten boycott in Florida. *New York Times,* p. A22.

Carnegie Council on Adolescent Development. (1989). *Turning points: Preparing American youth for the 21st century* (Report of the Task Force on Adolescent Development). Washington, DC: Author.

Carpenter, M. (1999, August 29). Back to school: Building good character through just a trait a week. *Pittsburgh Post-Gazette.* Retrieved March 10, 2006, from http://www.post-gazette.com/regionstate/19990825character2.asp

Carr, S. (2004, December 2). School must find another name. *Milwaukee Journal Sentinel.* Retrieved July 22, 2005, from http://www.jsonline.com/news/metro/dec04/280701.asp

Carter, G. R. (1997). Service learning in curriculum reform. In J. Schine (Ed.), *Service learning* (96th yearbook of the National Society for the Study of Education, Part I, pp. 69–78). Chicago: University of Chicago Press.

Character education. (n.d.). Raleigh, NC: Wake County Public School System.

Character educators applaud educators and community in winning national honor. (1999, October 25). Raleigh, NC: Wake County Public School System. Retrieved March 10, 2006, from http://www.wcpss.net/news/poston/character_education/index.html

The classroom as sacred space [Electronic version]. ASCD *Education Update, 43*(4). Retrieved June 15, 2001, from http://www.ascd.org/readingroom/edupdate/2001/june01/2.html

Coles, R. (1986). *The moral life of children.* Boston: Houghton Mifflin.

Coles, R. (1994, October 26). Putting head and heart on the line. *Chronicle of Higher Education,* p. A64.

Collins, M., & Tamarkin, C. (1990). *Marva Collins' way* (2nd ed.). New York: Jeremy P. Tarcher.

Colton, A. B. (1998). *The nature of two teachers' professional morality: Their interpretations and behaviors.* Unpublished doctoral dissertation, University of Michigan.

Colton, A. B. (1999). *The nature of two teachers' professional morality: Their interpretations and behaviors.* Paper presented at the annual meeting of the Association of Teacher Educators, Chicago.

Comer, J. P., Ben-Avie, M., Haynes, N. M., & Joyner, E. T. (Eds.). (1999). *Child by child: The Comer process for change in education.* New York: Teachers College Press.

Community School. (2000, March 16). *Community School graduates seven.* Retrieved December 7, 2000, from http://rockland.k2bh.com/School/Story.cfm?StoryID=2834

Connolly, T., Dowd, T., Criste, A., Nelson, C., & Tobias, L. (1995). *The well-managed classroom: Promoting student success through social skill instruction.* Boys Town, NE: Boys Town Press.

Core Knowledge Foundation. (2005a, June 22). *School profile renewal forms.* Retrieved July 22, 2005, from http://www.coreknowledge.org/CK/schools/index.htm

Core Knowledge Foundation. (2005b, June 22). *State alignments.* Retrieved July 22, 2005, from http://www.coreknowledge.org/CK/schools/statealign.htm

Cuddy, D. L. (1994, June 17). You can't get around it: Underlying beliefs make all the difference [Letter to the editor]. *The News & Observer*, p. A15.

Damon, W. (1988). *The moral child: Nurturing children's natural moral growth.* New York: Free Press.

DeBrosse, J. (1993a, December 19). Dad's whip formed principal's views. *Dayton Daily News*, p. 6A.

DeBrosse, J. (1993b, December 19). An "A" in values: Scores up, woes down at school. *Dayton Daily News*, p. 1A.

Delpit, L. (1986). Skills and other dilemmas of a progressive Black educator. *Harvard Educational Review, 56,* 379–385.

Delpit, L. (1988). The silenced dialogue: Power and pedagogy in educating other people's children. *Harvard Educational Review, 58,* 280–298.

Delpit, L. (1995). *Other people's children: Cultural conflict in the classroom.* New York: New Press.

Delpit, L. (1999). A letter to my daughter on the occasion of considering racism in the United States. In T. B. Jelloun (Ed.), *Racism explained to my daughter* (pp. 175–193). New York: Free Press.

Dewey, J. (1980). *Democracy and education.* In Jo Ann Boydston (Ed.), *John Dewey: The middle work* (Vol. 9). Carbondale: Southern Illinois University Press. (Original work published 1916)

Edwards v. Aguillard, 482 U.S. 578 (1987).

Egan, K. (1990). [Review of *The moral and spiritual crisis in education*]. *Curriculum Inquiry, 20*(1), 121–128.

Elbow, P. (1986). *Embracing contraries: Explorations in learning and teaching.* New York: Oxford University Press.

Emmons, C., & Carberry, B. (1999). I can fly. In J. P. Comer, M. Ben-Avie, N. M. Haynes, & E. T. Joyner (Eds.), *Child by child: The Comer process for change in education.* New York: Teachers College Press.

Engel v. Vitale, 370 U.S. 421 (1962).

Epperson v. Arkansas, 393 U.S. 97 (1968).

Exodus 2000. (n.d.). Retrieved March 10, 2006, from http://www.citizenreviewon line.org/news/stories/exodus.html

Exstrom, M. (2000, October/November). Yes, ma'am, Louisiana kids are respectful. *State Legislatures*. Retrieved December 5, 2005, from http://www.ncsl.org/ programs/pubs/1011res.htm

Fenstermacher, G. D (1986). Philosophy of research on teaching: Three aspects. In M. C. Wittrock (Ed.), *Handbook of research on teaching* (3rd ed., pp. 37–49). New York: Macmillan.

Fineman, H. (1994, June 13). Virtuecrats. *Newsweek*, pp. 30–33, 36.

Fitzgerald, T. (1994, February 26). Chastity "made the cut" [Letter to the editor]. *The News & Observer*, p. A15.

Freedman, S. (1999). Other people's children [Review of *Other people's children*]. *Radical Teacher*, No. 57, 22–27.

Gadamer, H. G. (1975). *Truth and method*. New York: Crossroad.

Galley, M. (2003, October 15). MD service learning: Classroom link weak? [Electronic version]. *Education Week*. Retrieved July 28, 2005, from http://www .edweek.org/ew/articles/2003/10/15/07mdservice.h23.html?querystring =MD%20 service

Gatto, J. T. (n.d.). *The 9 assumptions of modern schooling*. Retrieved November 25, 2003, from http://www.sepschool.org/edlib/v1n3/gatto.html

Gauld, J. W. (1993). *Character first: The Hyde School difference*. Bath, ME: Hyde Schools.

Gauld, J. W. (1996). Meeting each student's unique potential: One approach to education. *NASSP Bulletin, 80*, No. 583, 43–54.

Gee, R., & Quick, J. (1997). *Wisconsin citizenship initiative: Program guide* (Bulletin No. 97178). Madison: Wisconsin Department of Public Instruction.

Genovesi, A. A. (1994, May 17). School survey's flip side [Letter to the editor]. *The News & Observer*, p. A12.

Giroux, H. (1988). *Teachers as intellectuals: Toward a critical pedagogy of learning*. Granby, MA: Bergin & Garvey.

Goldsmith, S. (1995, June 23). The community is their textbook [Electronic version]. *The American Prospect, 6*(22).

Goodlad, J. I. (1994). *Educational renewal: Better teachers, better schools*. San Francisco: Jossey-Bass.

Goodlad, J. I., Soder, R., & Sirotnik, K. A. (Eds.). (1990). *The moral dimensions of teaching*. San Francisco: Jossey-Bass.

Grace Covenant Christian School. (n.d.). Retrieved July 15, 2001, from http:// www.gccschool.com

Greer, C., & Kohl, H. (Eds.). (1995). *A call to character: A family treasury*. New York: HarperCollins.

Griffith, G. (1991). [Review of *The moral and spiritual crisis in education*]. *Convergence, 24*(3), 90–92.

Hansen, D. T. (1998). The moral is in the practice. *Teaching and Teacher Education, 14*, 643–655.

Hansen, D. T. (2001a). *Exploring the moral heart of teaching.* New York: Teachers College Press.

Hansen, D. T. (2001b). Teaching as a moral activity. In V. Richardson (Ed.), *Handbook of research on teaching* (4th ed., pp. 826–857). Washington, DC: American Educational Research Association.

Harrington, D. (1992). Reaching beyond the self: Service learning for middle schoolers. *American Educator, 16*(2), 36–43.

Hart, D. (2001, March 18). School at home. *Chapel Hill News,* pp. A1, A10–11.

Hatch, B. (1999, February 11). *Community School to present expansion plans.* Retrieved December 7, 2000, from http://rockland.k2bh.com/School/Story.cfm?StoryID=947

Haynes, C. (1998). *Talking about religion in American life: A First Amendment guide.* Ashville, TN: The First Amendment Center.

Heartwood Institute. (2001a). *Teaching materials.* Retrieved July 24, 2001, from http://www.heartwoodethics.org/curriculums/teacher_materials.html

Heartwood Institute. (2001b). *Design of a Heartwood lesson.* Retrieved July 24, 2001, from http://www.heartwoodethics.org/curriculums/hwd_design.html

Heartwood Institute. (2004). *The Heartwood story.* Retrieved November 25, 2005, from http://www.heartwoodethics.org/5about/story.asp

Henriques, D. B. (2003, September 2). Rising demands for testing push limits of its accuracy. *New York Times,* p. A1.

Hirsch, E. D., Jr. (1987). *Cultural literacy: What every American needs to know.* Boston: Houghton Mifflin.

Hirsch, E. D., Jr. (1988). *The dictionary of cultural literacy.* Boston: Houghton Mifflin.

Hirsch, E. D., Jr. (1991). *What your first grader needs to know: Fundamentals of a good first grade education.* New York: Dell.

Hirsch, E. D., Jr. (1993). The Core Knowledge curriculum—What's behind its success? *Educational Leadership, 50*(8), 23–25, 27–30.

Hirsch, E. D., Jr. (1996). *The schools we need: And why we don't have them.* New York: Doubleday.

Hirsch, E. D., Jr. (2000, February 2). The tests we need. *Education Week,* pp. 64, 40–41.

Hirsch, E. D., Jr. (2005). General introduction to the Core Knowledge Series. In E. D. Hirsch, Jr. (Ed.), *What your fifth grader needs to know: Fundamentals of a good fifth grade education* (pp. xxi–xxvi). New York: Doubleday.

Howe, H. (1997). Forward. In J. Schine (Ed.), *Service learning* (96th yearbook of the National Society for the Study of Education, Part I, pp. iv–vi). Chicago: University of Chicago Press.

Hoyle, J., & Slater, R. (2001). Love, happiness and America's schools: The role of educational leadership in the 21st century. *Phi Delta Kappan, 82,* 790–794.

Jackson, D. (1997, February 19). Chapel Hill schools' service rule is upheld. *The News & Observer,* p. A1.

Jackson, P. W., Boostrom, R. E., & Hansen, D. T. (1993). *The moral life of schools.* San Francisco: Jossey-Bass.

Jacobson, L. (1999, July 14). A kinder, gentler student body. *Education Week*, pp. 1, 22–23.

Kane, E. (2004, December 18). Marva Collins explains: She just wanted her good name back. *Milwaukee Journal Sentinel*. Retrieved July 22, 2005, from http://jsonline.com/news/metro/dec04/285361.asp

Katz, J. (1997). *Virtuous reality: How America surrendered discussion of moral values to opportunists, nitwits, and blockheads like William Bennett*. New York: Random House.

Kessler, R. (2000). *The soul of education: Helping students find connection, compassion, and character at school*. Alexandria, VA: Association for Supervision and Curriculum Development.

Kimball, B. A. (1995). *Orators and philosophers: A history of the idea of liberal education*. New York: College Entrance Examination Board.

Kleiner, C. (2000, June 12). Test case: Now the principal's cheating [Electronic version]. *U.S. News & World Report*. Retrieved July 12, 2005, from http://www.usnews.com/usnews/news/articles/000612/archive_016180.htm

Kline, B. (1996, September 14). Dayton parents upset: Vow to keep Allen principal. *Dayton Daily News*, p. 1B.

Koenig, A. (1994, November 20). Rights and wrongs. *Lancaster [PA] Sunday News*, p. A1.

Kohn, A. (1997). How not to teach values: A critical look at character education. *Phi Delta Kappan*, 78, 429–439.

Kotecki, J. S., Jr. (1994, May 21). Character education [Letter to the editor]. *The News & Observer*, p. A17.

Kozol, J. (1991). *Savage inequalities: Children in America's schools*. New York: Crown.

Kozol, J. (1995). *Amazing grace: The lives of children and the conscience of a nation*. New York: Crown.

Kozol, J. (2005). *The shame of the nation: The restoration of apartheid schooling in America*. New York: Random House.

Kranz, C. (2002, July 24). School reacts to Collins' criticism. *Cincinnati Enquirer*. Retrieved December 5, 2005, from http://www.enquirer.com/editions/2002/07/24/loc_school_reacts_to.html

Lancaster Catholic High School. (2004). *Philosophy of Lancaster Catholic High School*. Retrieved July 25, 2005, from http://www.lchs-yes.org/about

Lickona, T. (1991). *Educating for character: How our schools can teach respect and responsibility*. New York: Bantam.

Lickona, T. (1993). The return of character education. *Educational Leadership*, 51(3), 6–11.

Lickona, T. (1998). A more complex analysis is needed. *Phi Delta Kappan*, 79, 449–454.

Lickona, T. (n.d.). A 12-point comprehensive approach to character education. Retrieved August 10, 2005, from http://www.cortland.edu/character/12pts.html

Lickona, T., & Davidson, M. (2005). *Smart and good high schools: Integrating excellence and ethics for success in school, work, and beyond*. Retrieved July 27, 2005, from http://www.cortland.edu/character/highschools

Lundstrom, M. (1999). Character makes a comeback. *Instructor, 109*(3), 25–28.

Lyman, I. (1998, January 7). *Homeschooling: Back to the future?* (Cato Policy Analysis No. 294). Retrieved November 26, 2003, from http://www.cato.org/cgi-bin/scripts/printtech.cgi/pubs/pas/pa-294.html

Mackley, T. A. (1999). *Uncommon sense: Core knowledge in the classroom.* Alexandria, VA: Association for Supervision and Curriculum Development.

Magnuson, P. (2000, February). High-stakes cheating [Electronic version]. NAESP *Communicator.* Retrieved July 7, 2005, from http://www.naesp.org/ContentLoad.do?contentId=151

Mann, H. (1957). Twelfth annual report to the Massachusetts Board of Education. In L. A. Cremin (Ed.), *The republic and the school: Horace Mann on the education of free men* (pp. 79–112). New York: Teachers College, Columbia University. (Original work published 1848)

Maryland Student Service Alliance. (n.d.). *What does a service learning project look like?* Retrieved July 26, 2005, from http://www.mssa.sailorsite.net/define.html

Mauro, T. (2000, June 19). *Supreme Court bans student-led prayer at football games.* Retrieved July 27, 2005, from http://www.freedomforum.org/templates/document.asp?documentID=12727

McClellan, B. E. (1999). *Moral education in America: Schools and the shaping of character from colonial times to the present.* New York: Teachers College Press.

McCreary County, Kentucky v. ACLU of Kentucky, 125 S. Ct. 2722 (2005), 162 L. Ed.2d 729 (U.S. 2005).

McGoogan, G. (2002). Around the world in 24 hours. *Educational Leadership, 60*(2), 44–48.

Medina, J. (2003, March 28). Top-performing school teaches art of test-taking. *New York Times,* p. D3.

Midobuche, E. (1999). Respect in the classroom: Reflections of a Mexican-American educator. *Educational Leadership, 56*(7), 80–82.

Meier, D. (1995). *The power of their ideas.* Boston: Beacon.

Meier, D. (2000, February/March). Educating a democracy: Standards and the future of public education. *Boston Review, 25,* 1–16.

Merriam-Webster Online Dictionary. (2005). Retrieved December 3, 2005, from http://www.m-w.com/dictionary/heuristic

Molnar, A. (1997). Editor's preface. In A. Molnar (Ed.), *The construction of children's character* (96th yearbook of the National Society for the Study of Education, Part II, pp. ix-x). Chicago: University of Chicago Press.

Moore, R. S., & Moore, D. (1981). *Home grown kids: A practical handbook for teaching your children at home.* Waco, TX: World Books.

Moore, R. S., & Moore, D. (1982). *Home-spun schools: Teaching children at home— What parents are doing and how they are doing it.* Waco, TX: World Books.

Muncey, D. E., & McQuillan, P. J. (1993). Preliminary findings from a five-year study of the Coalition of Essential Schools. *Phi Delta Kappan, 74,* 486–489.

Muncey, D. E., & McQuillan, P. J. (1996). *Reform & resistance in schools and classrooms.* New Haven, CT: Yale University Press.

Muncy, J. (1994, June 2). *Understanding Christian homeschoolers.* Retrieved July 25, 2005, from http://www.hstuac.org/muncyjim.html

Nash, R. J. (1997). *Answering the "virtuecrats": A moral conversation on character education*. New York: Teachers College Press.

Nash, R. J. (2002). *Real world ethics* (2nd ed.). New York: Teachers College Press.

National Commission for Excellence in Education (NCEE). (1983). *A nation at risk* [Electronic version]. Washington, DC: National Institute of Education. Retrieved July 12, 2005, from http://www.ed.gov/pubs/NatAtRisk/risk.html

National Commission on Teaching & America's Future. (1996). *What matters most: Teaching for America's future*. New York: Columbia University, Teachers College.

National Education Association. (1975). *Code of ethics of the education profession*. Retrieved July 28, 2005, from http://www.nea.org/aboutnea/code.html

National Science Teachers Association. (1996). *Standards for science teaching*. Retrieved July 19, 2005, from http://books.nap.edu/html/nses/3.html

National Service-Learning Clearinghouse. (2005). *Welcome to service learning*. Retrieved July 26, 2005, from http://www.servicelearning.org/welcome_to_service-learning/index.php

Noblit, G. W., & Dempsey, V. O. (1996). *The social construction of virtue: The moral life of schools*. Albany: State University of New York Press.

Noddings, N. (1984). *Caring: A feminine approach to ethics & moral education*. Berkeley: University of California Press.

Noddings, N. (1988, December 7). Schools face "crisis in caring." *Education Week*, p. 32.

Noddings, N. (1992). *The challenge to care in schools: An alternative approach to education*. New York: Teachers College Press.

Noddings, N. (1995). Teaching themes of care. *Phi Delta Kappan, 76*, 675–679.

Noddings, N. (1998). Teachers and subject matter knowledge. *Teacher Education Quarterly, 25*(4), 86–89.

Noddings, N. (2000, March 23). [Interview with Marty Kirschen, co-editor of newsletter *Teaching from Our Hearts*]. Caring or coercion? What are the costs of high stakes testing and other methods of coercing students? Retrieved March 10, 2006, from http://teachers.net/archive/testing032300.html

Noddings, N. (2001). The caring teacher. In V. Richardson (Ed.), *Handbook of research on teaching* (4th ed., pp. 99–105). Washington, DC: American Educational Research Association.

Noddings, N. (2002). *Educating moral people: A caring alternative to character education*. New York: Teachers College Press.

Nord, W., & Haynes, C. (1998). *Taking religion seriously across the curriculum*. Alexandria, VA: Association for Supervision and Curriculum Development.

O'Keefe, J. M. (1997). Children and community service: Character education in action. *Journal of Education, 179*(2), 47–62.

Oldenski, T., & Carlson, D. (2002). *Educational yearning: The journey of spirit and democracy*. New York: Peter Lang.

Oser, F. K. (1986). Moral education and values education. In M. C. Wittrock (Ed.), *Handbook of research on teaching* (3rd ed., pp. 917–941). New York: Macmillan.

O'Toole, K. (1998, February 4). Noddings: To know what matters to you, observe your actions. *Stanford Report* [Electronic version]. Retrieved January 4, 2001, from http://www.stanford.edu/dept/news/report/news/february/

Palmer, P. (1993). *To know as we are known: Education as a spiritual journey.* San Francisco: Harper & Row.

Palmer, P. (1998). *The courage to teach: Exploring the inner landscape of a teacher's life.* San Francisco: Jossey-Bass.

Pariser, E. (1990). A day in the life: The Community School. *SKOLE: The Journal of the National Coalition of Alternative Community Schools, 6*(1), 1–18. (ERIC Document Reproduction Service No. ED 360 126)

Pariser, E. (1998, April). The Community School. *New Perspectives,* Issue #51 (Woodbury Reports Archives). Retrieved August 4, 2005, from http://strugglingteens.com/archives/1998/4/np02.html

Pariser, E. (1999). *Relational education: An antidote to school-induced despair.* Retrieved August 5, 2005, from http://www.thecommunityschool.org/relational.htm

Paulson, A. (2000, October 10). Homeschoolers are an increasingly diverse crowd. *Christian Science Monitor,* p. 18.

Perkins-Gough, D., Lindfors, S., & Ernst, D. (2002). A curriculum for peace: A conversation with Sir John Daniel. *Educational Leadership, 60*(2), 14–17.

Peterson, B. (1994). Coping with TV: Some lesson plans. In B. Bigelow, L. Christensen, S. Karp, B. Miner, & B. Peterson (Eds.), *Rethinking our classrooms: Teaching for equity and social justice* (pp. 80–81). Milwaukee, WI: Rethinking Schools.

Peterson, B. (1995). La Escuela Fratney: A journey toward democracy. In M. W. Apple & J. A. Beane (Eds.), *Democratic schools* (pp. 58–82). Alexandria, VA: Association for Supervision and Curriculum Development.

Peterson, R. E. (1991). Teaching how to read the world and change it: Critical pedagogy in the intermediate grades. In C. E. Walsh (Ed.), *Literacy as praxis: Culture, language, and pedagogy* (pp. 156–182). Norwood, NJ: Ablex.

Pierce, N. R. (1995, September 10). America's schools: How bad? What next? *The News & Observer,* p. A28.

Portner, J. (1994, April 27). Youth service day brings new challenges to district mandates [Electronic version]. *Education Week.* Retrieved August 1, 2005, from http://www.edweek.org/ew/articles/1994/04/27/31youth.h13.html

Portner, J. (1996, June 5). Father Flanagan's gospel. *Education Week,* pp. 27, 30, 32–34.

Purpel, D. E. (1989). *The moral & spiritual crisis in education: A curriculum for justice & compassion in education.* Granby, MA: Bergin & Garvey.

Purpel, D. E. (1991a). Moral education: An idea whose time has gone. *Clearing House, 64,* 309–312.

Purpel, D. E. (1991b). Education as sacrament. *Independent School, 50*(3), 45–54. A revised version of this essay (same title) appears in D. E. Purpel, *Moral outrage in education* (pp. 173–186). New York: Peter Lang.

Purpel, D. E. (1997). The politics of character education. In A. Molnar (Ed.), *The construction of children's character* (96th yearbook of the National Society for the Study of Education, Part II, pp. 140–153). Chicago: University of Chicago Press.

Purpel, D. E. (1999). *Moral outrage in education*. New York: Peter Lang.

Reedstrom, K. (1997, June). [Interview with Marva Collins]. *Full Context*, 9(10). Retrieved November 26, 2003, from http://www.fullcontext.org/people/collins_intx.htm

Richardson, V. (2001). *Handbook of research on teaching* (4th ed.). Washington, DC: American Educational Research Association.

Ricoeur, P. (1987). *Hermeneutics and the human sciences* (J. B. Thompson, Ed. and Trans.). Cambridge, England: Cambridge University Press.

Risman, B. J., & Kane, R. B. (1994, June 17). If "character education" means narrow values, it isn't healthy [Letter to the Editor]. *The News & Observer*, p. A15.

Roberts, T., & the Staff of the National Paideia Center. (1998). *The power of Paideia schools*. Alexandria, VA: Association for Supervision and Curriculum Development.

Rose, L. C., & Gallup, A. M. (2003). The 35th annual Phi Delta Kappa/Gallup poll of the public's attitudes toward the public schools. *Phi Delta Kappan, 85*, 41–56.

Rudner, L. M. (1999, March 23). Scholastic achievement and demographic characteristics of home school students in 1998. *Education Policy Analysis Archives*, 7(8). Retrieved August 5, 2005, from http://epaa.asu.edu/epaa/v7n8/

Ryan, K. (1981). *Questions and answers on moral education* (Fastback No. 153). Bloomington, IN: Phi Delta Kappa.

Ryan, K. (1986). The new moral education. *Phi Delta Kappan, 68*, 228–233.

Ryan, K. (1996, May 29). Guidelines from a character-education "manifesto." *Education Week*, p. 31.

Saks, J. B. (1996). *Character education in the classroom: How America's school boards are promoting values and virtues*. Alexandria, VA: National School Boards Association.

Schaeffer, E. (1997). Character education: Focus on the Future. *Social Studies Review*, 39(1), 82–84.

Scherer, M. (1992/1993). On savage inequalities: A conversation with Jonathan Kozol. *Educational Leadership, 50*(4), 4–9.

Schine, J. (Ed.). (1997). *Service learning* (96th yearbook of the National Society for the Study of Education, Part I). Chicago: University of Chicago Press.

Schine, J., & Harrington, D. (1982). *Youth participation for early adolescents: Learning and serving in the community* (Fastback No. 174). Bloomington, IN: Phi Delta Kappan Educational Foundation.

Schlesinger, A., Jr. (1998). *The disuniting of America: Reflections on a multicultural society* (rev. and expanded ed.). New York: Norton.

School Development Program. (2002). *Overview of the School Development Program*. Retrieved October 30, 2003, from http://www.med.yale.edu/comer/about/

Schulte, B. (2000, June 28). Penalties urged in MD test scandal. *Washington Post*, p. B1. Retrieved September 7, 2000, from http://www.newslibrary.com/deliverppdoc.asp?SMH=53405

Scott, C. L. (1992). Shaping character. *American School Board Journal, 179*(2), 28–30.

Sergiovanni, T. J. (1992). *Moral leadership.* San Francisco: Jossey-Bass.

Silberman, T. (1993, November 29). A question of character. *The News & Observer,* p. A1.

Silberman, T. (1994, June 10). Wake panel OKs 8 value traits for schools. *The News & Observer,* p. B1.

Simon, K. G. (2001). *Moral questions in the classroom: How to get kids to think deeply about real life and their schoolwork.* New Haven, CT: Yale University Press.

Sizer, T. R. (1973). *Places for learning, places for joy: Speculations on American school reform.* Cambridge, MA: Harvard University Press.

Sizer, T. R. (1984). *Horace's compromise: The dilemma of the American high school.* Boston: Houghton Mifflin.

Sizer, T. R. (1992). *Horace's school: Redesigning the American high school.* Boston: Houghton Mifflin.

Sizer, T. R., & Sizer, N. F. (1999). *The students are watching: Schools and the moral contract.* Boston: Beacon.

Sockett, H. (1993). *The moral base for teacher professionalism.* New York: Teachers College Press.

Sockett, H., & LePage, P. (2002). The missing language of the classroom. *Teaching and Teacher Education, 18,* 159–171.

Solomon, D., Watson, M. S., & Battistich, V. A. (2001). Teaching and schooling effects on moral/prosocial development. In V. Richardson (Ed.), *Handbook of research on teaching* (4th ed., pp. 566–603). Washington, DC: American Educational Research Association.

Spring, J. H. (1972). *Education and the rise of the corporate state.* Boston: Beacon.

Spring, J. H. (2000). *American education* (9th ed.). Boston: McGraw Hill.

Stallones, J. (2000a, November). *Democracy, community, and faith: A three-legged stool.* Paper presented at the annual conference on Curriculum and Pedagogy, Austin, TX.

Stallones, J. (2000b, November). *Religion in the social studies curriculum.* Paper presented at the annual conference of the National Council for the Social Studies, San Antonio, TX.

Stallones, J. (2000c, October). A new look. *The Lion's Roar: Newsletter of the Grace Covenant Christian School.*

Stallones, J. (2000d, November). What's wrong with Christian schools? *The Lion's Roar: Newsletter of the Grace Covenant Christian School.*

Stern, S. (2003, January 14). Muslims craft their own curriculum. *Christian Science Monitor,* p. 13.

Strike, K. A., & Soltis, J. F. (1985). *The ethics of teaching.* New York: Teachers College Press.

Strike, K. A., & Ternasky, P. L. (Eds.). (1993). *Ethics for professionals in education: Perspectives for preparation and practice.* New York: Teachers College Press.

Thomas, E., & Wingert, P. (2000, June 12). Bitter lessons. *Newsweek,* pp. 50–52.

Thompson, M. (2001). *Wilson Elementary School.* Retrieved April 4, 2001, from http://www.kusd.edu/schools/wilson/wilson_principal.html

Tom, A. R. (1984). *Teaching as a moral craft*. New York: Longman.

Townsend, K. (1992, December). Why Johnny can't tell right from wrong. *The Washington Monthly, 24*(12), 29–32.

VanOrden v. Perry, 125 S.Ct. 2854 (2005), 162 L. Ed. 2d 607 (U.S. 2005).

Verde, T. (1990, September 1990). Maine alternative school gives dropouts a way back. *Boston Globe*. Reprinted in *SKOLE: The Journal of the National Coalition of Alternative Community Schools*, 1991, 7(2), 93–98. (ERIC Document Reproduction Service No. ED 360 126)

Viadero, D. (1996, March 13). Unconventional wisdom: Two distinguished African-American educators dissent from the progressive ideology of contemporary school reform. *Education Week*, pp. 40–43.

Walsh, M. (2002, June 5). Home school enrollment surge fuels "cottage" industry. *Education Week*, p. 8.

Weber, M. (1949). *The methodology of the social sciences*. New York: Free Press.

Westheimer, J., & Kahne, J. (2000, January 26). Service learning required. *Education Week*, pp. 52, 32.

Why small schools are essential [Electronic version]. (1997). *Horace, 13*(3). Retrieved July 27, 2005, from http://www.essentialschools.org/cs/resources/view/ces_res/18

Wiese, K. (2005, July 3). Kansas school funding case holds lessons for Missouri. *Kansas City Star*. Retrieved July 12, 2005, from http://www.kansascity.com/mld/kansascity/news/local/12048494.htm

Williams, R. (1991). The impact of field education on student development: Research findings. *Journal of Cooperative Education, 27*, 29–45.

Winerip, M. (2003a, February 19). On education: Defining success in narrow terms. *New York Times*, p. B7.

Winerip, M. (2003b, October 8). On education: How a good school can fail on paper. *New York Times*, p. B9.

Winerip, M. (2003c, October 15). Trail of clues preceded. *New York Times*, p. B10.

Wisconsin Citizenship Initiative. (2004). Retrieved August 4, 2005, from http://www.dpi.state.wi.us/dpi/dlsea/sspw/citindex.html

Wiseman, F. (Director/Editor/Producer). (1994). *High School II* [Motion picture]. Cambridge, MA: Zipporah Films.

Wittrock, M. C. (Ed.). (1986). *Handbook of research on teaching* (3rd ed.). New York: Macmillan.

Wynne, E. A. (1982). Rigorous thinking about character. *Phi Delta Kappan, 64*, 187–188.

Wynne, E. A. (1985/1986). The great tradition in education: Transmitting moral values. *Educational Leadership, 43*(4), 4–9.

Wynne, E. A. (1988). Balancing character development and academics in the elementary school. *Phi Delta Kappan, 69*, 424–426.

Zahn, M. (1996). [Interview with Marva Collins]. Retrieved August 5, 2005, from http://www.jsonline.com/news/edu/marva/marvatranscript.asp

Zernike, K. (2002, September 3). Plaid's out, again, as schools give up requiring uniforms. *New York Times*, p. A1.

Index

Abington v. Schempp, 32
Academic
  achievement, 14, 15, 66, 71, 73, 75
  as common understanding, 24, 29, 37,
    101
  development, 7, 75
  disciplines, 19, 109
  excellence, 14, 45, 66
  growth, 4–5
  relation between moral and. *See* Moral/
    academic relation
  standards. *See* Standards
Academic Dominant (subcategory). *See*
  Dominant, Academic
Academic First (subcategory). *See*
  Sequential, Academic First
Accountability, 6–7, 12–15, 19, 61, 67, 82,
    112, 113, 130–134, 148
Adler, Mortimer, 38, 67, 75, 78
Adolescents, 55, 98, 108, 129
Advisors, 98, 109
Advisory group, 109
Aesop's Fables, 82
Agency, 141, 142, 150
Allen Academy, 45, 48–51, 61, 136
Allen, Jeanne, 7
Allison, Dorothy, 27
Amazing Grace, 74
Ambiguity, 26, 58, 121, 133
  in moral deliberation, 58
Amos, D. S., 85
Anderson, K., 21
Angelou, Maya, 83
Answering the "Virtuecrats", 147

Anthropologists and What They Do, 84
Apple, Michael, 17, 18
Archer, J., 91
Assertiveness training, 99
Association for Supervision and
    Curriculum Development,
    21, 128
At-risk children, 94
Attitudes, 64, 66, 73, 84, 85, 103, 106,
    126, 129
Austen, Jane, 82
Authentic assessment, 109, 121
Authority, 3, 4, 26, 27, 43, 93, 96, 126,
    141
Autonomy, 8, 31, 88, 91, 92, 121

Background knowledge, 86, 87
Ball, Deborah, 132, 148
Basic School, The, 17
Basic skills, 24, 29, 78, 140, 141
Bastard Out of Carolina, 27
Battistich, V. A., 12, 19
Beane, James, 17, 18
Behavior modification, 59
Belzer Middle School, 102, 104
Ben-Avie, M., 71
Bennett, William, 16, 45, 47, 48, 61, 63,
    142
Bernardo, Rodolpho, 47–51
Beyer, Landon, 41, 116, 119, 120, 125
Biblical
  mandate, 93
  orientation, 125
Biblically based education, 125, 126

Biggs, Terrence, 73
Block scheduling, 109
Bob Jones University, 93
Book of Virtues, The, 47
Booraem, E., 100
Boostrom, Robert, 12, 17, 41, 102, 103
Boyer, Ernest, 17, 18
Boys Town Model, 38, 67, 69, 71, 78
Brothers Grimm, 84
Brown, Mary, 4–5, 145
Buck, Pearl, 84
Bush, George W., 12

Cahir, B., 15
Candide, 84
Canedy, D., 15
Capitalism, 31
Carberry, Belinda, 72–73
Cardinal Principles, 110
Caring, 4, 16, 19, 21, 40, 48, 51, 52, 69–
    71, 79, 101–104, 111, 113, 120–122,
    141
  as relation between carer and cared-for,
    19, 101, 102, 113
  as virtue, 102
  centers of, 97, 103, 112, 141
  ethic of, 97, 101, 112
Challenge to Care in Schools, The, 17, 18,
    102, 103
Carlson, Dennis, 129
Carnegie Council on Adolescent
    Development, 55
Carpenter, M., 50
Carr, S., 85
Carter, G. R., 46
Case method of instruction, 58
Category scheme, 1–2, 8–9, 10, 23–30, 36–
    44, 60–65, 78–80, 94–96, 111–114,
    134–148
Catholic school, 89–91, 123
Center for Education Reform, 7
Center for the 4th and 5th Rs, 42
Central Park East Secondary School, 41,
    111, 116, 120–122, 149
Character
  -based literature, 49
  good, 46, 49
  six pillars of, 16
  trait(s) of, 2, 3, 20, 47–50
Character Counts, 6

Character education, 2, 3, 12, 13, 16, 17,
    20, 39, 42, 45, 47–52, 60–65, 70, 82,
    102, 136, 137, 143, 146
  broad approach to, 16
  expansive, 52
  making the case for, 47–52
  modeling for, 5, 58
  traditional, 51
Character Education Manifesto, 16
Character Education Partnership, 16, 136
Character First, 67, 68
Charter schools, 83, 107
Cheating, 4, 6–7, 59
Chekhov, Anton, 84
Child by Child, 70
Christian
  ethic of love, 127
  ethics, 90, 116
  homeschoolers, 88, 91–94, 96
  love, 131
  schools, 92, 125–127
  tradition, 125
Christian Homeschool Community, 92
Chronicles of Narnia, 125
Church/state, 10, 32–33, 82
Citizenship, 3, 62, 68, 76–78, 100, 109,
    122, 137. See also Civic
Citizenship Initiative, 41
Civic
  engagement, 63
  responsibility, 53
  virtue, 16
Civil rights, 35
Civil War, American, 84
Classical Christian Homeschooling, 93
Classical education, 48
Classical literature, 83–85
Classroom
  discipline, 49
  environment, 68, 136, 145
  management, 35, 59
Close-mindedness, 96
Coaching, 76, 121
Coalition of Essential Schools, 38, 41, 108,
    109, 113, 120
Code
  of conduct, 24, 49, 53
  of ethics, 56, 57
Codes of power, 24, 30
Coles, Robert, 17, 45

Collaboration, 67, 72, 108, 119. 150

Collins, Marva, 40, 81, 83–85, 87–88, 95–96, 110,

Colton, Amy, 4–5

Comer, James, 67, 71–73, 78, 142

Communication, 11, 24, 26, 36, 72, 76, 86, 99, 108, 109, 117, 124, 134, 144, 146

Community, 2–3, 6–7, 8, 16, 18, 20, 24–26, 30, 46, 48, 51–55, 64, 75, 78, 88–89, 98–99, 105, 107, 118, 127, 137, 141, 149

  cohesion, 126

  functional, 73

  in schools, 66

  moral, 116

  of discourse, 150

  of educators, 138, 149

  of learners, 119

  of mutual respect, 71

  of truth, 128

  -school relations, 78

Community School, The, 98–100

Community service, 18, 21, 52–56, 136

Compassion, 47, 106, 107, 122, 128

Competition, 75, 105, 128

Complexity, 2, 95, 112, 114, 143, 144

Concern for others, 68

Conference on Curriculum and Pedagogy, 126

Conflict resolution, 20, 26, 73, 99, 136

Connolly, T., 69

Consensus, 3, 8, 72, 105, 150

Consequentialism, 58

Conservative, 15–17, 30, 31, 46, 51, 63, 146, 147

Controversy, 2, 8, 31, 32, 86, 142

Cooperation, 79, 87

Cooperative learning, 35, 58, 119

Core knowledge, 29, 86–88, 95, 107, 108

Core Knowledge Foundation, 87, 88

Core values, 25, 50, 63, 136, 137

Courage, 2, 16, 47, 48, 50, 51, 68, 137

Courtesy, 20, 47

Creating Democratic Classrooms, 119

Crisis, 48, 105–106, 112

Criste, A., 69

Critical consciousness, 106

Critical thinking, 24, 107, 140

C-School. See Community School, The

Cuddy, D.L., 3

Cultural

  diversity, 10, 23, 31, 33–35, 87, 94, 148

  homogeneity, 95

  perspective, 142

  sensitivity, 78, 140, 143

Cultural Literacy, 86–88

Culturally diverse students, 74

Culturally responsive teaching, 67, 73–74

Culture

  dominant. See Dominant culture

  of peace, 22

  of power, 116, 124, 131

Curiosity, 68

Curriculum, 5, 65, 81, 125

  academic, 84, 97, 127, 136

  developing character through, 3, 18, 51, 136

  classical, 48, 76

  core knowledge, 86

  discipline-based, 69

  idea-based, 77

  life skills, 100

  multicultural 119

  religion in the, 33

  with moral impact, 10

Dahl, Roald, 84

Damon, William, 17

Dante, 84

Davidson, M., 137

DeBrosse, J., 49, 51

Decoding, 84, 86

Delano Elementary School, 83

Delpit, Lisa, 116, 122–125, 130, 143

Democracy, 18, 28, 75–78, 95, 116, 120, 121, 125, 139, 147

Democracy in America, 84

Democratic

  classroom environment, 136

  community, 35, 74

  dilemma, 126

  ethic, 128

  functioning, 24, 44

  participation, 131

  principles, 128

  schooling, 43, 148

  sensibility, 127

  society, 49, 111

Democratic Schools, 17, 18

Dempsey, V. O., 12
Denenberg, Dennis, 20
Deontology, 27
Dewey, John, 44, 76, 84, 86, 93, 131
Dialectic, 58, 77, 120, 141
Dialogic approach, 116
Dialogue, 64, 119, 141, 146, 148, 150
    across difference, 8
Dictionary of Cultural Literacy, 87
Discipline, 26, 48, 49, 91. *See also*
    Classroom, discipline
Dispositions, 16
Disuniting of America, The, 34
Divine Comedy, The, 84
Dominant (category), 1, 9, 10, 24, 38–40,
    43, 80, 81–96, 97–98, 110–111, 134,
    135, 138, 141, 143–145
    Academic, 9, 40, 81–88, 94–96, 110–11,
    114
    Moral, 9, 38–40, 80, 89–97, 104, 114,
    116, 125
Dominant culture, 34, 124, 142, 147
Dowd, T., 69
Drug
    use, 16, 26, 82
    -free programs, 137
Due process, 57–59

Early Adolescent Helper Program, 46, 55–
    56, 61
Eclectic approach, 10, 41, 136–137
Educating for Character, 136
Edwards v. Aguillard, 33
Egalitarianism, 76
Egan, Kieran, 114
Elbow, Peter, 44
Emerson, Ralph Waldo, 84
Emmons, Christine, 72
Empathy, 108, 121, 122
Engel v. Vitale, 32
Engelmann's Direct Instruction, 85
Engrossment, 102
Enlightenment, the, 31, 105
Epperson v. Arkansas, 32
Equal opportunity, 59
Equality, 59, 104
Equity, 14, 77, 79, 112, 117
Ernst, D., 22
Esposito, Ralph, 72
Establishment Clause, 33

Ethical
    failure, 7
    inquiry, 58
    reasoning, 60
    theory, 60
    training, 61
Ethic of caring. *See* Caring, ethic of
Ethics, 51, 56–60, 62, 64, 90, 137
    of teaching, 46, 56–65
Ethics Curriculum for Children, An, 51
Ethics of Teaching, The, 46
Ethnocentrism, 104
Evolution, 33, 90
Exhibitions, 109, 110, 149. *See also*
    Authentic assessment
Existential, 43, 104–105, 141
Exodus Mandate Project, 93
Experiential learning theory, 46
Exploring the Moral Heart of Teaching,
    130
Expressive awareness, 115
Exstrom, M., 20

Fairness, 13, 56, 79, 129, 136
Fair Test, 7
Faith, 26, 27, 36, 47, 54, 55, 89, 93, 94,
    125, 126, 148
Family, 79, 89, 92, 95, 100, 117
    decline of, 16
101 Famous Poems, 84
Fenstermacher, Gary, 19
Fineman, H., 48
First Amendment, 31, 33
First Amendment Center, The, 31
Fitzgerald, Tami, 2
"Five Words", 68
Flanagan, Father Edward J., 69
Freedman, S., 124
Freedom, 33, 77, 83
    of thought, 127
Free will, 26, 92, 93
Freire, Paulo, 105, 116–120

Gadamer, Hans Georg, 145
Galley, M., 53
Gallup, A. M., 12
Gatto, John Taylor, 92, 93
Gauld, Joseph, 67, 68–69
Gee, R., 137
Gender, 34, 36, 51, 95, 142

Genovesi, A. A., 3
Gerstner, Louis, 14
Giroux, Henry, 17, 105
Goals of schooling, 42
Goldsmith, S., 53
Good behavior, 47–51
Goodlad, John, 12, 17, 19
Good life, the, 68, 77
Grace Covenant Christian School, 116,
    125–127, 132
Great Books, 76, 78, 141
Great ideas, 24, 67, 140, 141
Greene, Maxine, 105
Greer, C., 16
Griffith, G., 105

Habits, 16, 24, 47, 107, 108, 109, 121,
    131
  of mind, 24, 29, 30, 97, 107–109, 112,
    121, 122, 140, 141, 145
  of reasoning, 132
Handbook of Research on Teaching
  3rd Edition, 19
  4th Edition, 19
Hansen, David, 12, 17, 19, 41, 56, 115,
    116, 129–130, 133, 149
Harrington, D., 55
Hart, D., 21
Hatch, B., 100
Haynes, Charles, 31–33
Haynes, N. M, 71
Headman, Jay, 6
Heartwood Institute, 45, 51–52, 61, 63
  lessons, 51
Henriques, D. B., 15
Hewitt, Janette, 70
High School II, 120
High stakes testing, 1, 7, 14, 88, 94, 112,
    150
Hinduism, 83
Hirsch, E. D., 38, 40, 86–88, 95, 96, 110,
    141
Homer, 84
Homeschooling, 20, 30, 89, 91–94, 96,
Home School Legal Defense Association, 93
Honesty, 2, 6, 25, 48, 51, 137, 146
Hooray for Heroes, 20
Hope, 51
Horace's Compromise, 108, 100, 111
Horace's School, 108, 109

Howe, H., 44
Hoyle, J., 12
Hugo, Victor, 84
Humility, 130
Hutchins, Robert, 76
Hyde School, The, 39, 67, 68–69, 78

I Know Why the Caged Bird Sings, 83
Ideal type, 10, 43, 136
Ideas, 18, 29, 30, 66, 75
  as curricular base, 77
  big, 29, 30
  moral, 8, 20
Identity, 24, 33, 34
  cultural, 148
  national, 33–35
  politics, 34
  primacy of, 24
  well-formed, 128
Ideological
  debates, 80, 145
  divides, 147
  stance, 26, 145–147
Ideology, 9, 26, 27, 35, 41, 64, 141, 146–
    148
Improved Student Learning and Discipline
    Act of 1999, 20
Incentive store, 50
Individuality, 105
Indoctrination, 10, 31–32, 33, 43, 62–65,
    96, 106, 111, 127, 143
Integrated (category), 1, 9, 10, 24, 38, 41–
    43, 114, 115–133, 134, 135, 138, 141,
    143–145
Integrity, 2, 15, 24, 46, 68, 127, 128, 129,
    131, 143
Intellectual
  freedom, 58
  skills, 76–77
Intelligence, 14, 71, 108, 131, 139
  in use, 108
  method of, 131
Interdisciplinary
  study, 44
  units, 102
Interpretation, 145–146, 148
Isadora Wexler School, 71–72

Jackson, D., 21
Jackson, Phillip, 12, 17, 41, 115, 129

Jacobson, L., 20
James Madison High School, 48
Jefferson, Thomas, 28, 33
Josephson, Michael, 16
Joyner, E. T., 71
Julius Caesar, 83
Justice, 16, 51, 62, 77, 149
  economic, 143

Kahne, J., 53, 62
Kane, E., 85
Kansas Supreme Court, 21
Karch, Karen, 6
Katz, Michael, 8
Kessler, Rachel, 116, 128–129, 133
Kimball, Bruce, 67
Kleiner, C., 7
Kline, B., 51
Koenig, A., 21
Kohl, Herbert, 16
Kohn, Alfie, 16, 136, 146
Kotecki, John, 82
Kozol, Jonathan, 17, 67, 74–75, 78, 143
Kranz, C., 85
Kushner, Harold, 21
Kwanzaa, 51

La Escuela Fratney, 116, 118
Lancaster Catholic High School, 89–91,
  92, 103, 125
Language, 11, 18, 24–30, 35, 67, 72, 73, 116,
  117, 119, 122, 132, 145, 148, 150
  as tool for metacognition, 118
  explicitly moral, 4–5, 11, 18, 27, 68
  moralistic, 71
  of schooling, 11, 74, 132, 148
  to integrate moral/academic, 11, 132
Leadership
  as quality of moral development, 68
  moral, 12, 17
Learning communities, 26, 35
Learning disabilities, 97
Learning environment, 60, 70, 71, 75, 123
LePage, P., 149
Les Miserables, 84
Levasque, Sister Lourise, 91
Lewis, C. S., 125
Liberal arts
  curriculum, 75, 102, 103, 116
  education for teachers, 85

Liberal education, 75–78, 102, 116
Liberal perspectives, 16, 46, 31, 51, 52, 63,
  119, 125, 146, 147
Liberation, 26, 29, 30, 118
Libertarian, 90–92
Lickona, Thomas, 17, 42, 45, 136, 146
Lievow, Dora, 98, 100–101, 111–114
Life
  experience, 42
  meaning of, *See* Meaning
  skills, 99–101, 112, 113
Lindfors, S., 22
Literature, 47, 49, 51, 52, 76, 83, 98
Littky, Dennis, 111
Little Women, 84
Lockwood, Alan, 146
Love, 12, 82
  of God, 27
Loyalty, 51
Lundstrom, Meg, 16
Lyman, I., 93

Mackley, T. A., 87
Magnuson, P., 7
Maieutic questioning, 76
Management skills, 98
Mandatory service, 21
Mann, Horace, 30, 42, 139–140
Marc Antony, 88
Marva Collins Story, The (television film), 83
Marva Collins' Way, 83–85
Maryland Service Learning Requirement, 46
Maryland Student Service Alliance, 52, 53,
  56
Mauro, T., 21
McClellan, Edward, 13, 16, 63
McCreary v. ACLU of Kentucky, 33
McGoogan, G., 22
McQuillan, P. J., 113
Mead, Margaret, 84
Meaning, 27, 83–84
  of life, 55, 93, 99, 148
  quest for, 105
Medina, J., 15
Meier, Deborah, 41, 111, 116, 120–122,
  125, 130, 132, 133, 149
Meritocracy, 73
Methodological belief, 44
Methodological doubt, 44
Methods course, 57, 59, 60

Midobuche, Eva, 67, 73–74, 143
Mill, John Stuart, 74
Milton, John, 32
Mind, 29, 96, 103, 109
  as functioning tool, 110
  habits of. *See* Habits of mind
Mission statement, 48, 125, 142
Molnar, Alex, 51
Moore, Raymond and Dorothy, 93
Moral
  aspects of teaching, 4, 5, 17, 104, 139,
    147, 154
  breakdown, 7
  climate, 49, 69
  codes, 81
  community, 116
  contours of schooling, 5, 9, 11, 13, 23,
    30, 35, 43, 119, 135, 140, 141
  decision-making, 104, 105
  deliberation, 32, 58, 61, 104–105
  development, 1, 4, 5, 7, 18, 19, 23, 23,
    36, 38, 44–45, 47, 51, 59, 65, 66,
    70, 74, 77, 83, 116, 126, 129, 145,
    146
  dimensions of schooling, 1–2, 5, 10, 13,
    17, 19, 20, 22, 23, 26, 35–37,40,
    42, 53, 61, 64, 71, 80–82, 86, 115,
    129, 134–136, 142–143, 146, 150
  domain, 20, 31
  education, 1, 3–5, 9–10, 12–13, 15, 17–
    20, 36, 48, 104–105
  issues in schooling, 8, 23, 61, 64, 134,
    144, 146
  judgment, 2, 6, 14, 26, 27, 34, 42, 61,
    62, 108
  language, 25, 26, 30–35, 74, 108, 132
  matters, 8, 10, 11, 12, 32, 56, 135–138,
    141, 142, 147, 149–150
  philosophy, 77, 130
  point of view, 8
  principles, 26, 27, 56, 66
  realm's interface with schooling, 12, 36,
    41–43, 147–148
  reasoning, 35, 38, 105
  renewal of schools, 10, 144
  responsibility, 59, 116, 131, 141
  stance, 27, 97
  stewards, teachers as 4
  truth, 78
  vision, 104–107, 114, 129, 131

Moral/academic relation, 9–11, 29, 30, 42,
    79–80, 100, 111–114, 120, 130–133,
    134, 136, 138, 145, 146, 148, 150
*Moral and Spiritual Crisis in Education,
    The*, 17, 18, 105, 106
*Moral Base for Teacher Professionalism,
    The*, 17
Moral Child, The, 17
Moral Dimensions of Teaching, The, 17, 19
Moral Dominant (subcategory). *See*
    Dominant, Moral
Moral First (subcategory). *See* Sequential,
    Moral First
Moral invisible domain, 13, 35, 46–47, 82,
    94, 112, 135, 138
Moralism, 73
Morality, 24, 67, 74
  private, 8
  teachers' professional, 4–5, 144
Moral Leadership, 17
Moral Life of Children, The, 17
Moral Transformative (subcategory). *See*
    Transformative, Moral
Moral visible domain, 12–13, 22, 23, 29,
    35, 46, 65, 138, 143, 144, 150
Morris, Rodney, 4–5, 144
Moving force, 37–38, 40, 79, 114
Multicultural education, 34, 73
Multiculturalism, 51, 52, 63, 118
Muncey, D. E., 113
Muncy, Jim, 93

Nash, Robert, 21, 27, 147
Nation at Risk, A, 13–16, 47
National Board Certification, 4–5
National Center for Fair & Open Testing, 7
National Commission for Excellence in
    Education, 13
National Commission on Teaching &
    America's Future, 21, 113
National Council for the Social Studies, 126
National Education Association, 56–58
National Governors' Association, 14
National Helpers Network, 55
National Paideia Center, 78
National Science Teachers Association, 60
National Service Learning Clearing House,
    60
National Society for the Study of
    Education, 64

Neal, J., 48–50
Neill, Monty, 7
Nelson, T., 69
Neutrality, 33, 43
New Consensus, 31, 33
New Testament, 90
Newman, Sara, 20
Noblit, George, 12
No Child Left Behind Act, 14, 88, 113
Noddings, Nel, 17, 19, 38, 40, 96, 97, 101–
    104, 106, 111–113, 121–122, 149
Nonconsequentialism, 58
Nord, Warren, 33

Odyssey, The, 84
O'Herlin, Buck, 99
O'Keefe, J.M., 54
Oldenski, T., 129
Old Testament, 90
Order, 79
Oser, Fritz, 19
O'Toole, K., 101
Oversimplification, 62–64

Quick, J., 137

Paideia Proposal, The, 38, 39, 67, 75
Palmer, Parker, 116, 128, 129
Parents
    as caregivers, 137
    role, 30, 58, 92, 103, 119
Pariser, Emanuel, 98–101, 11–114
Parochial school, 89–91
Patience, 129
Patriotism, 78, 140
Peer mediation, 20
Perkins-Gough, D., 21
Perseverance, 2, 3, 6, 47, 48, 82, 99
Perspective, 51
Peterson, Bob, 116–120, 125, 130, 133,
    143
Phi Delta Kappan, 146
Phonics, 84
Pierce, N. R., 14
Pilgrim's Progress, 83
Plato, 76, 84
Political
    action, 75
    analysis, 18
    commitment, 130

context, 5
correctness, 34
ideology, 8, 36
resistance, 140
spectrum, 146
Politics, 23, 30, 31, 63, 64, 123, 135, 147
    partisan, 30–31, 93, 150
Portner, J., 21, 70
Postmodernism, 96, 147
Potomac Elementary School, 6–7, 144
Poverty, 70, 82, 105, 139
Power, 14, 40, 106, 118–119, 124
    of the sacred, 128
    over students, 106, 141
    with students, 141
Power of Their Ideas, The, 121
Praxis, 120
Prayer, 21, 26, 32, 35, 54, 89
Pride, 82
Pride and Prejudice, 84
Pride Center, 73
Private school, 82–84
Problem-posing method, 118
Professional ethics, 39, 56. See also Ethics,
    of teaching
Professionalism, 19
Professional servants, teachers as, 4
Progressive teaching, 123, 124
Promptness, 49–50
Prosocial behavior, 4, 68, 71
Public school, 8, 32, 74, 75, 78, 91, 105,
    110
Punctuality, 48–50
Punishment, 58
Puritans, 32
Purpel, David, 17, 18, 63, 97, 104–107,
    111–114
Pythagoras, 83

Race, 14, 34, 36, 51, 74, 95, 142
Racism, 123
Rap music, 85
Rationality, 102
Real World Ethics, 27
Red flag, 4, 30–35
Reflection, 1, 11, 45, 53, 55–58, 62, 115,
    131, 136
Reflective equilibrium, 58–59
Rehnquist, William, 21
Reinforcement, 70

Relational education, 98, 101

Relativism, 33, 34, 47, 58, 63, 78, 133

Relevance, 82

Religion, 3, 8–10, 17–18, 21, 23–24, 26–
27, 30–33, 35–36, 42, 89–91, 94–96,
105–106, 125, 127–128, 131
and schooling, 126

Religious
belief in public education, 8, 33, 36, 127,
148
education, 96
faith, 26, 32, 126, 127, 131, 139–140
ideas, 74, 127
traditions, 24, 31, 126–127

Republic, The, 83

Respect, 2, 3, 6, 15–16, 20, 25–26, 56, 62,
67, 70, 71, 79, 91, 110, 119, 136,
137, 157

Response, 25, 27

Responsibility, 2, 4–5, 6–7, 8, 15–16, 25–
26, 46, 53, 56, 69, 83, 88, 99–100,
103, 109, 121, 131, 136–137, 149

Rethinking Schools, 116

Richardson, Virginia, 19

Ricoeur, Paul, 149

Right relation, 24, 25, 29

Rights, 22, 70, 80, 126

Risman, B. J., 3

Roberts, Terry, 77

Role-playing, 56

Rose, L. C., 12

Rousseau, Jean Jacques, 76, 86

Rudner, Lawrence, 95

Rules, 26, 48–49, 102, 146

Rural schools, 75, 88

Ryan, Kevin, 16, 17, 61

St. Mark's Elementary School, 46, 53–55

Saks, J. B., 17

Satan Deluder Acts, 30

Savage Inequalities, 17, 67, 74

Schaefer, Robert, 7

Schaeffer, E., 16

Schine, Joan, 55, 56

Schlesinger, Arthur, 33–35

School
as sociocultural setting, 142
climate, 70
funding, 17, 21, 44, 66, 67, 74–75
reform, 14, 101, 102, 107, 112

structure, 64, 71, 95, 108, 110, 139,
143, 145
uniforms, 21, 49

School Development Program, 67, 71–73,
78

Schooling as moral, 9, 13, 23, 42, 71

Scientific aspects of teaching and learning,
12

Secular humanism, 92

Secular perspectives, 32, 89, 91, 92, 93, 94,
95

Self
-concept, 74
-confidence, 99–100
-control, 54, 70–71
-esteem, 72

Self-Reliance, 84

Sendak, Maurice, 82

Separate (category), 1, 9, 10, 24, 37–39,
41, 43, 45–65, 79, 134–138, 141,
143–145
Academic First, 9, 39, 67, 75–78, 78–80
Moral First, 9, 39, 68–75, 78–80

Sequential (category), 1, 9, 10, 24, 38–39,
41, 43, 66–80, 134–138, 141–145

Sergiovanni, Thomas, 12, 17

Service
developing character through, 18
learning, 39, 45–46, 52–56, 60–65, 90

Sex education, 59, 91

Shakespeare, William, 83–84

Shame of a Nation, 75

Silberman, Charles, 2–3

Sirotnik, Kenneth, 17

Sizer, Nancy Faust, 111

Sizer, Ted, 38, 41, 96–97, 107–113, 120–
121, 142

Slater, R., 12

Small schools, 20

"Smart" and "good", 7, 24, 66, 69, 124,
134

Smart and Good High Schools, 137

Social class, 86

Social control, 30

Social justice, 24, 30, 106–107, 116, 120,
126, 131, 141

Social mores, 24

Social problems, 64, 82, 91, 105

Social skills, 107
instruction in, 69

Socioeconomic inequalities, 14
Sockett, Hugh, 17, 149
Soder, Roger, 17, 19
Solidarity, 79, 86
Soltis, Jonas, 46, 58, 59, 60, 61, 64
Solomon, D., 12, 19
Soul, 41, 116, 128, 129, 131
Soul of Education, The, 128
Southern Poverty Law Center, 20
Spiritual, 15, 26–27, 30, 48, 66, 92, 105–
    106, 125–131
  development, 128
  growth, 68, 77
  journey, 129
  point of view, 129
Spring, Joel, 139–140
Stallones, Jared, 116, 125–127, 128
Standardized tests, 6, 7, 12–15, 35, 88, 94,
    112, 149   ∘
Standards, 1, 7, 13–16, 24, 28, 32, 46, 61,
    84, 85, 88, 94, 111, 113, 140, 141,
    145, 149, 150
Stereotypes, 50
Strike, Kenneth, 46, 56, 58–61, 64
Student achievement, 50, 71
Students Are Watching, The, 111
Substance abuse counseling, 94
Supreme Court, 21, 32–33, 35

Tamarkin, C., 83–85
Teachers
  as caregivers, 136
  as moral educators, 8
  as morally influential, 5
  as technicians, 5
  education/training of, 57, 60, 71, 103,
    119
  ethics of, 56–60
  moral and academic language used by,
    25, 26, 28, 29
Teaching
  as moral endeavor, 8, 9
  as moral practice, 129–130
  as profession, 150
  as vocation, 85, 149
  to the test, 113
Teaching and Teacher Education, 129
Teaching as a Moral Craft, 115
Teaching Tolerance, 20
Ten Commandments, 30, 31, 107

Ternasky, P. L., 56, 62
Test scores, 50, 71, 88, 112
Thayer High School, 111
Thirteenth Amendment, 21
Thomas, E., 6
Thompson, Milt, 84
Thoughtfulness, 108, 110, 111
Tobias, L., 69
Tolerance, 26, 34, 121, 127
Tolstoy, Leo, 84
Tom, Alan, 115
Toqueville, Alexis de, 84
Townsend, K., 53
Tracking, 75, 104
Traditional
  academic disciplines, 122
  curriculum, 46, 69, 94, 100, 112
  liberal arts, 104
  moral inculcation, 35
  values, 45, 48, 85, 143
Transcendence, 128
Transformative (category), 1, 9, 10, 24, 38,
    40, 41, 43, 80, 97–114, 115–116,
    134–135, 138, 141, 143–145
  Academic, 9, 40–41, 97–98, 107–116,
    142
  Moral, 9, 38, 40, 68–75, 78–80, 96–107,
    115–116, 125
Trust, 70, 78, 101
Trustworthiness, 16, 136
Truth and Method, 145
Twain, Mark, 84

Uncertainty, 104, 111, 112
UNESCO, 22
Unique potential, 68, 69
Universalism, 105
Universal literacy, 87
Universal truth, 84
Urban school, 69–75, 88, 117–118, 120,
    122–125

Value-laden activity, 148
Value-neutrality, 5, 142
Values, 2, 5, 13, 25, 30, 31, 45, 51, 81–85,
    105, 110, 136–137, 142
  clarification, 35, 58
  core, 25, 63, 137, 139
  old-fashioned, 16
  traditional, 45, 49, 85, 143

Van Orden v. Perry, 33
Verde, T., 99
Violence, 16–17, 26, 32
Virtuecrat, 48
Virtue ethics, 100
Virtues, 2, 6, 15–16, 24, 45, 47, 48, 50–51, 62–63, 130, 141
Visual media, 118
Voltaire, 84
Volunteerism, 53

Wake County School Board, 2, 52, 144
Wall of Separation, 33
Washington Elementary School, 70–71
Watson, M.S., 12, 19
Weast, Jerry,
Well-Managed Classroom, The, 69–70
Westheimer, Joel, 53, 62
Westside Preparatory School, 86

When Bad Things Happen to Good People, 21
Wiese, K., 21
Williams, Natrice, 73
Williams, R., 46
Wilson Elementary School, 85
Wilson, Suzanne, 132, 148
Winerip, M., 15
Wingert, P., 6
Wisconsin Citizenship Initiative, 137
Wiseman, Fred, 1120
Wittrock, M. C., 19
Word of the Week, 49–50, 61, 136
Work-study, 53
Wynne, Edward, 16, 17, 38, 45, 47, 48, 61

YMCA, 51
Young Citizens, 54

About the Authors

Barbara S. Stengel is Professor of Educational Foundations at Millersville University (Pennsylvania) and former executive secretary of the Philosophy of Education Society. She is interested in the moral dimensions of teaching, learning, and leadership, and her professional activities reflect that interest. Her current focus is the intersection of fear, judgment, responsibility, and freedom in educational interaction. She is the author of *Just Education: The Right to Education in Context and Conversation* (Loyola University Press, 1991).

Alan R. Tom recently retired from the School of Education at the University of North Carolina at Chapel Hill, where he was Professor of Education. He also has held faculty appointments at the University of Arizona and Washington University in St. Louis. His teaching, program development, and research interests focus on the initial preparation of teachers and their career development. He has a special interest in the role of the moral in teaching, mentoring, and teacher education. He is author of *Teaching as a Moral Craft* (Longman, 1984) and *Redesigning Teacher Education* (State University of New York Press, 1997).

School?

make as effortless as possible for implicit learn
Effortful won't be life-learned as well

Funny how family + social decline is assumed to
be based on people's morals

severe

Xian upbringing robs a person of confidence
from harsh + neglectful treatment
"softens" you up for the
message of God's love
+ need for external rules